ALLEN LANE

GIORGIO E. VALERIO LARI

VOGUE
YOUNG BEAUTY
BRONWEN MEREDITH

ALLEN LANE
Penguin Books Ltd
536 King's Road
London SW10 OUH

First published

ISBN 0 7139 1346 0

Phototypeset in Linotron Sabon by
Western Printing Services Ltd, Bristol
Printed in Great Britain by
William Clowes (Beccles) Ltd, Beccles and London

Designed by Elizabeth Prior

CONTENTS

INTRODUCTION

Gaining confidence and self-assurance has a lot to do with how you look and how you feel about yourself. It works both ways: if you are happy with your looks, your spirits are high and you can face the world with optimism. It is not vain to want to be attractive, it is a positive approach to your body and is part of a disciplined attitude to life.

What is the right way to start caring for your looks? You need to learn about your body and its needs. Looking good today has more to do with health, fitness and energy than with camouflage. The emphasis is on improving, not changing, and you should think more about care than about cosmetics.

The following pages take you step-by-step through all aspects of body and beauty care. Here are hundreds of practical suggestions, all of which have been tried out by a real live teenager – my daughter Arabella. She has worked her way through the book and you can read her comments. Some things were fun, others were a bore, but she gave everything a try. You can do it too and you'll learn how to make the most of yourself and acquire rewarding habits that will stand you in good stead for the rest of your life.

YOUR BODY

The body is a remarkable machine.
It is also beautiful, sensitive,
resilient and adaptable.

You probably give little thought to the complex and refined systems that keep you going. It's time you did. To look after one's body is a basic personal responsibility. If you don't do it, who will? You can only fully understand how to maintain the health of your body if you understand how the organs work and interrelate. Comparisons are often made between the human body and mechanical objects. For example, you may read in textbooks that the brain is like a computer, the heart like a pump, the eye like a camera. Although this may lead to easier understanding of the organs and their functions, it loses sight of the fact that the human body is built and works on a far more complicated and efficient level than any man-made machine. Most important is the close relationship between the body and the mind. The two work in absolute harmony. You can think of the body as divided into sections according to function, but remember that no organ is independent of the rest and the health of every organ depends on the health of the rest.

BODY TYPES

Which one are you?
You might be able to change your shape,
reduce or increase weight, trim bits off here and there,
but you are limited by your basic body type

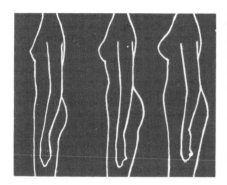

In your teens the dimensions of your skeleton are settled, muscles have matured and the amount of fat covering is determined. Some people are definitely bigger than others, and it is important right at the start to accept that you can never change your body type. You have to learn to work within the range of possibilities open to you.

Body type has nothing to do with height. It is to do with width and depth. There is naturally a degree of overlapping from one type to another.

It would appear that people come in thousands of shapes and sizes, but these can all be boiled down to three fundamental frame types.

Ectomorph – small frame
Small-framed, light-boned, narrow in width and depth – the side view slender. Shoulders and hips are narrow, little muscle or fat; some bosom shaping.

Mesomorph – medium frame
Medium-to-large frame, an athletic type of build with a certain degree of narrowness throughout the ribcage, waist and hips. This is a big look with a lot of muscle and bone, not much fat, often broad-shouldered and firm bosomed.

Endomorph – large frame
A heavy, often chunky, build but not always a large frame. The body is rounded with a thick middle section; it can be well-covered but firm with trim muscles. Often shoulders are narrower than the hips; bosom well developed.

THE SKELETON

The body's framework –
bones determine your basic shape

Guess how many bones you have? The answer is 206, though you may be surprised to hear that you were born with over one hundred more – many fuse together during early childhood. Bones make up much of the body's weight and strength. Their growth and final size depend on genes (hereditary traits from your parents) and girls usually reach maximum height by sixteen.

Bones form a firm frame around which the rest of the body is arranged. They give shape and support, they protect the more delicate internal organs and provide an anchor for muscles. Your skeleton determines your basic shape – the width of your shoulders, the length of legs and arms, the contour of your torso, the general impression of your whole body. You are stuck with it for life as nothing can change it. You may be able to reduce fat and trim muscles, but there's nothing you can do about your skeletal frame.

The unusual thing about the skeleton is that some parts are fixed and rigid (the pelvis, the ribs) whilst others are extremely flexible (hands and fingers). The most flexible of all is the spinal column which is the main bone structure – and despite its amazing agility, actually supports the whole body.

The spine consists of thirty-three little cylindrical bones called vertebrae, which are strung together, rather like a necklace, by means of a common central canal. Between each bone is a spongy material (cartilage) which makes the spine elastic and shock absorbent. Running down either side are ligaments that hold it together.

Your ribs (twelve pairs) are attached to the spine, curving round to the front where the upper ribs join the breast bone. This makes a sort of cage that acts as protection for the heart and lungs. Your limbs are also attached to the spinal column; there are special structures for this – the legs have the pelvis (those large bones that stick out below the waist) while the arms have the shoulder blades. The pelvis, which is shaped similar to a shell, holds and protects the organs of the abdomen. As you know, limbs are very mobile; their freedom of movement comes from ball-and-socket joints. The skull is also attached to the spinal column. It is therefore easy to see that the spine is the focal point of your body's activity as all parts of the skeleton are attached to it. Its good condition is vital to the health of the entire body.

BACK AND SHOULDERS

Good carriage of the back and shoulders is a very simple way to improve the look of the whole body dramatically

The spine is a very unstable and fragile structure, yet it has to cope with incredible strain every day. It is the pivot of all movement and can all too easily suffer wear and tear with each unbalanced or badly executed gesture. Once the back has been weakened, it rarely returns to peak condition because it would require weeks and weeks of rest on a board to put it right. It is only in the very young that the spine has its healthy normal curves. The teenage years are crucial. Take care of your back now and prevent trouble later. Follow the posture positions and exercises on page 12. Do regularly the exercises on pages 68–9 to help strengthen the back and make it more flexible.

The shoulder joint is a freely moving ball-and-socket joint. The ball is the bone of the upper arm, and the socket is made up of the shoulder blade (at the back) and the collar-bone (at the front). Shoulders should not be held back and rigid in the soldier manner, but down and relaxed, allowing the neck to stretch upward.

POSTURE

Good posture gives a better figure instantly

For most of us our natural posture is disastrous. We slump and stoop. The best posture, no matter what you are doing, is one that puts the least strain on muscles and backbone. It involves holding the body erect so that the curvatures of the spine at the neck and at the bottom of the back are not lost. The aim when standing, sitting, walking, even sleeping, should be to keep these natural curves. Many body defects are in fact postural – they can be changed by awareness and practice.

Standing and walking

Take off your shoes and stand with feet slightly apart. Sway slightly back and forth, finally placing your weight on the balls of the feet. Think of your spine as a long necklace with a thread running through it that is being pulled up taut from above your head. Shoulders back but relaxed, neck stretched upward, head in line, and your chin parallel to the ground; pull in the tummy, tuck under the bottom. Test your posture against a wall – your shoulder blades and buttocks should touch it. If only your shoulders touch, you are round shouldered. If only your back touches, your posture is bad because the spine is overly curved.

This posture is also for walking – stride around the room with head high, arms gently in swing following the body naturally and easily. Movement should come from the thighs, not the hips. Try to walk like this as often as possible but don't force the correct posture. As you consciously practise, posture will gradually improve and finally become automatic.

Sitting

Before sitting, be sure your back is to the chair and, keeping the back straight, lower yourself by bending the knees – not by pushing down the bottom. Place your bottom right back in the seat. Legs look better with knees together – either in front or to the side; try not to cross legs.

When you are studying, work will mostly be in front of you. The natural inclination is to bend the head over your work. However, the weight of the head pulls the body forward, straining the back and neck – this can be the cause of severe backache. Try to keep the back upright, using the shoulder joints to move the arms back and forth as you need them. If you are writing, you don't need to move your body, only your arms and wrists. Keep the head up – it's better for your eyes too – and if you have to bend forward do so from the hips without bending the spine. To relax the spine, after your class or work is over, stretch your arms high over head, sitting as tall as possible.

Lying down

Approximately one third of your life is spent in bed, and though you might think that the spine cannot be harmed while lying down, you're wrong. It's a question of checking your mattress. A downy, soft mattress is bad for the back; a firm one is much better. Even if you don't have any back trouble – and the chances are that as a teenager you don't – it's wise to sleep on a hard mattress to prevent strain. It also means that you will get so used to a firm bed that you'll find a soft one most uncomfortable. Thus a good habit will have been formed for life.

MUSCLES

You need them for every body function; some you control – others work automatically

You have 556 muscles, all of which exist at birth and grow in size, but not in number. Each muscle consists of many fibres; connective tissue binds them together and attaches them to the bones.

Muscles work when each fibre stretches and then contracts. Muscles are built up and made stronger only through continual work. When muscles are not used they become weak and slow to perform. If you have ever been ill in bed for more than a few days, you will remember how difficult it was to walk at first and you probably felt very 'weak at the knees'. Our bodies can be built up to a peak of physical performance only by constant exercising of the muscles.

There are two kinds of muscles – voluntary and involuntary – and they work just as their names suggest. Voluntary muscles are those that you consciously direct, such as the ones needed for moving legs and arms, raising and lowering your body, turning your head, and all physical movement. Involuntary muscles work without your even knowing it. They are tucked away in the body and do such things as push food through the stomach, pump blood, regulate breathing. Each movement – voluntary or involuntary – involves a different group of muscles.

Keep muscles in condition

Here are a group of movements that are more controlled than the exercises you're probably used to. They are specially worked out to strengthen muscles which are often neglected; they also help circulation and promote energy; they are fun to do – and they teach you balance.

Body roll

Sit on the floor, knees bent and up near the chest. Clasp hands under knees. Now roll backwards until knees are either side of the head. Back to starting position, and immediately roll backwards again. Repeat ten times.

Knee stretch

Lie flat on the floor, spine relaxed, knees bent, toes turned slightly inward. Breathe in and pull left knee towards your chest, foot tightly flexed. Breathe out, flatten tummy and push your leg up until it is straight and parallel with the thigh of the bent leg. At the same time lift head slightly and stretch arms. Spread fingers tightly, keep foot flexed. Hold to a count of five (count in your head). Relax and return leg to floor in bent position. Repeat five times with each leg.

Squatting

It's very difficult to balance the body, but it's so good for the muscles of the legs, thighs and back that it's well worth mastering this exercise. Start by squatting, keeping feet as flat on the ground as possible, bottom down near the heels, arms hanging in front to help balance. Put hands on knees and push body to a standing position. Raise the toes, then slowly lower the body keeping back straight and hands in front in a 'praying' position; finally sit on heels, hold for a second, then lower heels to relax in the squatting stance, arms in front. Breathe in as you raise the body on tiptoe; breathe out as you bend. Try to do this five times.

Hip swing

Lie on your back with knees bent, arms at sides, palms down. Swing bended legs over to one side, trying to touch the ground with the knees without lifting the spine at all. Return to the centre, then swing legs to other side. Swing from side to side fifteen times.

Back stretch

Stand straight and clasp hands behind your back. Lift arms away from the body and at the same time stretch backwards arching the back. Hold to the count of five. Now slowly bend forwards bringing arms up as high as possible, bending low. Hold to the count of ten. Repeat three times.

BLOOD AND CIRCULATION

The body's transport system: blood carries life-giving nutrients to all cells and carries waste products away

Your blood makes up 10 per cent of your body weight and on the average there are ten pints of blood in your body in constant motion. It is pumped through the system by the heart. The heart never stops pumping during life (though it can skip a beat or two) and beats about seventy times a minute, ejecting a cupful of blood with each beat.

The heart is actually not very big or heavy. It's the size of a fist and weighs less than 1 lb (0.45 kg). You most likely think of it as being on the left side of the chest because of the tradition of placing a hand there in times of passion or agitation. Actually the heart is fairly near the centre of the chest with one third of it going over to the right. It has two pumps; one sends blood through

This makes my heart beat faster

the respiratory system to deposit carbon dioxide and pick up fresh oxygen; the other pumps blood through the body to deliver the oxygen and pick up waste products from cells. It is quite remarkable to think this goes on every minute of our lives.

In fact blood is a very busy agent. Its most important job is transportation – and if you add up all the arteries, veins and capillaries (tiny, microscopic blood vessels) the entire highway would stretch thousands of miles. Apart from being the messenger for oxygen and carbon dioxide, during its travels it carries water (vital to all cells), nutrients, hormones and antibodies. It takes care of waste products and modulates temperature. Blood is literally involved in every function and reflects your general health level better than any other organ. This is the reason why a blood test is the first and best way to detect any illness.

Have you heard of blood pressure? Probably. But do you know what it means? It is the force of the blood measured in relation to the tension (elasticity) in the walls of the arteries. High blood pressure is more common than low, and has to be continually watched. Fainting is due to a decrease in blood flow to the brain – that is why the face first goes white as it drains of blood.

Blood itself contains many elements: red cells, white cells, platelets and plasma. These names may not mean much to you, but this is what they do. The red cells (or corpuscles) pick up oxygen from the lungs and deliver it to the tissues of the body. When carrying oxygen they are bright red. The white cells are almost transparent and they mainly combat infection. Blood platelets make the blood clot, keeping us from bleeding to death from a nick or cut. (Actually you can lose a quarter of your blood without severe consequences.) Plasma is mostly water but contains many nutrients and antibodies.

BREATHING

Your body needs oxygen to survive

Respiration is the term used for inhaling and exhaling, including the distribution of oxygen around the body and the expulsion of the unwanted carbon dioxide. All cells need oxygen. Life depends on it. You breathe in about ten to fifteen times a minute. If you are doing strenuous exercise you need more air, so you breathe in many more times, pausing only a second between each breath – hence the familiar 'panting' noise.

Breathing is controlled by the diaphragm, a large flat muscle which moves down when you breathe in and is pushed up when you breathe out. Air is taken in through the nose or mouth or both. It is better to breathe in through the nose as the hairs in the nostrils clean the air and make it more suitable for entry into the lungs. The lungs are two large, soft, spongy, pink bags filling most of the chest cavity. They consist entirely of little air sacs. Their most important property is elasticity; in getting air in and out of the body, they act like an efficient pair of bellows. Oxygen is transported from the lungs to the tissues of the body by red blood cells and as blood flows through the lungs a gaseous exchange takes place: the circulating blood gives up its carbon dioxide (which is breathed out) and in exchange picks up the fresh oxygen.

Learn to breathe properly

Very few of us breathe correctly. It is such an automatic action that you most likely have never thought if you were doing it properly or not – or that it mattered. It does. Most of us are lazy and take such shallow breaths that the lower parts of the lungs are never aerated. Good breathing brings vitality to the entire body, providing energy for mental and physical activities. Correct breathing is the basis of yoga, the very special body discipline that comes from the East. Try these breathing exercises; try to do one or more daily – and it's best to do them in front of an open window or outside.

Sitting cross-legged

Make yourself comfortable with legs crossed, spine straight, head balanced. Place hands on the knees. Sometimes it is easier to concentrate on breathing when eyes are closed. Take a long slow breath through the nose, hold it while mentally counting to five; exhale through the nose by jerking your stomach forcing it to push out air; don't let go of all the air at once; pause for a second, release more air, pause, then push out all the air until the lungs are empty. Repeat ten times.

Lying down

Lie flat on the floor, knees bent, toes slightly turned in, heels slightly apart. Make sure your spine is straight and very relaxed. Place your hands on your stomach. This time breathe through your mouth, shaping your lips as though sucking through a straw. Breathe in deeply and slowly, pushing the tummy

Do you know that:

Laughter is deep breathing followed by spasmodic breathing out?

Yawning is an extended deep breath to give the body more air to revive it?

Sighing is an extra heavy breathing out?

Hiccups are spasmodic inhalations which end in a click because the vocal cords are suddenly closed?

Opposite: OLIVIERO TOSCANI
Overleaf: BRUCE WEBBER, PATRICK DEMARCHELIER
Facing page 17: ERIC BOMAN

upwards and being sure not to lift your spine off the ground. Now breathe out by pulling in the stomach and pushing the air upwards and out. This is very difficult to do at first because it is exactly the opposite of what you are usually told – breathe in and hold your stomach in. This yoga breathing is not only a better way to aerate lungs, but at the same time strengthens tummy muscles. Continue breathing in this manner for two minutes. It will take many days before you can do it properly.

On the move

Start by kneeling and sitting on your legs, then curl over with arms at the sides, relax. Breathing through the mouth, inhale deeply, pushing out the stomach. At the same time raise the body and arms; hold breath for a second or two; now breathe out and slowly return to the curling position – lower arms first, then sit on your legs, then curl over. Inhale immediately and start again. This rhythmic sequence should be repeated six times – and as smoothly as possible.

DIGESTION

Food provides energy and body-building elements; here's how it's converted into usable units

Digestion is the process that breaks down complex food materials into simple substances that can be readily absorbed and used by the body. It is rather like a conveyor belt set-up. Think of the digestive tract as being a tube which runs through the body (twisting and turning) beginning at the mouth and ending at the anus. Food enters the mouth and takes from fifteen to twenty-four hours to pass through the body. During its journey it has many things added and removed by reaction with various chemicals and enzymes. The organs that help activate these processes are the liver, kidneys, pancreas and spleen.

Food is swallowed by automatic contractions that work even when you are upside down. On entering the stomach the three elements of food – proteins, carbohydrates and fats – are broken down by digestive juices and are changed into tiny particles of protein, glucose, amino acids, fatty acids and glycerine easily assimilated by the body.

The liver is essential to the processing of food. In fact the liver is essential to life (hence its name) and is the body's central organ of metabolism dealing with as many as five hundred jobs. It is the biggest single organ and weighs about 4 lb (1.8 kg).

The kidneys act as the body's filter and elimination system getting rid of waste products and forming urine. You have two, sitting either side of the spine just above waist level.

GLANDS

These body regulators manufacture substances called hormones, which control such things as growth, size, weight, sexual activity, reproduction and temperament

There are several hormone glands that have far-reaching effects on the body. Together they are called the endocrine system and they act as a team. The leader is the pituitary gland, but the mastermind is the brain. All glands secrete hormones which are passed directly into the bloodstream and influence areas quite distant from the gland itself. The hormones work in perfect rhythm and harmony like members of an orchestra.

As well as pointing the way for other glands, the pituitary also regulates growth, controls development and affects sexual functions, including menstruation. The adrenals are in touch with the nervous system, emotions and sex glands. The thyroid organizes the body's supply of oxygen and therefore influences your energy level. The parathyroids control the amount of calcium and phosphorus in the body – both very important minerals. The gonads regulate the reproductive cycle. The pancreas is also a gland – part of it produces the hormone insulin, which makes sure the sugar level in the body is under control.

What have you learnt about your body?

Can you now answer these questions?

● What body type are you – ectomorph, mesomorph or endomorph

● How many bones do you have?

● What are the two types of muscles? And what is the name of the muscle that controls breathing?

● Can you remember how many pints of blood are in your body?

● Is your liver the biggest single organ in your body or not?

● What is the name of the 'leader' gland, the one that directs all others?

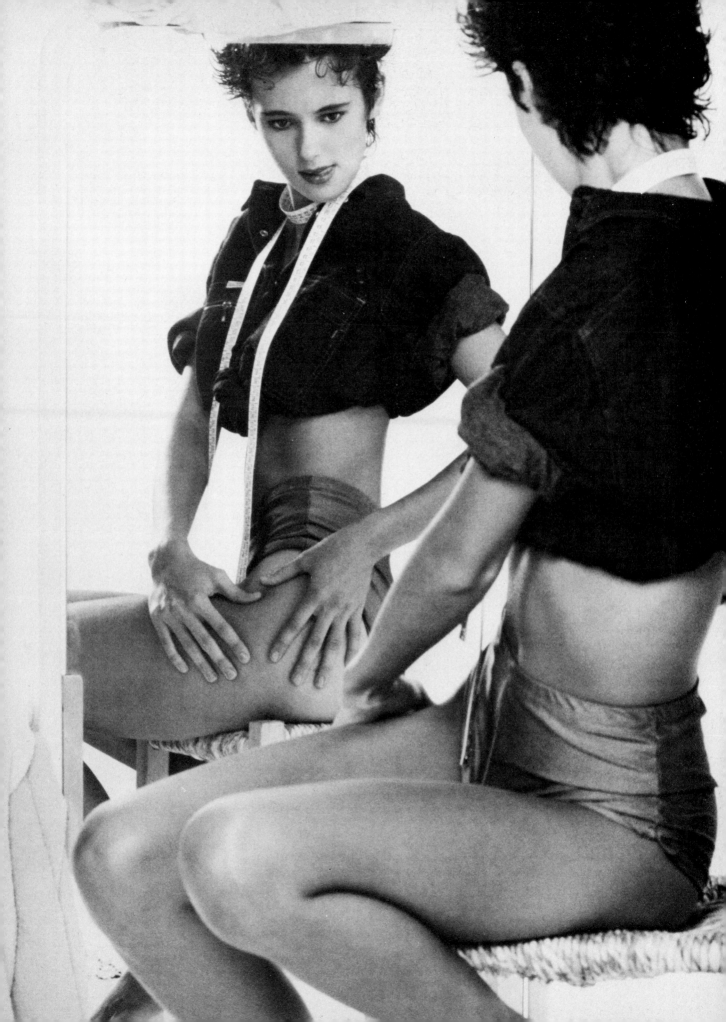

MIND AND EMOTIONS

The mind is the centre of your being.
Without it none of your body functions would work.

The mind directs all outward movements such as mobility of limbs and all involuntary internal activity such as digestion and circulation. It brings you in touch with the world around you through the senses. It registers your individual response to what you see, hear, touch, smell and taste, and stores the information for future reference. The mind is the control tower for moods and emotional responses. It enables you to learn and remember, to think and make decisions. Through sleep, it forces the body to rest and recuperate physically and mentally. In fact your state of mind influences everything you do. It needs to be tranquil, clear and constructive. You can do a lot towards achieving this. First of all you need to know something about how the mind works. Do you have any idea of the size or structure of the brain? Why is it that some people are brighter than others, and why do some people remember everything and others always forget? Your mind can actually be drilled and trained to function at its maximum level. You can learn to be conscious of what is going on in your mind and put it to your advantage. Your mind is not a mystery, but it is the most complex part of your body.

BRAIN POWER

The brain controls all body activity, physical and mental; it works like a computer, collecting information and feeding it back

In the matter of basic body functions that keep us alive and moving, the brain works the same for everyone. It operates on a two-way system: messages are received from various parts of the body and the outside world and an immediate response is sent back. These messages are relayed through the blood or nervous system and are either chemical or electrical. Chemical messages are connected to body metabolism, so it's the blood that hurries them to the brain. For example, if you eat a big rich meal, the brain tells the organs of the digestive system how to cope with it. Electrical messages are directed by the nerves in the manner of an electrical charge. For instance, if you touch something very hot, the brain knows in a flash and consequently does something about it.

As you can see, the brain performs on a massive scale (mental ability aside) to keep the body running efficiently, and it does so through various separate sections. A particularly important part is the hypothalamus, an area the size of a finger joint yet responsible for an incredible variety of operations including appetite, thirst, weight control, sleep, emotions, temperature and water balance. Another section controls muscles, another deals with sensations such as touch, sound, sight, taste and smell.

The body's nervous system works in direct contact with the brain. Its central runway is through the spinal cord, to which all nerve channels are attached. Nerve messages travel in two directions – to and from the brain – but all have to pass through the central spinal system.

For example, if you step on a nail, the electrical impulse goes up your leg, through the spine and into the brain.

What about intelligence?

This varies with each individual and it is the fore-brain (or cerebrum) which decides its level. This area is very large, in fact is over five sixths of the total brain. All higher functions occur here – the functions responsible for skills that put us apart from and above other members of the animal kingdom. This is where we think, remember, learn skills, speak, read, write, etc. Here lies our conscious and subconscious mind; some philosophies profess that here we also have a higher mind, a superconsciousness which has special spiritual powers if only we can learn to harness it.

Some facts about your brain

- Its size has nothing to do with ability.
- It is a soft mass of 14,000,000,000 cells and on the surface looks like a jigsaw puzzle.
- It weighs about 3 lb (1.4 kg).
- It is actually full of water and if not supported would flop over like a jelly.

Did you know that it is your brain that makes you shiver?

It is very important that your body keeps a temperature balance (normal is 98.4°F; 36.6°C) and it is the brain that keeps track of this. Shivering is an automatic muscle movement of very quick contractions that makes heat if your body's temperature drops too much.

MEMORY

Why do we forget some things and remember others?

What you don't remember is actually still in your mind waiting for something to trigger it into recall. Scientists today claim that the brain and its storage capabilities are far better than we ever thought. Most of us use only a very small portion of our full mental capacity. But why some people have better memories than others is still not known; however, it is believed to have a lot to do with the mind's level of concentration at the time when it took in the information. Distracted thoughts while learning lead to muddled thinking and it is not fair to expect the memory to systemize and recall clearly.

A rule for studying

For best results take regular breaks from five to ten minutes between study periods of twenty to forty-five minutes. This gives the brain an opportunity to reorganize what's just been put into it.

Different kinds of memory

Even instinctive actions such as breathing and sleeping are controlled by memory. The strongest memory is usually sensory, the one which is based on sight, sound, touch and smell. There is semantic memory, which is the one to do with word skills such as reading, writing and learning languages. The memory that recalls events in your life is called episodic (from 'episodes'), while your factual memory recalls facts which are not actual events.

How to improve your memory

The mind remembers things better by relating them to existing memories. It is also easier to remember something that is visual and funny in some way. To help you remember, try to conjure up some association that is either visual or amusing, anything from tying a knot in your hanky (that has worked for years) or making up a rhyme. If you do it regularly it becomes a habit and a real aid.

Here are some mental exercises for you to try if you have difficulty in concentrating on one thing at a time, or paying complete attention in class. You can exercise your mind just like you exercise your body. You can train it to perform at its highest capacity. In time, thinking will become less muddled and you will be less influenced by outside distractions. At first the mind will wander, but persevere.

Visualize one object

Sit on the floor cross-legged and with eyes straight in front look at any object around you; look at it hard, really thoroughly taking in everything – its size, its form, its colour. After a minute close your eyes and try to visualize it in your mind as though on a TV screen between your eyebrows. It will appear

Learn how to concentrate
- It can help to improve memory.
- It builds up mental energy.
- It makes you think more clearly.

It helps to remember names by rhyming them with something.
Arabella says 'I remember her name's Mary because I rhyme it with scary'

quite clearly, but then will slowly fade. Open eyes, stare at it again for a minute. Close the eyes and again put the object in your mind. When it fades, look again; continue looking and recalling until you are able to hold the object visually for two minutes.

Recall one scene
Walk into a room – or down a street – and make yourself very conscious of the surroundings. Think of your mind like a camera. When you leave the scene, carefully try and recall as many pictures from it as possible – places, people, colours, actions, etc. Make your mind work, force it further. It sometimes helps to write down everything – rather like the childhood game of objects-on-a-tray.

Remember a day's events
Can you recall what you did yesterday? Did it rain, was it sunny? What did you see, whom did you see and talk to? You can probably remember the highlights, but the purpose of this exercise is to reconstruct the entire day in your mind – re-enact the exact order of happenings as if you were doing them on a stage. At first you'll forget quite a lot, but if you push your memory, with practice everything should come back.

YOUR SENSES

Sight, sound, touch, smell, taste – these are your contacts with the outside world

Literally your sensations, the five senses keep you in constant touch with the environment and help you to distinguish between pain and pleasure. You may not realize how much you rely upon them, but imagine being without just one. Which would you choose? Difficult, isn't it? All the senses send electrical impulses to the brain through the nervous system. Compared to animals our senses are not really so acute – they usually see, hear and smell better than us. However, our sense of touch is far superior. We have thousands of sensory organs which are able to perceive the slightest variant in pain, heat and cold. In our fingertips there is an incredible concentration of these sensory nerves which accounts for our manual dexterity and makes us unique among all animals. After all, who else can write?

EMOTIONAL REACTIONS

To achieve a well-balanced mind you need to recognize emotions for what they are worth

Emotions are your mental response to all that is going on around you. It is your senses that give the external messages to the brain, which in turn relates them to all past information and to your basic character traits – and out comes your reaction. Some responses are more sensible and balanced than others. At times you will be happy, pleased, exhilarated, excited, etc. At other times you will be sad, upset, depressed, gloomy. Then one day you can love, another hate. You can be frightened or full of bravado. You can be jealous and envious, or content, even smug. There is such a wide range of emotions that it's impossible to list them – however, to some degree you have them all in you.

In putting together your inner self, in building your personality, the most important thing is harmony. You have to learn to balance and cope with your emotions. Extremes are not advisable as they cause strife and conflict within your mind and can eventually affect your general health pattern. It is vital, however, to remember that you cannot battle too much against your true nature and get away with it. Be yourself and learn to stand up against the tides of life with strength. You shouldn't let emotions get out of hand; even at a young age exercising restraint and control brings tranquillity and satisfaction.

Today everyone comes under stress and it greatly affects our emotions

Adolescent girls are often under stress. What is it? It's a word you are probably very familiar with as everyone talks about the stresses of modern life – the pace, the complexities, the uncertainties. Becoming an adult is stressful because you are faced with so many new situations and feelings, and you have to start making decisions on your own. Stress essentially is a demand on the body – physically or mentally – that is more than it can cope with. Our reaction is an instinctive one that dates back to our animal ancestry when survival meant fight or flight. The brain orders the release of a hormone, called adrenalin, into the bloodstream and this causes the nervous

Do you cry?

A good weep is good for you and don't let anyone persuade you otherwise. You shouldn't be afraid to cry – it's a fine way to unleash feelings, get them out of your system and start afresh. As a child maybe you were encouraged not to cry and bravely held back the tears. Sometimes crying makes you understand your emotions, whether you are crying for someone or something, or out of self-pity. And another plus: it helps to give the eyes a good wash and clean them out. Ever thought of that before?

Do you blush?

In the teenage years you are prone to blushing and it is very embarrassing. There's nothing you can do about it. As you gain confidence in yourself, it will slowly go away. It is an automatic reflex action to a stimulus – usually embarrassment, guilt or desire. The face, neck and sometimes other parts of the body become pink, as blood rushes to the surface of the skin. Many people (adults, of course) think it looks attractive. Doubtless you don't.

response of tensed muscles and raised blood pressure all ready for action. Of course, you are not going to run away or stay to have a fist fight, but having created all that energy for a physical plunge, your emotions are affected in a negative manner. You could become tense, anxious, afraid, furious, tearful, etc.

A small amount of stress is good for you. If you are young and healthy, increasing the stress can increase the quality of performance – in games, for example, you often play better in competition. The stress of an exam can bring out the best in you and half-forgotten facts can suddenly be brought out of the back of the mind. Some people always work better under pressure – in fact find it difficult to achieve anything without it. Unfortunately all too often the opposite can happen. When stress is great, many of us can't manage and we go into a temporary decline. Stress levels are individual, each of us has a limit as to how much we can stand before the brain is alerted and changes take place in the hormones.

Anxiety is common, but it should be recognized as being different from fear because you are invariably worried about something that probably won't happen. If you are afraid you are going to fail an exam or make a mess of your first date, for example, that's anxiety. When you are frightened, there is real danger at hand – in a small boat when a gale blows up, alone in a heavy thunderstorm. To help you to stop being anxious, try to look on the positive side, thinking about the good things that could happen and not the bad. A great number of people go through life worried to death about things that never materialize – the 'what shall I do if . . .' thought. You can decide what to do when the 'if' happens – which it almost never does – and this will help you to stop worrying about it.

Unbalanced emotions can cause great stress. To hate to extreme is one example, to be jealous or envious are others. Jealousy is probably one of the most destructive emotions. It can cause damage to health and mind. You could be jealous of a person, a thing, a situation, and it can eat away at you, distorting all other thoughts. Your energy is better directed into doing something positive.

BODY RHYTHMS

Life's ups and downs relate to your energy and physical peaks which are influenced by nature

Why do you feel full of zest one day and useless the next? You've probably been told 'that's just life' but there are interesting explanations for it. Our bodies have a definite rhythm which is controlled by nature. We are influenced by the moon as it goes through its cycle, while the position of the sun affects our daily living pattern. Of the twenty-four hours it stands to reason that the night is the least active period, but the metabolism of our bodies slows down too: temperature, pulse rate and blood pressure fall and nervous activity decreases. In deep sleep you are almost hibernating. Just before waking, a specific hormone level begins to rise and reaches its highest point around noon when the sun is at its zenith. This is the time you are usually able to do your best work. Of course, there are some exceptions, and quite a few people are chemically geared to work best at night.

There's another aspect of body rhythm that concerns fluctuating supplies of energy. It's a relatively recent theory but there is quite a lot of evidence to support it. The body is said to have three energy cycles: the physical, which goes on twenty-three-day cycles and determines health, stamina and vitality; the emotional cycle, which spans twenty-eight days and affects your moods, emotions and creativity; and the intellectual cycle, which lasts thirty-three days and controls mental ability and concentration. Each cycle is rather like a mountain with the valley rising to a peak and going down again on the other side. When you are at your peak you are at your best in that particular cycle. There are several times in life when all cycles are at their respective peaks at the same time – you are then in superb form, excelling in everything, or rather, having the potential to excel, depending upon what effort you put into it. All cycles commence at birth. There are experts who can map out your body rhythm chart.

SLEEPING AND DREAMING

Sleep revives the body; dreams recharge the mind

You no doubt accept the fact that sleep rests your body, giving it a break from all its physical exertion. You would literally drop on your feet without it. But sleep has another essential quality. When you sleep you dream, and through dreams you get rid of any tension and work out inner emotional problems without consciously knowing it. You wake up feeling both physically and mentally refreshed and ready for anything.

There are two kinds of sleep – light and deep; you dream during deep sleep and underneath those closed lids your eyes are making rapid movements. The two types alternate all during the night. Sleep isn't necessarily peaceful. Most people change position from twenty to sixty times a night. You toss and turn when you are particularly agitated about something. How much sleep do you need? An adult requires eight hours a night but an adolescent usually requires more – ten or even twelve hours are necessary, depending on the amount of energy expended during the day.

Do you sleep well? Can you get to sleep easily?

Here are some tips to get you to sleep fast and to sleep soundly – and wake up raring to go:

1 Get into a nightly routine. Habit is very calming as you feel satisfied and relaxed that all is in order. When it's time for bed, wash your face, brush your teeth, open your window a bit (fresh air is vital for sleeping hours), turn out the light, slip into bed. If you do the same things in the same order every night, you train yourself to fall asleep on cue.

2 Have a tired body before you go to bed; an energetic day will cause this naturally – all you want to do is collapse.

3 The right bedtime snack: a warm milk drink is perfect in cold weather – camomile tea too if you can acquire the taste. In summer take a handful of strawberries or make a strawberry milk drink. All these will make you more lethargic.

4 Sleep in a cool room but a warm bed, and try not to go to bed with cold feet.

5 Don't ignore that old friend the teddy bear you cuddled as a child. It's a great comforter in bed and contact with such a familiar item is reassuring.

6 If an unpleasant dream wakes you up, make yourself wake up properly otherwise you might go right back to it. Comfort yourself, stroke your arms, cuddle that toy – this helps to break the electrical passage of the dream and enables you to drop off to sleep with a clear mind.

Bedroom tips

1 Make your room as pretty and as personal as possible, a joy to retreat to, a pleasant place to dream in.

2 Colours make all the difference – blue is calm, yellow is cheery, pink is cosy, white is fresh and can be sexy. Keep away from dark and cold colours.

3 Be tidy – fighting your way through chaos before you find the bed is not conducive to the soundest sleep. And always have the bed properly made, the pillows plumped.

SEXUALITY

The word 'sex' basically refers to the fact that people come in two kinds – male and female; girls mature and develop faster than boys and the biggest changes happen between eleven and sixteen.

At birth the sexes don't differ very much except in the areas that will be used later on to express sexuality. A baby boy has his sex organs showing; a girl's sexual parts are hidden but the opening leading to it (the vulva) is visible as a fold or slit. Children's bodies are more or less the same, but with the approach of adolescence, the two sexes start to differ. Girls develop quicker and between eleven and sixteen the body changes shape; the most marked development is between the ages of thirteen and fifteen. How fast you develop depends on your genes (the hereditary factors) and how well fed you are. In Western societies we are adequately nourished, so the determining factor is your internal clock which is situated in the hypothalamus, a part of the brain. At a certain point – usually when you are eight or nine – this clock goes into motion and messages are sent from the hypothalamus to the pituitary gland, which is in control of all sexual functions. The pituitary gland starts producing hormones which in turn are responsible for your changing shape and for establishing your menstrual cycle in preparation for having a baby.

BODY CHANGES

Your shape gradually changes and your female sexuality develops

The first change is in the development of your breasts and curves. Hips get rounder and a definite curve indicates the waist. Hair starts to grow under the arms and around the sex organs. The skin also starts to produce a mature lubricant, which can cause spots and pimples on the face and elsewhere.

All these things are part of growing up and you need time to get used to a new body. Adolescence is probably the most difficult period of life for anyone to go through. It is worse for girls than boys, because your body changes so much. Maybe you think your breasts appeared too early and too big, or too small and too late, or are just too odd in shape. Everyone feels strange during these years and you must accept that there is no one standard shape or ideal, despite what you may see in magazines. Your developing body is an integral part of your developing personality. You will in time become quite comfortable with it. At this point in your life your body is probably growing faster than your mind and emotions, so there is bound to be some inner conflict and anguish.

The whole process of puberty lasts approximately five years, and one of the most significant moves to maturity is when the pituitary gland releases a hormone to the female sexual organs (the ovaries) where it stimulates the growth of sacs containing eggs. These can be fertilized by male sperm to produce a baby. The supply of eggs (ova) is already complete at birth, but it is during puberty that the body makes them available for reproduction. If eggs are not fertilized you will shed one a month and that is what your period (menstruation) is all about. You are simply getting rid of one of your eggs. While the eggs are being prepared for possible impregnation, the ovaries are releasing a hormone called oestrogen, which is vital for women of all ages. It is the hormone of sexuality, as it controls your female curves, your feminine traits, your sexual cycle. In fact it affects your entire body and it is the substance in your body that makes you a woman and completely different from a man.

The puberty programme
Your body advances by precise yet gradual steps from childhood to womanhood

● Hormones are produced.

      ● Your body becomes more shapely.

   ● Definite breasts form.

       ● Underarm and pubic hair appear.

   ● Skin becomes oilier and pimples can result.

        ● Menstruation starts.

THE BOSOM

Breasts are a prime symbol of sexuality; of all the changes that occur during puberty breast development is the most noticeable

Your breasts start developing around twelve and are usually fully mature by sixteen. Young women are more concerned about the shape and size of their breasts than about any other part of their anatomy. Few girls are entirely happy with the way their breasts look. You probably observe how your friends are developing and feel your breasts are different and not quite right. You are doubtless very self-conscious about them, and wish they'd conform to a set pattern.

The fact is that the shape of your breasts is as unique as your fingerprints. No one else's breasts are shaped quite like yours. However, there are two basic shapes – conical and rounded – and you probably come close to one or the other.

One shape is not better or more desirable, it is simply different. You may also find that one breast is larger or higher than the other. This too is perfectly normal.

Breasts are really meant for feeding the young. They are glands contained in fatty tissue, which is what determines shape and size. They are covered in fine skin connected by fibrous tissue and it is that which decides your bosom type as bouncy or firm. Breasts are supported by muscles called Cooper's ligaments and if these are stretched the breasts will never return to their original shape.

Breasts do change in size and appearance throughout your life. If your breasts are small you will be aware of these changes. However, if they are large you probably won't notice any variation. The most usual size change is caused by your monthly menstrual cycle. As your period approaches, hormonal changes cause the breasts to become fuller and tender. Pregnancy also causes breasts to increase in size, but they return to their original size afterwards. When you gain or lose weight, your breasts usually increase or decrease in size. Sexual stimulation can cause a temporary enlargement due to increased blood supply.

Will exercise increase the size of your breasts?

Exercise can improve the look of your breasts but not the size. It can increase the size and strength of the muscles that lie beneath the breasts, giving them a firmer, more prominent look. (See pages 72–3 for bosom exercises.)

During the adolescent years you may get pimples on your breasts. These can be treated like any facial breakout – washing well and dabbing with witch hazel or lemon juice. If they are persistent, you should consult a doctor. Hairs may be another problem. If you object to the hairs around your nipples, you can clip them with manicure scissors (don't pull them out with tweezers, it can be harmful) and any hairs between the breasts can be removed with a depilatory.

DO YOU REALLY NEED A BRA?

How do you decide if you do?
How do you choose the right one?
Here are the answers to all your questions about bras

You have to accept from the start that no matter how embarrassing it may seem, your breasts are growing and will finally need some support if they are going to retain a good shape. Throughout centuries the female breast has been a focus of attention and in the process – and usually in the interests of fashion – has been subject to much pushing around and reshaping. Think of the tight corsets of the last century, the flattened flapper look of the 1920s, the prominent curves of the sweater girls of the 1940s. Fortunately all that is now past, and today the natural look is in, along with the new emphasis on health, fitness and freedom of body movement.

A bra or not? It depends on your size

During adolescence, breasts are firm because they are developing and the tissue is new and strong. But this tissue is fibrous and stretches easily, so unless you are small, going without a bra will in time result in sagging. It is simply a matter of motion and gravity. The degree of sag will depend on the size and weight of the breasts. This is not likely to happen during teenage years unless your breasts are particularly large. Wearing a bra is a protection for the future, a way to help you keep those youthful, firm contours as long as possible. If your breasts are full, size B or over (see below for explanation), it's best to wear a bra.

What size are you?

Bras come in sizes that combine inches and cup measurement. The inches represent the approximate width of your back and chest and are categorized in even numbers (32 to 40). The cup size measures the fullness of your bosom and is indicated by the letters A, B, C, D – A being the smallest. You might have a narrow back and ribcage but a very full bosom, or a wide back and hardly any bosom at all; it therefore stands to reason that bras cannot be sized by a single measurement as two dimensions have to be considered.

How to determine your correct size

First measure your ribcage under your bust, not too tight but snug. Then add five inches, which will give your correct body size; if it's an odd number (like 33) go on to the next number (34).

Place your tape measure over the fullest part of the breasts and measure loosely. If this measurement is one inch more than your body size your cup size is A; two inches more, it is B; three inches more, C; four inches more, D.

How to shop for a bra

The first time you go to buy a bra, it is going to cause you embarrassment, so expect it. But bear in mind that there are lots of women and girls doing the same thing. Nobody enjoys it, and it doesn't necessarily get any better or any easier as you get older. A bra is about the worst garment to buy. Not only does it involve stripping down to the skin, but there's the nuisance of trying on dozens of styles before the right one is found. Don't give up and don't settle for anything that is less than perfect.

Don't go alone; it's best to go with your mother if you can, or take along a good friend. Nothing is more frustrating than being stuck in a changing room with all your clothes off and a pile of discarded try-ons – and not a salesperson in sight. You need someone to act as a liaison between you and the merchandise outside. Here are some guide rules:

Take a good look at the various styles
These are usually on show. Select many to try on as there's a vast difference in cut and fit between one make and another, even though the size might be the same. (See below for basic style information.)

The way to try on a bra
Slip the straps over your shoulders and bending forward ease your breasts into the cups, holding on to the sides of the bra. Straighten up, then hook it at the back, making sure the back band is low. Adjust the straps.

Check on the straps
These should never cut into the shoulders; they are not there to hold up your breasts but to keep the bra in place and to smooth the tops of the bra cups. Straps should not have to be shortened to achieve a proper lift. Uplift comes from the cut and design.

Look at the back band
This also aids uplift. It should never be higher than the front band. If the back is hiked up, then it is not the right design for you.

Is the undercup band too tight?
There should be sufficient give here – it should never feel as though it restricts breathing. Test by seeing if you can slide your fingers easily underneath the band.

Are there any wrinkles in the cups?
This happens when the bra is either too small or too big and means you need to try another cup size.

A bulge above the bra
This means the bra is too tight or too small (sometimes the bulge is at the sides under the arms). Either way, it's the wrong size.

The various types of bra

There is an incredibly wide variety of bras, but most can be grouped in the following categories. For young, developing breasts, the natural bras are by far the best as they are not restricting, are comfortable, are ideal for sports and give support with a natural line. Cotton is the healthiest fabric, particularly for active sports, but synthetic fabrics are used for the bulk of designs.

The natural bra

This is smooth, comfortable and usually unlined; it gives a sleek fit that looks natural. It moves with the body. It is difficult to tell whether you are wearing a bra or not, which for adolescents is ideal.

The stretch bra

Another bra which gives a natural-looking effect and is good for young figures. It is made of stretch fabric that clings to the body, and can be restrictive if you get too small a size – many come in one-size-to-fit-all, which means it's the cut and design that will make the difference.

The underwire bra

Here wire is inserted in the curved half-moon seam of the undercup section. It gives support for the fuller-breasted girl without the ugliness of a wide underband which the more substantial bras used to have (and some are still around). This design can also push up the breasts of small-breasted girls who wish to look more shapely.

The contour bra

This bra has a very thin interlining that's not exactly padding but has a cushiony feel and look. It provides shape without adding inches. It also gives a smooth line so the nipples don't show.

The padded bra

This has a substantial padded look either throughout the entire cup or just in the undercup area. It can make your figure about a size larger and is only for those who are really flat-chested and want to appear bigger.

MENSTRUATION

Your period can start any time between the ages of nine and sixteen. Twelve and a half is the average; however well prepared you may be, the reality can still be hard to accept

A baby girl is born with anything from 40,000 to 400,000 immature eggs (ova) stored inside the two ovaries. Every month an egg is released into the uterus. This is known as ovulation. It sits there, awaiting fertilization. It is embedded in a kind of nest that has been previously built up by the surrounding tissue. If the egg is not fertilized, it is discarded from the uterus together with its surrounding 'nest'. When these cells are shed there is bleeding from the vagina. This is called 'having a period' and happens about every twenty-eight days. The egg drops into your uterus about the middle of your menstrual cycle, and it is during the egg's first three or four days there that you are most likely to get pregnant if you have sexual intercourse.

Bleeding every month for a few days – usually three to five – is a nuisance and it is often referred to as 'the curse' for this reason. Periods are not always regular when they first begin. There is no set rule; everything depends on your own individual metabolism. When you start can vary: it can be any time from nine to sixteen. The average age today is about twelve and a half. If you have not begun to menstruate by sixteen, you should be seen by a doctor.

The first thing to understand is that a normal menstrual cycle covers a wide range of variations. In time you will come to recognize your own biological timetable. As soon as you get your period, make a note in your diary of the first day and the number of days it continues. A twenty-eight-day cycle is the average. Some girls have it every twenty-six days, others every thirty. But you will find that after the first erratic year you will most likely establish a definite pattern. So be sure to keep a note of the dates. The bleeding usually lasts for about four days, but for some it is only one, for others a week. It can vary from time to time, particularly during the first year, but there is nothing to be concerned about. You may have stomach cramps during a period, you may put on weight just before it or your breasts may swell and be very sensitive. You can become irritable and depressed, and suffer headaches. It's all quite normal. Stomach cramps can be helped with heat or by taking three drops of tincture of cinnamon in a glass of warm water – you can buy it at any chemist's. An aspirin will also help.

At first the amount of blood is small and it may be rather brown. To soak up the blood you can use a sanitary towel, a wad of cotton encased in gauze, that is placed over the vulva. You can also use a tampon, which is a special cylinder of absorbent cotton, which can easily be inserted in the vagina. It has a tail-like string on the end which is left hanging outside, so to pull out the tampon you just tug on the string. Young girls who have never had intercourse can use tampons, but they will probably need a small size. It is a clean and hygienic way of absorbing the blood. Instructions for inserting are on the pack; there may be difficulty at first, but this soon goes.

Pay no attention to old wives' tales that you shouldn't bath, swim, wash your hair or take part in active sports when you have your period. Do everything as usual. Having a period need make absolutely no difference to anything you do. It may be tiresome, but it's not an illness.

YOUR SEXUAL ORGANS

They are tucked away inside but there are sensitive external parts

Your sexuality centres around the parts that are visible – the breasts and the vulva (the opening to the vagina). Everything else is neatly hidden and you cannot see much of a girl's sexual equipment any more than you can see the tonsils. But if you open the lips of the vulva you can see the inner lips and the clitoris – a little, smooth knob that is very sensitive. In making love, women enjoy having it touched, and it has no function other than giving sexual pleasure.

You have two ovaries where eggs are matured. These are quite small, about the size of a bean, and from each a tube (called fallopian) leads to the uterus. Think of a letter T; the cross-bar is the fallopian tube with an ovary at each tip, the down stroke is the uterus. Each month an egg drops from alternate ovaries into the uterus to await fertilization.

Important sexual parts are the lubricating glands which cannot be seen. When you are sexually aroused, these glands moisten the lining of the vagina and the whole genital area can become quite wet.

The way into the vagina is usually partly closed by a little skin fold, called the hymen. When you have intercourse for the first time, the hymen gets torn or stretched and can bleed. In the past it was thought that on the first occasion of intercourse, there should be proof that the hymen was still intact and had to be broken. The fact is that the hymen can break for many reasons (sports, riding, athletics, etc.) early in childhood. Even a doctor can't tell for sure by looking at the hymen who has had intercourse and who hasn't.

Health check: it's important to know about sexual secretions and infections

There is always a certain amount of discharge from the vagina. This is perfectly normal and varies in density throughout the menstrual cycle. It is usually white or a yellowish colour. Every woman has it, so there is no need to be worried or embarrassed about it. However, there are times when an infection sets in, produced by the body's own bacteria. The discharge can become thicker and whiter, sometimes yellow; you may suffer itching and soreness, also burning when you urinate. Under such circumstances it is advisable to keep the body as cool and dry as possible, avoiding hot baths – fungus thrives on heat. Cotton underwear also helps prevent infection, as it allows air to circulate more freely around the vaginal area. You can use a douche: a spray that is put in the vagina, the liquid coming from a plastic bag with a tube attached to the spraying fitment. (You can buy a douche bag and nozzle in any chemist's.) The simplest solution to use in the douche is a tablespoon of salt in a litre of warm water. If heavy discharge and irritation continue, you should consult a doctor.

There are also infections of the sexual organs that can only be contracted through intercourse. They can be extremely dangerous if not treated in the early stages. They are called syphilis and gonorrhoea and are detected by constant discharge from the vagina, redness and sores around the genital area, burning during urination. Any of these symptoms should be reported to a doctor.

There are medical specialists, called gynaecologists, who deal with everything within the sexual reproductive system. After puberty it is a good idea to go to a gynaecologist for an annual check-up. He – or she – will give you a 'pelvic examination', which means he will either put a finger in your vagina to feel if everything is in order or he will insert an instrument called a speculum, which makes it possible to look inside. It is a strange feeling and something you'll have to get used to, but it doesn't hurt. There is nothing to feel shy about; a doctor has to be able to check your sex organs in just the same way as he needs to look down your throat.

BIRTH CONTROL

Teenage pregnancies are rising and it's better to be wise before the event than sorry afterwards

The only way of making sure you don't get pregnant is quite simply not to have intercourse. Many young girls find it hard to think about birth control because they feel that by choosing a method of contraception (a means of preventing conception) they are committing themselves to sexual intercourse, for which they may not be emotionally ready. Do you feel this way?

It is certainly better not to get yourself so involved before you are really ready to step over that fine dividing line between adolescence and woman-hood. You'll know when you are ready – both emotionally and physically. Nevertheless it is wise to think hard and seriously about contraception before-hand. Ultimately the responsibility rests with the woman and you cannot make an informed decision unless you know the facts.

There is no perfect contraceptive. Look at the chart on page 40 and you will see a summary of the various methods, explaining how they work and giving the advantages and disadvantages of each. You may think the Pill is the perfect solution. It isn't. Granted it is nearly 100 per cent effective and simple to take, but it can have bad side effects. More important, it interferes with your reproductive organs and cycle, and its long-term effects are still not known. You may want to protect yourself from an unwanted pregnancy but you also surely want to protect your body and the health of future children. Today, a lot of women are rejecting the Pill for these very reasons. They are also having second thoughts about the intrauterine device (IUD), a plastic – some have a copper coating – coil that is put in the vagina and physically irritates it. The common-sense approach is to use the barrier methods that have been around for a long time.

Barrier methods are the diaphragm and the condom; these form a physical barrier of rubber that prevents sperm from entering the cervix (the opening of the uterus). A diaphragm goes into the vagina and blocks off the entrance to the uterus. A condom goes on an erect penis and traps the sperm. They are certainly the best methods for young girls, and in addition they help prevent the transference of any sexual disease.

A diaphragm has to be fitted by a doctor, which is embarrassing – for you, but not for the doctor who is doing it every day. You have to learn how to put it in and take it out yourself. A condom can be bought in any chemist's, and other shops too, but that is usually considered the boy's responsibility.

There are foams, creams and jellies which also act as barriers against sperm invasion. These are called spermicides, but they are not effective when used alone – they should always be used with the diaphragm or condom.

Natural methods of birth control are for later years, for marriage or steady relationships. They rely on finding out your 'safe' period by means of temperature control and secretions from the vagina. It is difficult enough to work it out when you are mature, but it's almost impossible during adolescence, as your body has yet to establish regular rhythms and cycles. In addition, these methods carry a high risk of pregnancy.

CONTRACEPTION

METHOD	HOW IT WORKS	ADVANTAGES	PROBLEMS AND RISKS
The pill and minipill	The pill contains two synthetic hormones (oestrogen and progestogen). It prevents an egg from ripening and from being released from an ovary. If no egg is available, there's no chance of getting pregnant. There are many pills on the market, but all are taken the same way: one each day for twenty-one days with a break for seven days when you have your period. Some packets contain twenty-one pills, others contain seven extra dummies so there's a pill for every day. It is important to take the pills in correct sequence. The minipill contains only progestogen and is not so effective because it does not always suppress ovulation, but it does interfere with egg implantation and sperm mobility. The pill is almost 100 per cent effective. You need a doctor's prescription.	If you take the pill according to instructions it is the most foolproof method, but drugs or stomach upsets can cause unreliability. It is easy to take and does not affect sexual spontaneity.	Long-term effects are unknown and during adolescence it is most unwise to tamper with the body's delicate hormonal balance. Medical side-effects that are known include nausea, weight gain, headaches, bleeding, circulation problems and depression. The minipill has fewer risks.
IUD (Intra-uterine device, coil)	Intrauterine means 'inside the uterus' which is where the coil is fitted. Coils are small, flexible and flat, made of plastic, sometimes copper-coated; they come in various loop and curved shapes and have a couple of threads attached to one end. It is thought that they cause a localized inflammation which upsets timing of implantation of the egg and probably causes the uterus to reject the fertilized egg. Fitting is quite simple but it must be done by someone who is specially trained. It takes less than half a minute. It can hurt, particularly if you are tense. The threads hang down into the top of the vagina, which enables you to check if the coil is still in place. High-level effectiveness: the failure rate is only 2 per cent.	The coil can be put in and forgotten except for weekly personal checks of the hanging threads to see if it is still in place. It doesn't involve taking chemicals and doesn't affect sexual spontaneity. When you want to have a baby you can have the coil removed.	It can cause heavy and increased menstrual bleeding. It can also cause infections of internal sex organs. The womb isn't used to having anything solid in it, and so often tries to push the coil out. This can cause cramp pains and bleeding. It's very easy for an IUD to be pushed out and flushed away unnoticed, so you must check once a week to see if it's still there. Many doctors won't give the coil to young girls.
Diaphragm and cervical cap	A diaphragm looks like a small shallow bowl; the dome is made of thin rubber, the rim of flexible wire rolled with rubber. It fits inside the vagina and closes off the entrance to the womb so that the sperm stays in the vagina and goes no further. A cervical cap is basically the same, but is narrower and deeper; this fits snugly around the base of the cervix, completely blocking the entrance to the uterus. Both have to be specially fitted by a doctor as no two girls are the same size and shape inside. You will be shown how to insert it and how to take it out. (It is much more difficult to insert the cervical cap correctly.) A diaphragm or cap has to be inserted before intercourse and used with a spermicide (for details see below). After use, it has to be washed gently in warm water and checked for defects and tears. If correctly in place it is very effective, with a failure rate of only 5 per cent.	A reliable method of birth control if used properly and looked after carefully. There are no side-effects, since there is no interference with the body's normal mechanism. It doesn't affect sexual spontaneity.	Having to think about putting in a cap quite a while beforehand can be a drawback. It must not be removed for six to eight hours after intercourse and needs further applications of spermicide if intercourse occurs again within that time. If you get fitted for a cap before you've ever had sexual intercourse, you need to go for another fitting afterwards, as you may need another size. If you lose more than 7 lb (3.2 kg) in weight, you also need to check the fitting.
Condom	Also known as a sheath, rubber, french letter; it's made of very thin rubber and covers the man's penis during intercourse, catching all the sperm and preventing them from entering the vagina. There are several shapes and colours. It is most effective when used in combination with foams or creams, when the failure rate is about 5 per cent. Lubricated ones can make intercourse easier.	Easy to buy and simple to use. No side-effects whatsoever. They give protection against vaginal infection and sexually transmitted diseases.	Condoms do tend to dull sensation and interfere with spontaneity. Drops of semen that spill from the penis before ejaculation can cause pregnancy, so condoms must be put on before the penis approaches the vagina. The penis must be withdrawn from the vagina as soon as ejaculation takes place.

What you need to know

METHOD	HOW IT WORKS	ADVANTAGES	PROBLEMS AND RISKS
Spermicides	These are foams, creams, jellies and suppositories which provide a chemical barrier against sperm; most also contain a sperm-killing ingredient. They are not reliable on their own, and should be used in conjunction with the diaphragm, cap or condom.	They are inexpensive, no prescription is needed and there are no side-effects. Some actually help to prevent the spread of sexually transmitted diseases.	They are messy and must be inserted (with an applicator that comes with the product) shortly before intercourse. A new dose must be added each time intercourse occurs. The smell and taste are not very pleasant. The jellies don't disperse as quickly or as evenly as the foams, while the suppositories don't always melt in the right place. If they burn try another brand.
Natural method	By observing and recording your body's cyclic changes you can predict and recognize ovulation, and abstain from intercourse during unsafe periods. Temperature rises during ovulation and mucus of special density is secreted into the vagina before ovulation. Constant vigilance of secretions is essential, as well as taking note of regular calendar symptoms such as mid-menstrual pains. In time you can work out your cycle, but it could take a year.	No side-effects whatsoever; you have the satisfying feeling that you are conscious of the workings of your body and therefore have a degree of control over them.	A long-term proposition that requires a high degree of motivation and voluntary abstinence. It takes time and patience to learn correct interpretation of monthly charts and data. It is really a method for married couples or for those with an established relationship. The failure rate is very high – about 60 to 75 per cent.

ABORTION

The termination of a pregnancy before the foetus is capable of independent life

Medically, it is perfectly feasible to have an abortion, although there is a great deal of controversy on the moral issues involved. Also, having an abortion leaves you with a tremendous burden of guilt which is extremely difficult to overcome. No matter how much you may rationalize the positive aspects of your decision, this guilt can become so depressive that it negates everything else in your life. It is a very personal decision, requiring careful thought about the present and the future. If you are under sixteen, you need the written consent of your parents or guardians.

How safe is it? Any operation involves some risk, and an abortion is no exception. The sooner you have the abortion, the safer it is. Statistics show that it is actually safer to have an abortion than to have a baby. Out of every 100,000 women who have a legal abortion, about four die. Out of every 100,000 women who continue their pregnancy, about twelve die. There are sometimes complications: an abortion can cause an infected or damaged womb, or it may stretch the cervix and so make having a baby difficult in the future.

If you think that you may be pregnant, your first step should be to have a pregnancy test. A urine test will give fairly reliable results fourteen days (or more) after the date of the missed period. Examination by a doctor gives reliable results, but you have to wait until at least four weeks after the date when your period should have started.

There are several methods of abortion – the one selected depends on how many weeks pregnant you are. The method most commonly used up to twelve weeks from the beginning of your last period is called vacuum aspiration. A thin plastic tube is pushed up the vagina, through the cervix and into the womb. The other end is attached to a suction machine which draws out the contents of the womb.

Up to sixteen weeks you can also have a minor operation called a D and C (dilation and curettage). The cervix is stretched and the contents of the womb scraped out.

After sixteen weeks – and it should never be left as late as this – injections of salt solution can be given to make the womb contract so that it pushes out its contents. In young girls this is only done in the most exceptional circumstances.

HARMFUL HABITS

The things you do regularly every day make all the difference to how fit and healthy you are.

Good habits in eating, exercising, thinking and generally taking care of your body and looks can be learned and brought into a daily routine. Then there are the bad habits that can be unlearned, such as over-eating, laziness, nail-biting, etc. In fact an adolescent's resilience allows you to get away with almost anything, as the body and mind can recuperate amazingly quickly and get back on the right track. But there are some things you cannot get away with, certain habits that may start off harmlessly enough but are highly dangerous because in the long run the body cannot cope with such abuse. They are smoking, drinking and taking drugs. The most lethal of all, of course, is the drug habit, which is a killer at any age. It is so easy to get into and so tempting to just give it a try. You may do so out of bravado or curiosity, but this first step could take you down a long road of disaster. Smoking and drinking seem harmless at first, indeed in moderation they can remain that way, but if you go beyond the safety zone they take their toll later in life. In the teenage years it's a firm no to all three. You're not being a coward in this rejection, you're being sensible, valuing your health and respecting your body. It's important that you are aware what smoking, drinking and drugs can do to your system. You are often told not to do these things, here's why.

SMOKING

It's now smart not to smoke and if you don't acquire a taste for smoking in your early years, the chances are you never will

Despite widespread publicity about the dangers of smoking, more teenage girls are doing it. Why? Many of you may think of trying it for fun, in the belief that you can easily give it up. The problem is that you don't realize how habit-forming smoking is. Before you know it, you are hooked.

Maybe you can get away with it when you are young, but smoking will take its toll later in life. There is definite evidence that smoking causes lung cancer, as well as cancer of the mouth, throat, oesophagus, bladder and pancreas and other areas. It will undermine the functioning of the heart and, thinking ahead to the time when you have children, there's a strong likelihood they'll be smaller and weaker if you smoke.

What's in a cigarette? There are three active ingredients: nicotine, tar and carbon monoxide. When you inhale, there's an immediate tickling sensation as the smoke stimulates nerve endings in the mouth and lungs. **Nicotine** is responsible for this, and taken in small doses, it can act as a stimulant, making you more alert, sharper, receptive. Experiments have shown that the nicotine obtained from smoking three cigarettes an hour is indeed a way of sustaining mental activity over long periods of time. That is the positive side. The negative aspect is that nicotine causes a special hormone to be released into the bloodstream, one that increases blood pressure and mobilizes fatty acids. This means that the heart has to work harder and requires more oxygen.

"NOBODY SEEMS THAT IMPRESSED I'M SMOKING"

Tar is the element which increases the chance of chronic bronchitis and lung cancer. It damages the fine hairs of the windpipe and bronchial tubes, hampering them in their task of cleaning out the system of irritants or bacteria which have been breathed in.

Carbon monoxide is responsible for the connection between smoking and heart disease. When a filter tip is added to a cigarette it may reduce the tar and nicotine breathed in, but it increases the amount of carbon monoxide inhaled.

The fact is that stimulation through tobacco is not worth it. You are no longer considered a coward or weak if you refrain from smoking. There are other ways to show your sophistication. So if you've played around with smoking, stop. If you haven't, don't start.

DRINKING

Alcohol, like nicotine, is a drug
on which you can easily become dependent.
It does exhilarate and it's OK in moderation –
beyond that, NO

You should be aware early on that the pressures of today's society on women have greatly increased the number of women who drink too much. This is usually due to boredom, isolation or frustration, but it is no way out of any of them.

Drinking is a social pastime and as such when done in moderation can be very pleasant. Most doctors agree that a controlled amount of alcohol won't do any harm, but it's still best to stay away from it until you are over eighteen.

For future reference, then, wine is the most acceptable drink; indeed, it is said to be beneficial in that it aids digestion and relaxes the nervous system. It certainly brings more enjoyment to a meal. Spirits – whisky, gin, vodka, rum – are more concentrated alcohol and cannot be drunk in the same way as wine. Sweeter spirits such as sherry, port and vermouth are taken in small measures (and small glasses); so are liqueurs, which are drunk after dinner and often aid digestion.

What happens to your body when you drink? Why do you feel light-headed and not quite clear about speech and actions? Alcohol is quickly assimilated and almost immediately opens up the blood vessels, allowing it to enter the bloodstream. Within a few minutes half of it is in the blood and on the way to the liver. The liver can absorb about one third of an ounce of alcohol an hour. You feel 'high' when you drink more than the liver can cope with. What happens is that the blood pumps the excess alcohol around the body while it awaits its turn to get into the liver. It literally goes to your head and affects the brain, particularly the control centres, which is why if you drink too much you'll feel weak in the limbs and slow of speech; it also numbs your senses, which is why you are apt to do things you wouldn't dream of doing when your senses and mind are working the proper way. It is often difficult to judge time and distance, which is why it is terribly dangerous to drive after drinking.

When you take your first drink do so slowly; sip it, don't gulp it down. The more slowly alcohol is consumed the more easily the liver can keep pace with it, and so less will go to your head. A social drink is fine when you are mature; being drunk isn't any fun either for you or those around you. Go slow. And at first go slow even on wine; it is better to mix it with mineral water at the beginning. Leave the strong spirits for much later – they can be lethal.

DRUGS

Avoid at all costs; they can ruin your life and some can literally kill you

There is more drug addiction now than ever before and addiction often begins at school. To be aware of the dangerous consequences you should know about the various drugs and their effects.

Marijuana

It comes from the cannabis (hemp) plant and is known by many names – pot, weed, grass, hash, hashish, Indian hemp, etc. It is the weakest of all stimulants. A marijuana cigarette or 'joint' is easily distinguished from a tobacco cigarette. Marijuana is green; the joint has a home-made appearance and burns hotter and brighter.

Shortly after inhaling marijuana, you become 'high' and the senses of touch and perception and conception of time, distance and speed are greatly distorted. The heartbeat increases. It takes several hours for the body to return to normal.

'Lots of my friends smoke pot but I'm determined I never will. It's not easy to join the group, but I realized they only do it to be cool and half of them don't even enjoy it. What's more, they look stupid when they are "stoned" or pretending to be. Luckily it is very expensive, so they only ever really smoke it at parties, but I wonder what would happen if they got hooked.'

A SIXTEEN-YEAR-OLD

'Even if I could afford drugs or knew where to get them I would never, never do it. My brother was once caught with some dope, and it broke my parents' hearts. Also it's not considered so "with it" any more.'

A FIFTEEN-YEAR-OLD

Glue

Can you really get 'high' sniffing glue? Yes, you can, and what is more it can become addictive. It is the simplest way of getting an immediate kick, but the chemicals involved are not simple at all – they are complex compounds that can destroy your nasal tissue and seriously harm the whole breathing network.

Cocaine

This comes from the leaves of the coca shrub which grows in Peru and Bolivia. It is interesting to note that for centuries the leaves have been chewed by the natives for their stimulating effect. Cocaine is processed into a fine crystalline powder which is odourless and white; it is also rather fluffy, hence it is often called 'snow'. It is usually taken by sniffing, rarely by injection. The drug is absorbed through the membranes of the nose.

Under the influence of cocaine you are hyperactive and in a false world. There is a bad let-down after stimulation that often ends in a sort of stupor. Continual dosage can damage your lungs for life. Another horrific result is that after a very short while the lining of the nostrils can be completely destroyed and the nose tissue is attacked.

'It was OK while I was taking it (cocaine) which was usually in the evenings, but every morning I felt really ill and stayed miserable all day until I could have some more. So I took more and more . . . of course it's terribly expensive so after a few weeks I couldn't afford to go on. I looked really ghastly and felt worse all the time. I considered stealing in order to get more money but couldn't bring myself to do so (thank goodness). I knew that there were special homes and treatments for people like me but I could not bear the humiliation of doing 'cold turkey' (a special supervised diet with no alcohol or drugs for about two agonizing weeks) where people could see me suffering from withdrawal symptoms – and you really do suffer because your body cries out for more stimulants and you hurt all over when you don't take any more.

'Miraculously I managed to cure myself – one morning I took matters in hand by making myself realize that I was disgusting and unbearable and worth nothing, and that I had to start from scratch to get back to normal. With drugs I think it is the only way to stop – completely and suddenly.

'It took a year of hard discipline and frightening despair, but I made it and now I am back to my normal self and I feel so good. I had forgotten what it was like to wake up with a clear head, with the desire to get-up-and-go and above all, be in a good happy mood.

'Would I ever take any drugs again? No way. Not even smoke a joint? Never. I have seen what even a relatively mild stimulant can lead to. I have seen what hard drugs have done to myself and the worse effects they've had on friends. I know that if I try even a little it will all start snowballing again, so I just keep right away and have lost contact with my so-called "friends" who take a lot of drugs and don't like me managing to survive without them. They aren't much fun any more anyway. It's another world, a useless scary world. I count my lucky stars I had the strength to get out of it.'

A YOUNG EX-ADDICT

LSD

This is a chemical and is so potent that extreme reactions are inevitable, even when the drug is taken in the smallest doses. It is tasteless, colourless and odourless. The early physical effects are often distressing – nausea, vomiting, pain. During the LSD experience, or 'trip', blood pressure is raised and the sensory centres are stimulated to such a degree that they sometimes appear to interchange. There are reports of drug users 'hearing colours' and 'seeing sounds'. Dangerous hallucinations are also common. The experience can be so frightening that you could panic in an attempt to control the situation, and when this happens you could be on the borderline of suicide. There have been many appalling accidents as a result of taking LSD – jumping to death, killing, permanent brain damage. An overdose – which is very easy – can produce long periods of delirium and a 'flashback' of the original LSD experience.

'I had smoked marijuana and sniffed cocaine, and then it just happened at a party; along with friends I was talked into giving heroin a try, and within a very short time I was an addict. The last months have been spent trying to recuperate with the use of pills – and by going to a psychiatrist. I didn't intend to get hooked, I just did . . .'

AN EIGHTEEN-YEAR-OLD GIRL

Heroin

This is a derivative of opium and the most deadly of all drugs. Opium comes from the opium poppy and these fragile red, white or purple flowers grow best in a hot, dry climate. Opium is actually the dried juice obtained by cutting the unripe capsule or pods of the flower. This is done late in the evening and overnight the milky white juice oozes to the cut surface, oxidizes and thickens, changing its colour to reddish brown. It gradually hardens, forming gum-like balls. This is raw opium, and has a bitter taste and a heavy, sweet odour. In the East, raw opium is widely used as a narcotic, but in the West morphine is produced from opium by a chemical process, and from that comes the potentially fatal heroin. Heroin is twenty to twenty-five times stronger than morphine, so when you consider that morphine is used medically to reduce the most severe pain, imagine the power of heroin. It also has twice the addictive powers of morphine.

In its pure state heroin is a greyish-brown powder. Because of its strength the pedlar is able to dilute it many times with milk sugar (lactose) and still provide a potent drug. Heroin when 'cut' in this manner becomes white; it is odourless and has a bitter flavour; it is also more dangerous than the pure heroin. Yet it is this adulterated heroin which is usually sold.

The reason why young people take heroin in the first place is that it initially produces high spirits. But once one starts there is no end to it because of the degenerative progress of the drug. Beginners usually introduce the drug to their bodies through the nostrils by 'sniffing', which in itself can destroy the lining of the nose. But it is not long before the need for a greater kick leads to injections. Heroin enters the bloodstream immediately and its effect is instantaneous. It can be built up to this level very quickly as heroin is the most toxic of all the narcotics. The danger of addiction is greater than with any other drug because the body's tolerance builds up very rapidly.

Addicts can suffer extreme discomfort and pain if their injections are not taken three or four times daily, the dosage required just to maintain a relatively normal condition. The cost in hard cash is astronomical, yet a confirmed addict will do anything to get the money for the drug, and the price you pay could be your life.

The most horrendous point about heroin addiction is that it is almost impossible to cure it permanently – very few addicts can stay away from heroin for more than a few months after a cure. What is more, very few addicts are inclined to go on a cure and it is usually parents or relatives that have to enforce treatment. So be warned. It's a one-way street and it's up to you never to enter it.

'On average, those who start young will die before they reach thirty. The "cut" heroin can kill suddenly and those who use purer versions have more of a chance to live longer. Practically all beginners think they can control it, but there's little chance. An addict has to be slowly weaned off heroin, usually with synthetic drugs and often in combination with psychiatric counselling. It's a long patient process and there is always the likelihood that the addict will give up and return to the habit. Withdrawal symptoms are not pleasant, and can set in within six to eight hours, rising to a peak between eighteen and twenty-four hours. The physical symptoms are shaking, shivering, muscle cramps, a high temperature, vomiting, sweating and a feeling of great anxiety. Most addicts have little interest in food, so malnutrition is a major problem – a pallid look and an emaciated body is typical . . .'

A DOCTOR

Angel dust

A relative newcomer to the field of addictive drugs, it is one of the nastiest and is rapidly spreading. It is also known as crystal, hog, peace, weed, super grass or PCP. It is a chemical compound that is very easy to produce, even by back-street chemists. It is a crystalline powder that dissolves in water or alcohol, and pedlars offer it either as crystals or as a liquid. Angel dust can be taken in more ways than any other drug – smoked, sniffed, swallowed or injected. But it is most commonly taken as a cigarette – the powder being put on mint or parsley leaves, then rolled into a joint.

Only a quick puff is needed for intoxication. The first effects occur after two to five minutes, reaching their peak between fifteen and thirty minutes and going on for four to six hours.

The effect is apparently different from that of other drugs and, say users, impossible to describe. When high, you go into a zombie state quite detached from normal sensations. Hallucinations can lead to very violent behaviour completely out of character – to running wild, to crime, to murder. It is actually not addictive, but it can stimulate bizarre and gruesome behaviour. If you take large doses you may become unconscious. Some takers have suffered convulsions violent enough to tear muscles and break bones. Very high doses may knock out the part of the brain that controls breathing.

'It is insidious that the pushers or pedlars are trying to reach children at such a young age, in their early teens when they are unable to be responsible. The only thing we can do is constantly warn our children, be aware of what the drugs are and their effects. There is no point saying "don't" – it has to be backed up by the reasons why not . . .'

THE MOTHER OF A YOUNG ADDICT

Your life is at stake

Danger! Stay away from all drugs.

Answer these questions:

● *Do you want to ruin your health and your life?*

● *Do you think short sessions of make-believe are worth hours and days of pain and agony?*

● *Do you want to be at the mercy of an insidious drug that gradually takes over your life?*

● *Do you want to be desperate enough to steal or even murder for a drug shot?*

● *Do you want to be without your family, abandoned by all your friends?*

● *Do you want to die young?*

If you don't, let the truth sink in now: all drugs can lead to these disasters. Don't even give them a try; don't trust anyone who says 'It's fun, it's great, it's harmless.' And don't let anyone think you are a coward for not joining in. They are the losers, you are the winner.

49

GIORGIO E. VALERIO LARI

KEEPING FIT
AND HEALTHY

SPORT AND EXERCISE

**Sports keep you fit, but specific exercises
can get you trim and keep you that way.**

Fitness through sports can be an adventure. To get your body tuned to such a degree that it performs with stamina and accuracy is very satisfying. It is both a physical and a mental discipline. It's not only your body that will benefit – your energy level will rise, your health will improve and your skin will glow.

Of course, not everyone has the capability or the desire to be a great athlete. At least two dozen variables affect sports performance. If you have certain physical characteristics your chances of playing and winning in a sport can be increased. But even if you don't excel, that's no reason to stop doing something you enjoy. Winning shouldn't be more important than taking part anyway. But there is a vast difference between losers and those who don't try. Actually losers often try harder than anyone else, they are just less talented. Sports should be part of your everyday life, particularly those you are most likely to continue playing in the future.

Skip it!
All you need is a skipping rope and lots of stamina. It's a good way to keep yourself trim and in condition for any other sport, and you can do it all on your own without feeling silly. Start skipping slowly and work up to a hundred jumps a minute. Then vary the steps – hopping, running, and so on.

SHAPING UP

Get fit to play your sport
You'll enjoy your game more

Most athletes do extra exercises to put them in top form. For example, tennis and swimming champions often jog, run and cycle regularly; they also use weight-lifting to increase strength and, in warm-up exercises, yoga stretches for flexibility.

Have you good muscle tone? Do you feel less springy when you get out of bed in the morning? Even overnight you can lose some muscle tone though it's transient. If you are ill in bed for a while you always feel weak when you first stand up. This is not due to the illness but to a decrease in muscle function. One way to maintain muscle tone is continuous movement – if you're sitting for a long time in class, stretch your arms, flex your legs; get up and walk around between lessons. Regular exercise also builds and maintains muscle tone, but for strengthening muscles there's nothing like weight-lifting. For girls? Doesn't that build up too much muscle, you may ask. No, because if it's done properly, weight-training will not produce unsightly muscles. What it will do is build strength and a better figure. You will not get the bulky biceps of boys because it's male hormones that cause the extra development.

Weight-lifting for beginners

Do exercises every other day. Use 3 lb or 1.5 kg weights – the easiest are weighted plastic strips which wrap around wrists and ankles. They can be bought in any sports shop.

1 With a weight strapped on each wrist, stand in front of a high step or sturdy chair. Step up with one foot, bring up the other leg. Step down in the same way. Repeat 8 times. Rest one minute. Do the same putting the other leg first. Rest three minutes.

2 Lie on back, arms at shoulder level, elbows bent. Push alternate arms to the ceiling. Repeat 6 times each arm. Rest three minutes.

3 Stand with your feet slightly apart, knees relaxed, arms by your sides. Pull right arm up and bend body to the left without bending it forward. Then pull the left arm up, bending to the right. Repeat 6 times each arm. Rest three minutes.

4 Now put weights on the ankles. Lie face down on the floor, arms by sides. Raise right leg as high as possible, hold to the count of five, lower slowly. Repeat 6 times. Do the same with the other leg.

5 Lie on your side, supporting your body on your elbow, using the other arm for balance. Now raise the upper leg, hold to the count of five, lower slowly. Repeat 6 times. Turn over on to your other side and do the same.

Warm-up exercises give you flexibility

The greatest number of sports injuries happen because muscles are overtight. Stretching before you start exercising or playing any sport is essential. Take ten minutes minimum to do these exercises. It's also a good idea to stretch for several minutes after your sports activity.

1 Toe touch: stand with feet apart, arms at side. Bend over and try to put hands on floor, hold to the count of six. Repeat eight times – smoothly, don't bounce.

2 Overhead stretch: stand with your feet apart, arms relaxed. Raise your arms, reaching as high as you can and at the same time stand on the balls of your feet. Hold to the count of six. Relax to starting position. Repeat eight times.

3 Body lunge: from a standing position with hands on hips, step forward with a big stride using left leg, then bend the knee pushing forward from the right leg, keeping it straight. Hold to count of six. Repeat four times. Do the same with the other leg.

4 Knee bends: stand, feet apart, hands on hips, go down slowly to squat on heels, balancing on the balls of your feet, arms stretched in front. Hold to count of four. Return to standing position. Repeat eight times.

5 Thigh stretch: sit on the floor, knees out and soles of feet together. Hold your ankles with your hands and try to bring your body as close to your knees as possible, pressing knees on floor, bending the torso forward. Push then hold to the count of four, relax. Repeat eight times.

6 The big stretch: sit on floor with the legs very wide apart, hands on knees. Bending to the left try to put your head on your knee, hands clasping the ankle. Push down, hold to the count of four, relax. Repeat five times. Do the same on the opposite side.

What's your type? Which sport is for you?

Match the sport to suit your temperament and physical shape. First, are you a loner? There are many sports you can do on your own, such as running, swimming, cycling. If you need the challenge of an opponent, there's tennis and squash, which, if played energetically, are maximum fitness sports. Your body type indicates your physical suitability to certain sports, giving you a better chance to do well. Here are some indications:

Long arms

Standing with your arms by your side – if they reach below the middle of your thigh, you have long arms. You'll be good at any racket-and-ball game, particularly tennis.

Strong legs

If you can keep going on your feet all day and dance all night, you have strong legs. You would probably have no trouble with walking, hiking, cycling, skiing or riding.

Slight body frame

If you have small bones, light structure and little fat, you could try gymnastics, ballet, diving.

Body strength

If you have no trouble lifting heavy packages and carrying them, you most likely have the power to push yourself to speed and endurance in swimming and to play forceful strokes in tennis.

What happens when you get out of breath and why does your heart beat faster?

If you are not fit, you are bound to become breathless during sports. This is because your muscles suddenly require more oxygen to do the job you are demanding of them. The heart beats faster to send muscles more oxygen-carrying blood. For the blood to get more oxygen you have to breathe in more air – and this means quicker shorter breaths. Your heart normally beats at a rate of seventy to seventy-five times a minute. This is called your pulse rate. You can feel your pulse by putting the middle three fingers of the left hand on the inside of your right wrist. Count the beats for a minute. This is your resting pulse.

When you suddenly exert yourself the heart can beat as many as two hundred times a minute. This is too high and can strain your heart and also your lungs, which are over-working to bring in the air. This is where fitness training is so important, as you can gradually build up the strength of the heart so that it is able to pump enough oxygen to the muscles by beating between 120 and 160 times a minute. At this point you will no longer be gasping for air, but steadily breathing deeply. You can check your active pulse rate at the end of an exercise session by putting your fingers at the side of the throat – count for ten seconds and multiply by six.

Eat right for sports – a carbohydrate-rich diet gives quickest energy

Good foods for quick energy are potatoes, pasta, rice, grains, bread, peanut butter, low-fat yogurt and milk, and fruit.

When you use energy you burn up calories, so your food intake should meet your energy requirements. Carbohydrates (see chart on page 93) provide the immediate energy needed for the muscles to work well. The best way to have energy available is to eat about 60–70 per cent of your daily calorific intake in carbohydrates. Up to 15 per cent should be protein foods like meat, fish, chicken. The rest can be fats such as cheese, milk, butter. Avoid sweets and sugary foods of all kinds – it's a myth that these give you instant energy.

Don't exercise on a full stomach, but do drink plenty of fluids. Good snacks: bran muffins provide bulk and energy, bananas provide important minerals often lost during heavy exercise.

Sweating is good for you

Why do you sweat? It's a way of regulating internal body temperature when you are overheated from intense activity. As sweat evaporates it cools you down. Sweat itself doesn't smell; body odour results when perspiration comes in contact with bacteria on your skin. To make up for the loss of water, you need to drink lots of fluids – water and natural juices are best.

Hoop-la

A fun way to work up general fitness – it's good for heart, lungs and total coordination; in addition it's marvellous for trimming hips and waist. You must gyrate your hips to keep the hoop up and moving. Do it to music . . . do it with friends . . . do it for enjoyment as well as exercise.

Sports gear

What to wear for support and comfort

Clothing
Try to wear cotton clothes – cotton breathes as you sweat and prevents any trapping of moisture. Make sure nothing is too tight – you have to be able to move with ease: you'll need shorts, T-shirts, tracksuit and a spare sweater and jacket.

Bras
Bouncing bosoms can hurt and won't do your figure any good either. Preferably your bra should be in cotton with non-stretch straps. It must not ride up in front and should be supported on a band. Hooks must be padded inside for comfort.

Shoes
All sports require special shoes – ones that are right, not just for your feet, but for your ankles, knees and spine. Fit is the first priority. Ill-fitting shoes allow the body to get out of alignment. Try them on with the socks you'll wear. Look for layered cushioned soles. Avoid the synthetics – tops should be canvas, leather or suede, depending on the sport. Always go to a specialist sports shop. And remember you get what you pay for – and your feet are very precious.

What about exercise during your period?

You can carry on as usual; forget those old wives' tales that activity is bad for you at this time. You can even swim. For all sports it is advisable to use tampons for maximum security and confidence.

A big caution: watch the sun

If you are outdoors a lot in a sunny climate you do need a protective cream for your face. The combination of sun and snow can be just as harmful as those midsummer rays. Wind too can cause burns and roughness.

Take care of your feet

Callouses and corns are the result of pressure, friction of poorly fitting shoes. They are very painful and can hinder any sporting endeavour, so watch out for the early signs. Soak your feet regularly in warm salted water and rub away any hard spots with a pumice stone or skin-sloughing product. If they get bad you must have professional attention. There are special corn pads you can wear for protection – a ring of felt around the corn frees it from pressure.

Athlete's foot is very common. It's a fungus infection picked up by going barefoot in gyms, showers and swimming pools. It thrives on warm, damp skin, spreads easily and is highly contagious. It looks like a kind of ringworm and appears between toes and on the soles of the feet. At first there's an itchy rash, then splitting of skin between the toes and often blisters under the foot. Treatment consists of washing feet frequently, always wearing clean socks and applying fungus powders and ointments.

When you hurt a muscle

Very cold packs should be applied. Wrap ice in a towel and hold it on the injured area for half an hour. If there is swelling, prop up the leg and continue applying cold compresses for several hours. If the swelling is not down within six hours, take a soak in a warm, not hot, bath. Do several sessions of warm-up exercises before you go back to your sport.

When you sprain an ankle

Keep the ankle elevated as much as possible – the less pressure on it the better. Ice packs should be applied frequently over a period of twenty-four hours. Also strap with bandages and put no pressure on the foot or ankle. To get back into action, begin by making circles with the foot, then pushing it against a wall. Keep the ankle strapped and try to walk. If it's not too painful walk quite a way, it's the best method to get back to normal quickly.

THE BIG FOUR FOR FITNESS

- **walking / jogging / running**
- **swimming**
- **cycling**
- **tennis**

These are the best sports for overall exercise, for promoting stamina and for keeping weight under control. They are the best ways of training your lungs and heart to deliver oxygen-rich blood to the working muscles as fast as possible.

A programme of walking, jogging or running is the perfect build-up programme for other sports. Boring? Not really worth the effort? They may sound so to you, but a good walk could mean an interesting hike; learning to run through jogging could put you in the girls' athletic league, where competitive events are becoming more and more popular. All three provide great basic training for all other sports. They are the most natural and beneficial forms of exercise.

Walking

The more you walk the fitter you are – and there's a very good chance you'll enjoy it more and more. Walking is the simplest way to exercise and maintain your health. You can do it anywhere and at any time. Walking improves circulation, stimulates the heart and lungs and also benefits the parts of the body involved in digestion. When you walk you use more than half the body's muscles: all the foot, leg and hip muscles, also the back, abdominal and rib muscles; if you walk briskly and swing your arms, your shoulders, neck and arm muscles come into action. Try for an easy, continuous motion. It is not the speed at which you walk that affects fitness, but the endurance of long-distance rhythmic walking on a daily basis. How correctly do you walk? Your feet should point straight ahead and you should step down on your heel first, and then let your weight move along the outer side of your foot and across the ball to the big toe. Shoes are your vital equipment. Gym shoes are fine for easy ground, but not for tough walks. Running shoes are a good alternative because of the wedge under the heel. In the city or on paved roads, comfortable rubber-soled shoes are fine. Hiking boots are perfect for support, comfort and safety, but they need to be broken in. If you are going on a hike, thick socks are essential; if you wear several layers of clothing, you can adjust to climatic conditions.

Set yourself a three-month plan to increase your walking speed by degrees:

Month one

It is bad for you to walk for miles unless you are used to it. Even such a simple thing as a walking programme has to be built up gradually. Walk ten minutes three or four times a week and initially work at picking up your pace rather than aiming for extra minutes. Twenty minutes a mile (1.6 km) is slow, eighteen minutes per mile is moderate and fifteen minutes per mile is brisk. The next step is to walk for longer periods, aiming for four twenty-minute workouts a week, doing eight minutes at a slow pace and twelve minutes as fast as you can without becoming breathless. By the end of one month you should be able to do a $2\frac{1}{2}$-mile (4-km) walk in about forty minutes.

Month two

Increase your walking time and pace. You should aim to do four twenty-to-thirty-minute workouts a week, plus one of an hour – and remember to warm up by taking the first eight minutes at a slower pace. At the end of the month you should be able to walk $3\frac{1}{2}$ miles (5.6 km) in fifty-five minutes.

Month three

Continue to pick up speed, using the same system of four sessions of thirty minutes, walking slowly at first before going at your full capacity. Attempt one long walk each week of about an hour. By the end of the month you should aim to accomplish 5 miles (8 km) in an hour, or just a little over.

Once you reach this point you are very fit and in peak condition for any other sport. Maintain this ebullient level by doing four thirty-minute workouts and a one-hour walk a week.

Jogging

This is becoming one of the most popular and fastest growing sports. It is really walking speeded up but not as fast as running. It is particularly good for your heart and lungs, while it also tones up and strengthens the legs and has a firming effect on the muscles of the bottom. In all it helps to keep your figure trim. Anyone can jog, at any age, but a lot of girls are put off by their self-consciousness – you might feel very conspicuous, jogging alone while others merely meander along and often stare. Jogging may also seem like hard work – agonized expressions on some joggers' faces would seem to confirm this! Jogging is not for everyone but it can be fun and shouldn't be seen as some form of punishment.

The movement of jogging comes easily; just remember to land on your heels and take off from the toes. You do not have to reach any speed, nor is it necessary to jog every day. Always begin with five minutes of warm-up exercises (see page 68). At first just jog until you tire (could be no more than one eighth of a mile), and then walk until you feel energetic enough to jog again. You must never push yourself beyond your physical capacity. Build up stamina gradually, jogging for fifteen minutes three times a week to start with; you can soon build up to a 1–2 mile (1.6–3.2 km) trot – a two-mile trot should take no more than half an hour; young women in training can run from 4–6 miles (6.4–9.6 km). After you have finished, don't just flop as this could cause dizziness or even fainting – walk a little or do some light physical activity to cool off.

It is easier to run on grass or a dirt track than on cement. Shoes are most important and should be selected with great care. The best have reinforced pliable soles, instep support and good padding around the ankles. Avoid plastic. Blisters are often a problem, so wear two pairs of socks – one thin pair next to your skin and another thick pair to counteract any roughness in the shoes. Dress warmly in cold weather, in a tracksuit and sweater – sometimes even gloves and hats are necessary – and keep warm afterwards. In the summer, shorts and a T-shirt are adequate. Natural fibres are always best.

Running

For this you have to be fit and properly trained, in order to build up your stamina, endurance, muscle strength and ability to control speed. Because women's athletics are becoming more popular, many schools have athletics programmes, or you can join a club. When you run with other enthusiasts it is a very challenging and rewarding sport. You can prepare yourself on your own by building up stamina through walking and jogging.

Swimming

Swimming is excellent for breathing and circulation; it strengthens and firms all muscles and helps align the bones of the spine. Indeed, if you have any problems with your back, get into the water right away; it is such a relief for the spine to be horizontal and not in a supporting position.

Just as with walking or jogging you need to build up stamina slowly, but you will be amazed at your improvement if you train steadily and frequently. However, you have to learn in the first place as we humans do not naturally take to water. Unless someone in your family can swim very well, it is better to take lessons to learn the proper breathing and limb coordination. The most energetic stroke is the front crawl; the breathing is difficult as you need to use your mouth and water often flows in, but because you have to control it so well, you improve the performance of your lungs and circulation. Breast stroke is very good for your back and bosom, and for strengthening the legs.

Measure your proficiency by the number of lengths you can complete. One length is usually 25 yards or 25 metres. See how many lengths you can swim using the crawl. Rest a little and try to do it again. If you want to build up to a better performance you should practise three times a week for thirty minutes or so – and each week try to swim two lengths more than you did the previous week. Swim at a leisurely pace; don't worry about speed.

After two months, even if you started by being able to swim only one or two lengths, you'll be up to a distance of a quarter of a mile. Now is the time to start building up speed by sprinting (swimming as fast as you can) one length after you've swum three slowly, then pausing a minute and returning to slow strokes. If you build up your number of sprinting lengths, you'll soon be in the school team. You need to wear a one-piece swimming costume, a cap, and maybe goggles to protect your eyes from the chlorine in the water.

Cycling

Cycling is marvellous exercise for the legs, as it firms up the muscles and makes the entire leg more shapely. It helps the heart and the lungs and if you use a conventional straight handlebar bike (as opposed to a racing model) it encourages good posture. One good thing about cycling is that it can become part of your everyday life – and provide perfectly adequate exercise – without implying that you are a fitness freak. However, if you are going to concentrate on cycling as your only method of keeping fit (no other sports at all) then you should build up to thirty minutes of continuous cycling three times a week. You can slowly increase both distance and speed – an extra ten minutes a week – until you can manage about 25 miles (40 km) in about an hour and a half. There is something very exhilarating about being able to reach a speed of about 15 miles (24 km) an hour – you are flying with the wind. Country or park rides are far superior to city streets, as not only is it safer but you are clear of the hazards of pollution, which can put more foul than good air into your lungs.

Quick-check guide for ideal schedules

Sport	Weekly plan	Calories burnt per hour
Running	15–30 minute sessions 3 or 4 times weekly	approx 600
Cycling	20–45 minutes 3 or 4 times weekly	approx 400
Swimming	20–30 minutes 3 or 4 times weekly	approx 350
Brisk walking	20–30 minutes 3–5 times weekly	approx 300
Tennis	1 hour sessions 2 or 3 times weekly	approx 270

What kind of bike? The conventional 26-inch (66-cm) wheel bicycle is the best size – the small-wheeled modern bikes are only good for short trips. Bikes come without gears, or with three-, five- or ten-speed gears. Bikes without gears are often quite heavy. Three-speed bikes may be lighter and have narrower wheels. The super bikes are the five- and ten-speed ones, as they make going up hills much easier.

As for clothing, a track suit and an extra waterproof jacket are ideal for cold weather, and just shorts and a T-shirt in summer. Keep clothing bright so you can easily be spotted in the traffic; luminous bands or a bolero are essential in the city. Wear flat shoes or gym shoes. Avoid flapping trouser legs as these easily get caught in the chain.

A warning in warm weather: watch how you grip the handlebars. If you grip them tightly for a long time the constant pressure can cause numbness and you will lose coordination. So change your hand positions frequently or wear gloves.

Tennis

If solitary exercise is not for you, then by far the best sport for all-round fitness is tennis. An easy game of singles or doubles may be fun – and there's often lots of fooling around on a tennis court – but it's the hard game of singles that burns up calories, exercises the heart and lungs, increases flexibility, helps tighten stomach muscles and trims the legs. Tennis requires speed and mobility, and good players are often tall with long arms to generate power.

Select your racket according to the weight you can grip and balance in your hand – ask the advice of an expert. Coaching is essential for beginners and for more experienced players as well – if you are going to take your tennis seriously you need frequent check-up sessions with a professional. Learning tennis well in your early teens is a plus for later on, as it is a great social asset and you will make lots of friends (and admirers) if you play the game well.

To begin with you need half-hour lessons once or twice a week. Then try to spend at least two hours a week on the court, dividing your time between practising your shots and playing games. You can do this with a partner of more or less your own ability or better. Many courts, clubs and school grounds have practice walls to play against – a great way to improve your shots and assess your own ability.

Improve your serve
Accuracy is not enough – you need to serve with speed so there's less chance of your partner pounding it back. You won't get as many in as with a weak serve, but it's the speed and force of a serve which will win you points.

Work on a powerful forehand
This is usually your most aggressive shot, where the ball is hit hard and accurately. The weight of your body – not just your arm – has to be put behind each stroke. Learn accuracy first and then bring up the speed.

Build up that weak backhand
This is usually a beginner's weakest stroke and your inclination may be to avoid using it at all. Make your partner send you plenty of backhand shots.

TEN POPULAR SPORTS

Recreational sports can be much more pleasurable than solitary runs or swims. They are slightly less beneficial to health, but they bring you into social contact with others and it's a great combination to have fun with others and exercise at the same time. Find the sports you like best and stick to them.

Schools provide plenty of opportunity to take part in team games and if you want to continue playing them after school you can join a club. Usually, however, it is easier to continue with the sports which you can do on your own or with a small group of friends, such as those mentioned here.

Different sports exercise different parts of your body; tennis strengthens your arms and tightens your bottom, riding helps hips, squash promotes agility, while the social sport of disco dancing exercises the whole body.

Badminton

This is a fast and exhilarating game. It requires agility more than anything else because it is often necessary to change direction very swiftly and to jump quickly for the high shots. There are often long rallies that demand intense concentration. You have to learn to vary your strokes from a touch that just flicks the shuttlecock over the net to a smash that slams it down. If you play tennis as well it takes a little time to adjust to the lightness of the shuttlecock and to using the wrist rather than a powerful arm swing. Badminton can be played indoors on a wooden-floored court or outside on grass, but any trace of wind can ruin the game.

Badminton can build up your endurance level, and it is especially good for strengthening the back and shoulders and improving posture. It also helps to make your body much more supple.

Dancing

Although not exactly a sport, dancing can be an energetic pastime. In fact all forms of dancing are excellent exercise and it is probably one of the most enjoyable and social ways to fitness. Dancing helps flexibility, suppleness and coordination. It is very relaxing and takes your mind off your problems. If done with gusto it will certainly help you to keep trim.

Ballet

Ballet is the most demanding as it calls for discipline and control. It is best to start at an early age, but in your teens your body is still pliable enough to follow the exacting routines. Even if you are not thinking of becoming a dancer, it is marvellous exercise and a wonderful way to keep your body in shape. There are ballet studios with classes catering for women of all ages who simply want the exercise for health and shape. You need leotards, tights and ballet shoes.

Folk and country dancing

This is usually organized by local clubs and the approach is much more informal and social. Nobody is particularly concerned about mistakes –

except in competition of course – and beginners can pick up the steps at any age and classes are often available. As for the exercise value, it's a way of waking up all your muscles and improving circulation, nothing more. But you'll make lots of friends.

Jazz, modern and disco dancing

These provide the opportunity to express your individuality and your natural response to music. All can be exhausting with movements based on gymnastics and continuous body action. This means that they are very good keep-fit routines, helping shape, fitness and weight loss. You need to be flexible and relaxed; you need to have imagination and be uninhibited; you need to go with the rhythm of the music.

Golf

You probably think that golf is for the middle-aged and elderly, and that is true to a degree. But there's a new young enthusiasm in golf, particularly among girls, due to recent competitions and the increased interest in women golfers. It can be very enjoyable at any age; the fact that it is an expensive sport probably discourages young would-be players, however. It is preferable to be a member of a club (though there are public courses). You will need lessons from a professional and you will need some clubs. When you are choosing your clubs – you should try to buy them second-hand – ideally, you need the advice of a professional. If you are left-handed you will need left-handed clubs. Special spiked shoes are also necessary and a left-hand glove (right-hand if you are left-handed) for a better grip.

You can compete against another person or join with a partner to play against two others. The emphasis is on skill rather than strength and the main fitness benefit is from the walking involved, though swinging the club is good for the waistline. Scoring is based on a handicap system which means that players of different ages and with different levels of ability can still enjoy playing together. More teenage players are needed in golf – get out and have a try.

Gymnastics

Over the past few years there has been amazing growth in the popularity of this sport among teenage girls. It is doubtless due to the successive Olympic Games which have shown how graceful and visually appealing gymnastics can be when performed well. It involves a combination of strength, dexterity and artistry. It calls for determination and consistency, but the reward of finally doing something well is exhilarating. Gymnastics is best started when young, as you are more agile, though once a level of competence is achieved you can continue to enjoy it for many years. Careful coaching is necessary, and you can find this in various clubs and gymnasiums. Girls perform on the floor, beam and asymmetric bars, and also use vaulting equipment. Work on the floor is mostly creative, while apparatus calls for strength and endurance. You need to wear leotards but your feet are usually bare.

Gymnastics will give you a finely tuned sense of balance and rhythm, and will develop mobility, strength and muscle endurance to a very high degree.

Opposite and overleaf: GEORGIO E. VALERIO LARI
Facing page 65: BRUCE WEBBER

The joy comes from the creative side and the absolute satisfaction of realizing you can control your body. It's one of the best ways to be in touch with your body, to discover how it works and coordinates.

Ice skating

A fun sport that brings many benefits without your ever realizing it. It is exhilarating and good for mobility, circulation, posture and balance. It also helps to shape your body into firmer lines. Skates and boots are the essential equipment; they can be hired but it is better to have your own as they need to fit well and support your ankles. Wear them with thin tights or socks as you need very close contact between your feet and the boots in order to control movements. It's quite possible to teach yourself skating by watching others – but an initial lesson does help, if only to give you confidence on that slippery surface. Once you've got the hang of it, speed skating is the most energetic and beneficial.

Riding

Equestrian sports are enjoyed all over the world. The particular satisfaction comes from being in close contact with an animal and in coordinating its body and mind with yours. To ride well you need to have a good sense of balance together with technical skills which you can only learn from a teacher. In fact it is essential to have lessons at the beginning – you simply cannot just get on a horse and go without endangering you both.

To ride well you have to acquire good control and the sooner you begin the better, as this helps you get a 'natural seat'. You do need a certain amount of courage, particularly when the horse gallops and for jumping. The physical benefits of riding are minimal, though your legs have to grip the flanks of the horse, so it does encourage strong, firm thighs.

Roller-skating

This keeps your muscles working because you are constantly on the move. It is very good for strengthening the legs – and it is fun. You need a good sense of balance and at first your legs seem to run away with you. When you start, go to a rink and hire skates as you will get advice about fit and learn how the skates should feel. Then you can buy your own – there are different types for racing and dancing. For roller-skating or roller disco dancing, you can wear body stockings, leotards or jump suits.

Skiing

A marvellous sport and one of the best for all-round fitness. You must be fit and you need to have a good sense of balance, suppleness and strength; it involves the whole body because you have to twist, bend, pull, push and control; it is particularly good for the legs as you constantly have to flex knees and ankles. Skiing is quickly learned but you must go to a school otherwise you get into bad habits and incorrect postures, which could cause an accident. Many accidents would be avoided by learning properly in the first place, skiing with caution and making a point of being in good physical condition before taking to the slopes. Boots and skis can be hired at a ski resort, and it's better to hire this equipment the first time you ski, just in case you don't like the sport. Boots should fit tightly, especially around the ankle. Waterproof nylon suits are the best ski wear – a sweater is warm underneath – plus gloves, hat and goggles.

In most countries there are dry ski schools where you can get into training and practise skiing before you go to the resort.

Squash

This is one of the fastest games you can play. It makes great demands on your physical stamina – it will help you to keep trim and will make you more supple and faster on your feet. It really is a game for those who want to maintain a high level of fitness. Speed is actually more important than style. Squash is played indoors with a single opponent. You will need a white shirt and shorts (or skirt) and white tennis shoes; eyeshields are recommended to protect the eye socket from being hit by the hard, fast ball.

Water-skiing

You must be able to swim to participate in this sport. You also need a good sense of balance and a strong back. It is very good for your arm and leg muscles. Water-skiing is performed on calm water, and you need quite a stretch of it so that the boat can pick up speed. The best way to learn is to take lessons, which are usually for half an hour; you hire the skis, boat, driver and instructor – and it's advisable to wear a light life-jacket. Skis are made of wood or fibreglass; your feet slip into rubber pouches and can easily be freed should you lose your balance and fall into the water – which you will do many times at the beginning. Water-skiing is a summer sport, but you can train on land in the winter. When experienced, it is possible to ski at a considerable speed, swaying and criss-crossing from side to side, and it can be very exhilarating.

EXERCISES

Do you really need them?
It depends what you want and expect

There are few bodies that can't benefit from some exercise. Any physical jerks will benefit your health, but certain exercises will benefit your shape. They may not drastically change your shape as you can only trim within the limits of your body type, but if you systematically do a certain group of exercises you will get results. Everyone is interested in slimming down specific spots – stomach, waist, thighs, hips, etc . . . and the following pages give you many alternatives to help all these areas. Exercise won't produce instant miracles – it takes at least three weeks or more of regular daily exercise to produce a noticeable change. And maybe you only need firming up, in which case inches lost are minimal. Some spots respond quicker than others. All exercises involve muscle control which draws your body inwards, giving you a better posture. If you're proud of your figure you'll carry it better, you'll walk with a springier, more jaunty air. Your total look: in top form.

*From the following pages
select about twelve exercises
and do them regularly every day
for only ten minutes.
You'll feel good, you'll look great.*

FLEXIBILITY

Before doing any exercises it's a good idea to get your body going and in the mood for more precise movement by doing a quick series of warm-ups. This whole routine can be done in five minutes and it should be done in continuous rhythm. Off you go!

1

1 To warm up, stand with legs apart, arms above head. Pushing your bottom out, bend over to touch the floor with your palms; swing upwards; bend over again, pushing your arms between your legs this time. Repeat ten times.

2 Sit on the floor, with your left leg straight, your right leg bent heel to bottom, clasping your right ankle with both hands. Straighten your leg, pulling up as high as possible; hold to the count of three; return to bent position. Repeat three times with each leg.

3 Sit upright, legs wide apart, arms outstretched at shoulder level; swing forward to touch your left foot with your right hand, then vice versa. Repeat twenty times in continuous rhythm.

4 Sit with your legs bent, soles together, heels against buttocks; clasp your hands over your feet and slowly bend over, aiming to touch your feet with your forehead; hold to the count of five; relax. Repeat three times.

5 Lie on your back with your legs straight; pull your right knee towards your chest, hold to the count of ten; slowly lower. Repeat three times. Do the same with the other leg.

2

3

4

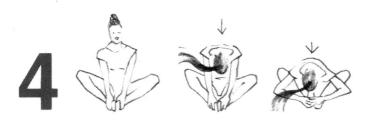

5

6 Lie on your back, arms at sides, palms down; raise your legs over your body, then lift yourself high and straight, supporting your body on your hands; push up, pointing your feet, and hold to the count of five; slightly bend your knees and lower to touch your forehead; uncurl and relax. Repeat three times.

7 Stand with your feet apart and link your hands behind head; keeping your elbows well back and your back straight, bend first to the right, then to the left. Repeat twenty times.

8 Stand with your feet apart, legs straight, arms curved over head; extend your right arm and bend over to the left, at the same time pushing your left arm down your left leg; hold to the count of five; return to starting position and repeat three times each side.

9 Stand with your legs a little apart and your hands clasped behind your back; lean backwards, throwing the head back, and then bend forwards, dropping your head and pushing your arms up as high as possible; hold to the count of five; return to standing position and repeat three times.

10 Stand on tiptoe, legs slightly apart, arms high over head; stretch up and then slowly curve the back forward, bend your knees, bring down your arms and lower your heels; relax completely. Repeat three times.

WAIST

Your waist dimensions are determined by your skeleton proportions. Muscle control is not involved here, but fat deposits can be whittled away with exercises that twist and turn the midriff area.

1 Sit with your legs as far apart as possible, feet flexed, back straight and arms held high. Inhale twisting to the right, exhale bending towards right leg; come up, and inhale twisting back to original position. Relax to the count of three. Four times each side.

2 Lie on back with your legs bent together, hands at sides, palms down. Stretch out your right arm and leg at the same time, toes pointed, fingers stretched. Hold to the count of five. Work alternate sides, six times each.

3 Starting with your feet apart, body bent, arms hanging down, turn to the right, making your left hand touch the right ankle, while bringing up your right arm; hold to the count of ten. Repeat on the other side. Work both sides six times each.

4 Stand with your feet apart, body at ease, arms at sides. Bend to the left from the waist, reaching down the left leg with the left arm and bending the elbow of the right arm to raise it a little. Push further down the leg, finally bringing the right arm over the head. Don't lean forwards, the movement is entirely sideways. Hold to count of ten. Do the same movement to the right. Repeat three times each side.

5 Start with your feet apart, knees slightly bent, arms held in front at shoulder level. Twist the torso from the waist up by swinging your arms to the right; count to five. Swing to the left; count to five. Repeat eight times. Now twist from the hips, bending the left knee when you go to the left, the right knee as you go to the right. The other leg is straight. Twist eight times on either side.

6 Sit with your legs spread wide, feet flexed, hands clasped over head. Bend forward and try to touch the left toes; push and bounce over leg six times. Return to starting position. Bend over to touch right toes; push and bounce six times.

BOSOM

No exercise routine will make your bust larger, but exercises can improve its shape and resilience. It is necessary to keep the pectoral muscles in good condition; these lie either side of and underneath the breasts.

1 Lie flat on your back, knees bent and hands clenched on your chest. Take a deep breath and then let it out slowly, pulling in the stomach muscles and at the same time stretching up one arm, hands unclenched, with fingers pushing up to the ceiling. Hold to the count of five.

2 Stand with your feet a little apart, arms bent and palms together in front of your chest. With your weight slightly forward, breathe in deeply and then exhale, pushing the palms hard together and consciously tightening your buttocks. Hold while you count five. Relax. Repeat six times.

3 Sit with your legs straight out in front, feet flexed, thighs taut. Hold your arms straight, thumbs turned inward. Inhale; then exhale, raising your arms; inhale again, lowering your arms in front of you, fists clenched, thumbs up; exhale, stretching your arms apart and back, keeping them at shoulder level. Repeat six times.

4 Fold your arms and grasp each arm below the elbow with the opposite hand. Push your hands towards the elbows – you'll feel your bosom muscles jerk. Push twenty times.

5

5 Lean forwards with your legs apart. Keeping your legs straight and your arms at shoulder level do ten crawl strokes with each arm.

6 Lie flat on your stomach with your arms bent, palms facing down under chest, chin on the floor. By pushing on your palms, slowly raise your head, then shoulders, then chest and finally upper abdomen if you can; hold the head back and count to ten.

6

STOMACH

This is an area where muscle control is absolutely essential. If your stomach muscles are well-toned, your stomach will be flat and remain so. Even when sitting, walking and standing you should consciously hold in these muscles.

1

1 Sit holding your bent left leg; contract the muscles of your stomach and buttocks. Then slowly curve the back and lower until your waist touches the floor; free your arms and stretch them out in front of you; breathe in and hold to the count of five. Lower your body three inches (8 cm) nearer the floor; then raise it. Repeat five times with each leg.

2 Lie flat on your back, head and shoulders on the floor, arms by your sides, palms down; bend your legs, raise your knees to your chest; slowly extend your legs, and then lower them and hold at 45°. Count three. Bend your legs back to your chest. Repeat six times.

2

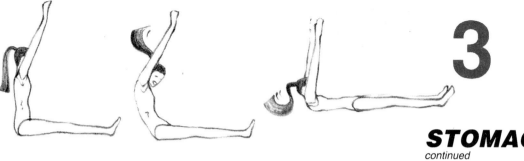

3

STOMACH
continued

3 Sit straight with your legs stretched out in front and your arms above your head. Inhale. Exhale, lowering your chin to your chest. Contract your stomach muscles and slowly lower yourself to the floor. Inhale and bring yourself back up to the starting position; repeat eight times.

4 Lying on your back, with your feet gripped under a couch and your hands folded on your stomach, raise and lower yourself three times. Relax to the count of ten. Repeat five times.

5 Lie on the floor, clasping your ankles, knees bent towards chest. Inhale, pulling in knees; then exhale, stretching out legs at an angle, feet flexed and arms stretched towards your ankles. Hold to the count of five, relax and return to starting position. Repeat five times.

6 Lie flat on the floor, legs straight and arms outstretched at shoulder level; raise your right leg, keeping the knee straight; slowly lower your leg to the right, aiming to touch your right hand. Hold to the count of five. Bring leg up and return to starting position. Repeat five times with each leg.

4

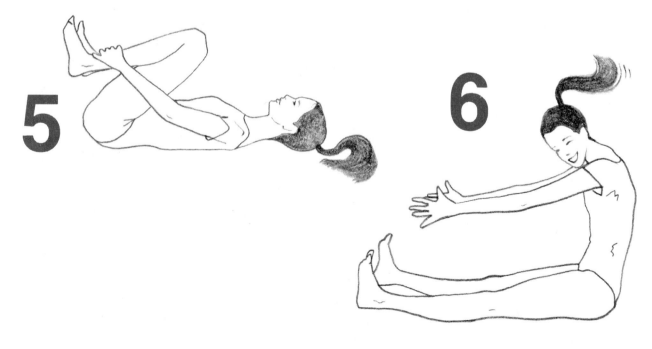

5

6

THIGHS

Most girls are inclined to put on weight between the knees and the hips — it is a natural biological fact. The exercises are intended to firm the fat rather than reduce it, as it is difficult to lose weight in this particular area, and excess dieting is never a good idea.

1 Lie on back, knees bent, arms flat at sides; raise your pelvis; hold to the count of three and then raise your left leg, extending it till straight, toes pointed; hold to the count of five; return to second position; repeat three times; relax. Do the same with the right leg.

2 Kneel on the floor, back straight, arms held out in front at shoulder level; tighten and pull in your bottom; slowly lean backwards as far as possible, feeling the pull on your thighs; hold to the count of five, return to vertical position. Repeat eight times.

3 Stand with your feet slightly apart and your arms straight, palms on front of thighs; go on tiptoe; then bend your knees, pushing outwards to a crouch position, and hold to the count of three; straighten your legs and lower your heels. Repeat ten times.

4 Kneel on all fours; bend your left knee, bringing it up to your chest, then push it backwards so that the leg is in a straight line with the back; hold to the count of five; without touching the floor again with your left knee, repeat ten times. Do the same with the other leg.

5 Lie on your back, legs up and together, arms by sides; keeping the knees straight, open your legs as wide as possible; hold to the count of five and then very slowly pull your legs together; repeat five times.

THIGHS
Continued

6 Crouch on tiptoe with your fingers touching the floor for balance and your body leaning forwards; stretch your right leg to the side and, turning from the hips, walk your hands to the right, pulling your head on to your right knee; hold to the count of five; return to first position. Repeat four times with each leg.

BEHIND

The shape of the buttocks can be improved with exercises. It is a matter of controlling the muscles at the top of the legs at the back and at the outer sides of the thighs. This helps prevent spreading of the upper thighs and will give your behind a tight, rounded line.

1 Lie on your stomach with your legs apart and your arms a little away from your body. Raise your right leg, keeping it straight, and hold to the count of five; bring up your left leg; with feet touching, bend your knees together and apart five times. Repeat with other leg.

2 Lie flat on your stomach, knees bent and apart, feet held together; push pelvis to floor, contracting your buttocks; without arching your back lift your knees and thighs off the floor. Hold to the count of ten, balancing your chin on your wrists. Return to the starting position and repeat six times.

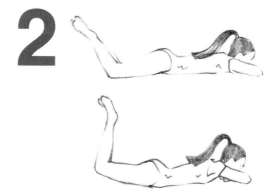

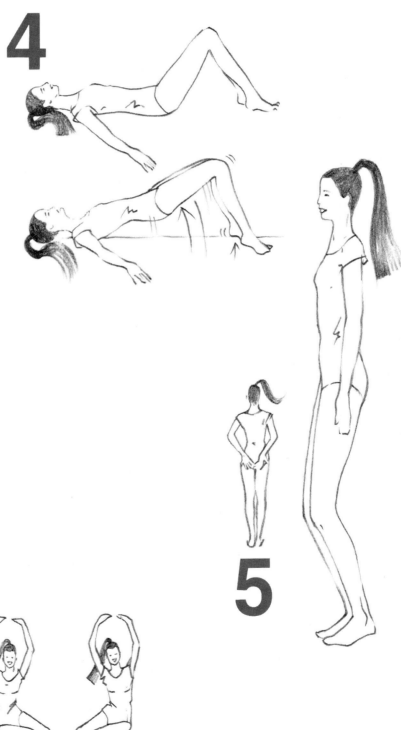

3 Lie on your right side with your knees tucked up in front of you; support your head with your right arm, balancing with your left. Stretch your left leg, foot flexed, in front of your body, lift it a few inches and hold to the count of three; repeat ten times; lift again and draw ten circles in the air. Repeat with each leg twice.

4 Lie on your back, knees bent, arms outstretched and palms down; raise your buttocks off the floor and raise your heels at the same time; hold to the count of five; lower; relax to starting position. Repeat ten times.

5 Stand with your feet parallel, a tiny bit apart. Using the muscles in front of your thighs, pull up knee caps. Place your palms over your buttocks and slowly draw the buttocks towards each other; when as tight as possible hold to the count of six; relax. Repeat six times.

6 Kneel on the floor with your arms arched overhead and lower your buttocks to touch the ground on the left; then swing to the right. Go back and forth ten times.

HIPS

One of the first places where fat is deposited is on the hips and it is only through regular exercises that they can be kept in trim. Most of the exercises use leg and hip swings which tighten the muscles and control the outline.

1 Lying flat on your back with your arms outstretched and your palms down, cycle in the air with your legs pedalling twenty-five times; consciously hold in your stomach muscles.

2 Lie on your back, arms outstretched at shoulder level, knees bent together at chest. Swing your knees, first to the left, then to the right, trying to touch the floor. Swing to each side ten times.

3 Lie on your right side with your right arm outstretched and your left arm in front of your chest for balance; raise your left leg and make two complete anticlockwise circles in the air, keeping your entire body straight; then make two clockwise circles. Repeat five times. Lie on your left side and do the same with the other leg.

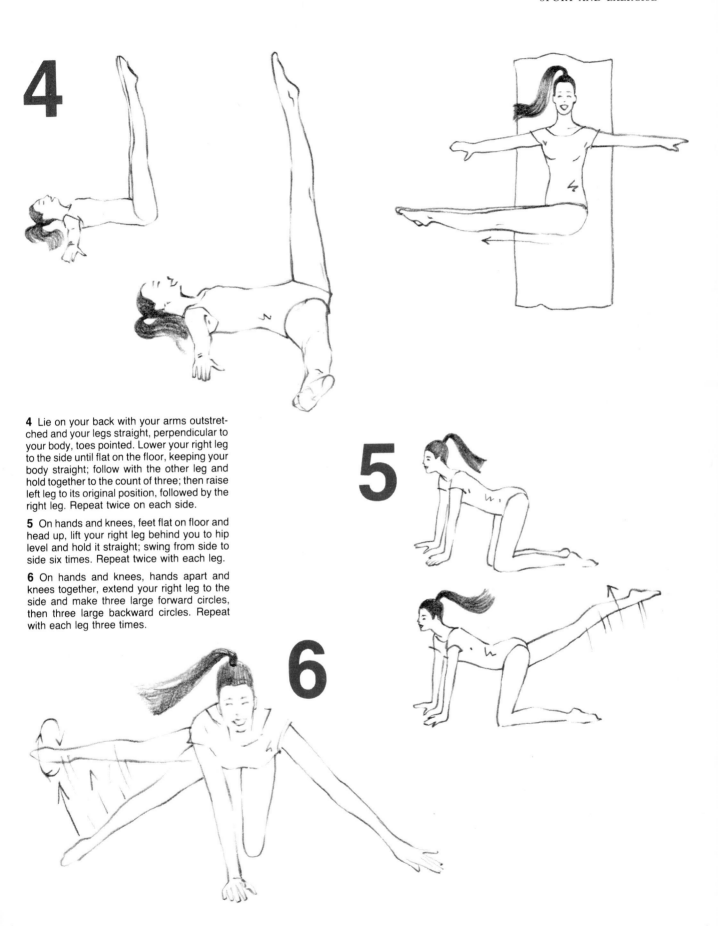

4 Lie on your back with your arms outstretched and your legs straight, perpendicular to your body, toes pointed. Lower your right leg to the side until flat on the floor, keeping your body straight; follow with the other leg and hold together to the count of three; then raise left leg to its original position, followed by the right leg. Repeat twice on each side.

5 On hands and knees, feet flat on floor and head up, lift your right leg behind you to hip level and hold it straight; swing from side to side six times. Repeat twice with each leg.

6 On hands and knees, hands apart and knees together, extend your right leg to the side and make three large forward circles, then three large backward circles. Repeat with each leg three times.

LEGS

The first thing to bear in mind is that the actual shape of your leg – the curve of your calf, the proportions of your ankle – cannot be altered. The leg exercises are intended to give flexibility and to trim the problem area round the knees where fatty deposits can start even in your teens.

1 Crouch down, knees bent, hands on floor, palms down; push your legs back, knees straight; hold to the count of five; return to the crouch position. Repeat ten times.

2 Lie on your left side, using your left arm to support your head and your right arm in front for balance; slowly raise your right leg as high as possible, keeping the knees straight and toes pointed; hold to the count of five; lower slowly and repeat ten times. Do the same on the other side with the other leg.

3 Place your foot on a support slightly higher than your hip; standing on tiptoe, raise your arms above your head and slowly bend forward to touch the toes of the raised leg; bring head to knee and hold to the count of five, remembering to keep both knees straight. Repeat three times with each leg.

4 Sit with legs spread wide, feet and knees out, palms on inside of thighs; raise your arms to shoulder level; bend your body forward, trying to clasp your ankles; hold to the count of ten; relax. Repeat five times.

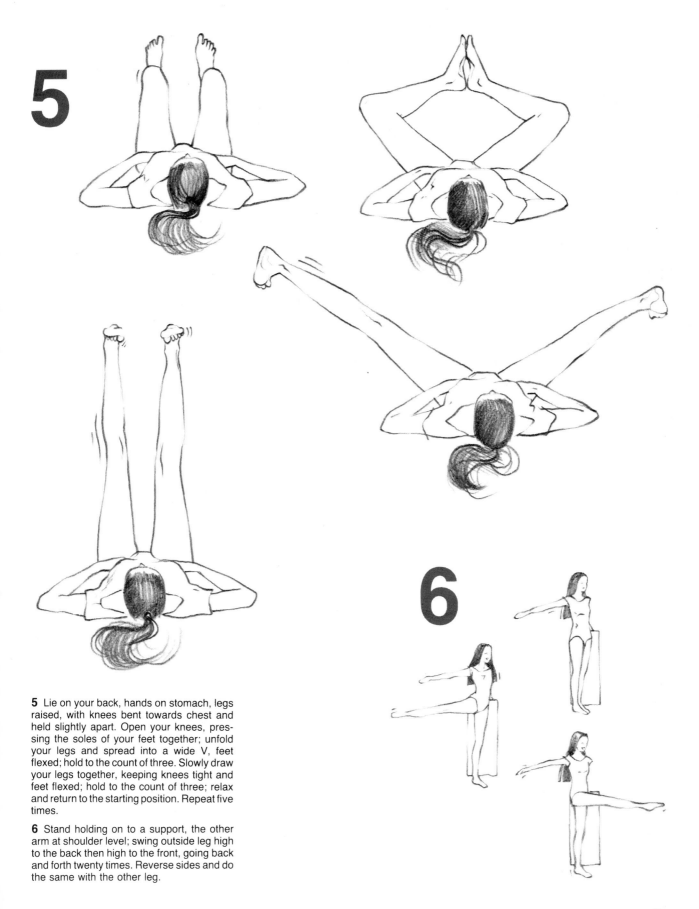

5 Lie on your back, hands on stomach, legs raised, with knees bent towards chest and held slightly apart. Open your knees, pressing the soles of your feet together; unfold your legs and spread into a wide V, feet flexed; hold to the count of three. Slowly draw your legs together, keeping knees tight and feet flexed; hold to the count of three; relax and return to the starting position. Repeat five times.

6 Stand holding on to a support, the other arm at shoulder level; swing outside leg high to the back then high to the front, going back and forth twenty times. Reverse sides and do the same with the other leg.

EATING RIGHT

For good looks you need good health, and for good health you need good food.

You are very much what you eat, and if the right eating habits are acquired during your adolescent years, you'll be set for life. You will also have no problem controlling your weight. There is no substitute for fresh produce: packaged, processed and convenience foods are never of the same nutritional value, no matter what anyone says.

The type and quality of food not only affects your health but also determines your vitality level, your moods and your thinking capacity. Adolescence is a time of swift and dramatic change; energy needs are at an all-time peak in order to cope with growth spurts and body development.

Energy is released when food is burnt up and the amount of energy a food produces is measured in calories. If you take in more food than you release as energy, you will store it as fat. A teenage girl needs between 2,100 and 2,400 calories a day. This varies depending on your height, bone structure and level of activity.

Don't make the mistake of thinking only in terms of calories. It is the type of food that's really significant. Sugar – sweets, chocolates, pastries, biscuits, jams, tinned fruits – provide calories but no nutrients whatsoever. Fats – butter, meat fat, oils – have twice as many calories as lean meat, fish, vegetables, grains and cereals yet have minimum nutrient value. A healthy balance of nutrients is very important during teenage years.

A HEALTHY APPETITE

Three things influence our eating pattern:
- *hunger*
- *appetite*
- *habit*

What makes us eat?

The body sends automatic hunger signals to the brain by which it indicates that eating is necessary. These pangs of hunger don't mean that you are starving for food, but that you are ready for more. You could easily live off stored fat for many days, and few people in western societies know the feeling of real hunger pains. The more you eat, the more your stomach expands and the more you want to eat.

Your appetite is stimulated by the sight, smell and taste of food. It is regulated by the brain, and you have probably often had a great longing for food when you smell something really good cooking.

Habit influences your choice of food. Eating habits date back to childhood when you obviously acquire the eating habits of your family. You probably eat more or less the same things all the time. Ice-cream, cakes and rich puddings are most likely special treats, yet these are not nutritious at all. To change eating habits is not easy, particularly when you're not doing the shopping or the cooking. But sit back and think about what you eat. Check with the 'Eat Right Guide' on pages 85–6. Is your daily diet anything like it? No? Well, try to change slowly, shifting the emphasis from the wrong foods to the right ones.

What should you eat?

Eating well is really a matter of ordinary common sense. Nature provides an abundance of food and if animals thrive on what is at hand, why shouldn't we? There is no need to tamper with food too much; the nearer the natural state the better the nutrients are. Refined products such as white flour and bread, white sugar and treated cereals are empty foods. So is everything made from them – sweets, pastries, cakes, biscuits, many puddings. Nutritionists divide food into three categories according to type and function: proteins, carbohydrates and fats. All provide energy and all have some vitamins and minerals, the two nutrients essential to life.

Proteins

These are found in meat, fish and poultry, in dairy products – milk, yogurt, cheese and eggs – in grains, nuts and seeds and in some vegetables, e.g. avocado pear. Proteins build and repair body tissue, provide energy, help the digestive system and supply essentials to the blood. In fact they have so many functions it's impossible to list them all.

Carbohydrates

There are three different types – sugars, starches and cellulose (fibrous matter). The sugars are fruits, honey and, of course, sugar; they provide energy quickly. The starches are the whole grains (and wholewheat bread), cereals, pasta and rice, root vegetables, such as potatoes, carrots, turnips, etc., beans, peas and other seed vegetables, such as lentils. All these are a source of heat and energy. The cellulose carbohydrates are most vegetables – stalk (celery), root (onions, fennel), leaf (cabbage, broccoli, cauliflower) and fruit (tomatoes, zucchini, cucumber). Fruits contain both cellulose and sugar carbohydrates. All the cellulose carbohydrates provide the bulk and fibre necessary for the digestive tract. Fibre is the structural part of a plant.

All carbohydrates are rich in vitamins and minerals. As long as your weight is OK, there's no such thing as eating too much of the carbohydrate foods. They are great foods, but make sure they are natural, fresh and non-refined.

Fats

There are two types of fat: saturated fats which are solid at room temperature and come mostly from animal sources – butter, lard, suet; unsaturated fats are liquid and come from vegetable sources – olive oil, corn and various seed and nut oils. For health it is better to limit animal fats (only a little butter on bread) and use the vegetable oils for salads, cooking and baking. Fats are stored in the body as reserve energy. They protect vital organs. They protect your body against cold and they act as carriers for fat-soluble vitamins.

What you should eat:

- fresh is best
- eat masses of vegetables and fruits
- eat fibre-rich foods and whole grains
- eat more fish than meat
- cut sugar to a minimum
- cut back on fat
- avoid processed and refined foods

EAT RIGHT GUIDE

Your basic daily plan

First the basics, then the frills; if you follow this guide you will be eating a well-balanced, healthy diet and getting all the essential nutrients. Select from the four main groups in the quantities indicated. Consider items in the fifth group as minimum additions – and only if you must. Out of habit you probably have cravings for cakes and sweets, but try to cut down on these. It's not only what you eat – when and how you do is also important. The rule is: sensible breakfast, hearty lunch, light evening meal.

Do you eat snacks instead of proper meals?

Fast, snack foods were originally designed as an occasional alternative to regular meals. Now they are often the staples of a teenage diet. Snack foods, chips, biscuits, sandwiches, cakes, waffles, etc. – are high in fats, sugars, calories, additives and salts. They are nearly always low in vitamins, minerals and fibre; they are usually heavily processed. Try to stop eating them. True, you can make a nutritious sandwich from whole-grain bread, a lean meat, cheese or eggs plus a salad – but make it, don't buy it packaged. Snacks should be just that – a nibble to keep you going between nourishing meals. Good snacks are fruit, cheese, raisins, nuts.

Muesli:

The best breakfast food

This is a recipe that comes from one of the leading health clinics in Switzerland. A big bowl of muesli will give you a nourishing breakfast – it's a meal in itself. Here's how you make it:

2 tablespoons oats
juice of ½ lemon
a little milk
2 tablespoons wheat germ
4 tablespoons water
2 tablespoons honey

Soak the oats overnight in water. In the morning add lemon juice, honey and wheatgerm, and mix well. Add the milk. Then on the top pile on any fresh fruit – shredded apple is particularly good. You can also add raisins, nuts and, finally, some natural yogurt. It's delicious.

Make time for breakfast

Starting the day with a good breakfast does count – it's not just mother nagging. Eating fruit in the morning wakes you up and it's more satisfying than juice. Try a whole orange, half a grapefruit, a cup of strawberries, half a melon. All these provide vitamin C. Soft-boiled eggs give you iron and the B vitamins. A chunk of cheese provides protein and calcium. Wholewheat bread and honey (plus a little butter) give you energy. A glass of milk contains protein and the B vitamins.

FOOD PLAN	AMOUNT
1. Vegetables and fruits	five servings daily
Vegetables: those with intense colour – bright greens and oranges are the most nutritious – broccoli, spinach, kale, sprouts, cabbage, green peppers, dark salad greens, alfalfa sprouts, turnips, carrots, potatoes with skin left on, tomatoes **Fruits:** the berry group are good food value – strawberries, blackberries, black currants, also apricots, the citrus fruits (orange, lemon, grapefruit) and peaches; also cantaloupe melon	A serving is about 1 cup of vegetables, which is the average vegetable portion. For fruits, one of medium size (apple, pear, orange, banana), a cup of berries, grapes, half a melon
2. Grains, cereals, beans and seeds	four servings daily
Grains: wholewheat bread, pasta, oats, brown rice **Beans and seeds:** all seed beans, fresh or dried, lentils	A serving is about 1 cup of cooked grains such as pasta or rice; ½ cup cooked oats, 2 slices of bread, ½ cup cooked beans or seeds.
3. Dairy products	three servings daily
Milk: hot or cold **Eggs:** raw or cooked **Cheese:** hard varieties, cottage cheese **Yogurt:** natural low-fat	A serving is a glass of milk, one egg, 2 oz (55 g) cheese, 1 carton yogurt
4. Meat, poultry, fish and nuts	two servings daily
Meat: liver, kidney, lean veal, lamb, beef **Poultry:** chicken and turkey **Fish:** number one choice in this group: all varieties, shellfish **Nuts:** peanuts, pine nuts, almonds, pistachios	A serving is 4–6 oz (115–70 g) of fish, poultry or lean meat, ½ cup nuts
5. Fats and sweets	minimum amount

These are pleasure foods and should be considered rewards only if you have included all the above basics. Foods in this group are high in calories and low in nutrients. Take a little butter for bread, sugar or honey if you need sweetening, vegetable oil for cooking and salads. Cakes and sweets should be rare treats.

FOOD FACTS

You are what you eat

Your diet and your eating habits are very important, for both your mental and your physical energy are affected by what you eat. So make sure that your diet contains enough of the essential nutrients. Even vegetarians can get a well-balanced diet with care.

To feed your brain you must eat at regular intervals

Everything you eat affects your brain and its capacity to function. Haven't you ever heard someone say 'fish is good for the brain'? Well, it is. Why? Because it is a particularly good source of protein with special elements that nourish the brain – and it is high in vitamin A.

The brain also needs a regular and even supply of glucose, which is its chief fuel. All carbohydrates (see chart, page 93) are converted into glucose. When meals are skipped glucose (more commonly called blood sugar) goes down and there is an immediate reaction in the brain. You might feel uneasy, nervous or weak. These symptoms are quickly reversed by eating some fresh fruit or drinking fruit juice. Don't suck a sweet, although you may have been told to do this. It merely provides false energy, depleting the body of vitamins. And vitamins are vital to the brain – if you eat right, you'll get enough.

For brain power eat a lot of fish, liver, kidney, citrus fruits and berries, green vegetables, whole-grain cereals, milk, cheese and eggs (but no more than six eggs a week).

What is energy and how do you get it?

You need more energy between the ages of twelve and sixteen than at any other time in your life. Energy is vitality. It is body power, both physical and mental, that enables you to move, to think, to accomplish things at a certain speed. Some people seem to have boundless energy, while others tire easily. It all has to do with what you eat because energy is directly related to your food intake.

The energy that your body runs on is measured as calories in your food. It doesn't matter what you eat or drink, everything has its calorific value. If these energy units are not used up right away, they are stored for the future.

A minute amount of energy is present in every cell ready for instant use. The bulk of your energy for immediate use is stored as glycogen (a starch) in the liver and muscles. Energy units are also stored as fat deposits – but the body uses this only when the instant energy sources are depleted. This is the reason why to lose weight you have to eat fewer calories in order to force the body to draw energy from your fatty deposits, thus burning them up.

Some foods provide faster energy than others. These are certain carbohydrates – the fruits, the whole-grain cereals and breads. Pure sugar in the form of sweets, cakes and chocolates may give you an initial spurt, but shortly afterwards you will feel tired and lethargic. Fat is the richest source of energy, but if you don't use it all up, the excess is stored as fat. It all comes down to

Some facts on sugar

- It's the number one enemy of good nutrition.
- To take in sugar, your body uses vital vitamins and minerals to fight the invasion.
- Excess sugar can make you tired and irritable.
- Sweets and chocolates are a habit acquired in childhood – learn to do without them.
- Sugar corrodes teeth – you'll need more fillings.
- Soft drinks are full of sugar – avoid them.
- You don't need to sweeten foods, most taste better without the addition of sugar.
- Liking sweet things is not natural – you have a sweet tooth because you eat sweet things regularly.
- We eat ten times as much sugar as we did a hundred years ago.
- Sugar is responsible for many diseases later in life.
- If you must sweeten food, use honey.

What about vitamin C?

A lack of this vitamin is especially harmful to young women because it is essential for iron absorption. It also helps combat virus infections. It is not stored in the body, so you must watch that each day you take foods that are good sources of vitamin C. These are: citrus fruits, watercress, broccoli, cabbage, green peppers.

one basic fact: if you eat more food than you burn up as energy, you will put on weight. The body of a healthy, slim young girl is usually 25 per cent fat.

Fibre – what it is; why it is so important

Fibre is the rough part of your food (in fact it used to be called roughage) that the body cannot digest. Nevertheless, it is very useful because it provides bulk, which means you often eat less because it fills you up. It also helps food to work its way faster through the digestive system; because it works like a sponge, absorbing water, it makes elimination from the bowels much easier. If you don't eat enough fibre foods your digestive system will suffer and because elimination of toxic matter is not made easy, you slowly poison your body. Good fibre foods are: whole-grain bread, bran, artichokes, blackberries, broccoli, apple with skin, beans, peas.

All about vitamins

Vitamins regulate body functions and that is why they are so important. If you are short on vitamins your body cannot perform properly. Vitamins are not body builders nor do they provide energy. They are rather like managers – busy telling everyone what to do and occasionally taking part themselves. They work as a team, which means that if one is deficient it may well affect the efficiency of the others.

There are sixteen known vitamins altogether and they are usually called by letters of the alphabet. This is because when first discovered their composition was unknown. Now they are often given chemical names, and the B group has many components, which have been revealed one by one over the years. New vitamins are being discovered and named but their properties and functions are not fully known.

Vitamins can help you to resist disease and scientists are now saying that they are probably our best protection against environmental stress and pollutants.

There are two groups of vitamins: those soluble in fat (A, D, E and K) which are stored in the fatty deposits of your body – these can always be called on for use; and those soluble in water (C and the many B vitamins) which must be taken in every day as, if not used, they leave your body in the urine.

If you take vitamins from fresh natural sources every day, you will get a perfectly adequate supply. Many people take vitamin pills, but if you eat right this is not necessary. It is very difficult to test for vitamin deficiency, as only when it is at an advanced stage do visible symptoms occur. Sailors, for example, used to suffer from scurvy (a skin disease) because they lacked fresh foods on long voyages – particularly vitamin C.

Most of the vitamins that we need come from the carbohydrate foods in our diet.

Minerals are necessary

It may come as a surprise to hear that we actually have minerals in our body. Well, we do, and we need them. They occur in minute quantities but they are

Lack of vitamin A is a teenage problem

If you live on snacks and don't eat right you're not going to get enough vitamin A. Eat every day either one dark green vegetable like broccoli or a deep yellow one such as turnip.

essential to body processes. They are not actually used by your body but their presence makes things happen – rather like a catalyst in a chemistry experiment. It is as though they are presiding over an operation and when it's done they contentedly leave the body through sweat or urine. They need to be replaced – but only by taking the right foods. Mineral supplements in capsule form can be very dangerous – the amounts required are so tiny and the dividing line between the required amount and an overdose is very fine. Minerals are obtained mostly from vegetables, grains and fruits – they come to you second-hand as the plants that provide the food extract the minerals from the soil.

What's a vegetarian?

If you are vegetarian, it means you eat no meat or fish at all. Why do people eat this way? There are two reasons: some vegetarians believe that a diet based solely on plant life is healthier; others that it is cruel to kill animals for food. It is actually quite possible to get all the nutrients you need from a vegetarian diet, though you have to watch what you eat very closely. For example, protein is essential in any diet and as this usually comes from animal foods, vegetarians must be sure that their daily intake includes sufficient protein. Dairy products provide protein, but some vegetarians (vegans) refuse to eat any food of animal origin – this means that all their food has to be of plant origin only and they need to be very conscious of the nutrients in food to be properly nourished.

You could be short on iron

Adolescent girls need more iron because of quick growth and the onset of menstruation. An insufficient supply can bring on fatigue and lack of energy; it can also contribute to overweight. You need liberal amounts of liver, kidney, shellfish, egg yolks and watercress.

WHAT DO YOU DRINK?

Water is the best, milk and juices are nutritious
Soft drinks are out

Liquid is the body's prime need. You could survive for weeks without food, but you can't survive more than a few days without water. Your body is actually nearly two thirds water by weight. Surprised? An adequate and regular fluid intake is vital for good health. You cannot drink too much water – any excess is quickly and efficiently removed by the kidneys and leaves the body as urine. It is good to drink at least a pint (three glasses) of water a day. If ordinary tap water seems dull, try the sparkling mineral waters or add a fizzy vitamin tablet to ordinary water. It all helps to keep your body free of any toxic food.

What about soft drinks?

There's nothing good to say about them except they are refreshing and taste rather nice. Nutritionally they are way down – most have added chemicals, colourings and flavourings. They also have a high sugar content, which encourages tooth decay. It is better to make your own juices and then add sparkling water, soda or tonic.

Warm drinks – which ones?

Tea, coffee or cocoa? All are stimulants, but tea wins out, particularly the herb teas which are healthy. Camomile tea can help digestion and induce sleep; peppermint tea also aids digestion but in addition revitalizes the mind. Better stay away from coffee; cocoa in milk is a nourishing breakfast or bedtime beverage.

Energy drinks

Pineapple crush

1 pt (6 dl) milk
8 oz (225 g) crushed fresh pineapple, chilled
2 fl oz (0.6 dl) fresh orange juice.
3 teaspoons lemon juice
liquid sweetener to taste

Combine pineapple with fruit juices and liquid sweetener. Add milk and stir well. Serve immediately.

Ginger water

1 large piece ginger root, peeled and grated
1 tablespoon honey
4 cups water
1 orange, sliced

Combine ginger, sugar and water. Refrigerate for 24 hours. Strain and discard pulp. Serve over crushed ice in sugar frosted punch cups. Garnish with an orange slice.

Lemon and ginger ale

2 large lemons
sweetener to taste
finely chopped mint
1 small bottle ginger ale

Peel the lemons, slice and mix with sweetener and chopped mint and 1½ cups boiling water. Allow to cool, pressing the lemon slices occasionally. Strain, add ginger ale. Stir and decorate with fresh lemon or lime slices.

Tropical special

3 oranges
1 grapefruit
2 lemons
liquid sweetener
1 bottle (7½ fl oz, 2 dl) low-calorie tonic water
crushed ice

Squeeze juice from fruit into a jug, add sweetener and tonic water. Mix and pour on to ice when serving.

Fruit punch

juice of 4 oranges
juice of 2 lemons
juice of 1 small grapefruit
1 tablespoon clear honey
2 bottles (7½ fl oz, 2 dl) soda water
some orange segments

Mix together the citrus fruit juices and stir in the honey. Chill for 1 hour. Add soda water and orange segments.

Chocolate milk

2 pints (1.1 l) fresh skimmed milk
1 cup dried skimmed milk
2 tablespoons olive oil
1 tablespoon carob powder or 2 tablespoons cocoa

Mix in a blender.

Peanut milk

1 cup milk
1 cup plain yogurt
1 banana
1 tablespoon peanut butter

Combine and mix in a blender.

Extra protein milk

1 egg yolk
½ pint (3 dl) milk
2 teaspoons olive oil
1 tablespoon wheat germ
1 teaspoon honey

Beat the egg yolk into the milk and slowly add the other ingredients. It is more easily done in a blender.

Raspberry milk

1 oz (30 g) blackberry juice
1 oz (30 g) raspberry juice
¼ pint (1.5 dl) milk
1 teaspoon honey
1 teaspoon grated lemon rind

Mix in a blender, leave for 30 minutes and serve cold.

DIETING

***Adolescent girls often put on a good deal of fat,
but usually grow out of it by the late teens***

During teenage years, a healthy balance of nutrients is the most important thing, so if you are less than 15 lb (6.8 kg) overweight you should not try to limit calories strictly. Instead you should eat a well-balanced and nutritious diet (following the Eat Right Guide on pages 85–6) and step up exercise. A moderate programme like this means you get the necessary nutrients for growth and development, and your extra poundage is gradually adjusted to your new proportions.

There is no magic formula for avoiding overweight; you need to eat as much food as you burn, and no more. To lose weight you have to decrease your food intake and increase your energy output through physical activity.

Gradual weight loss is best. Drastic diets are harmful and, what's more, they don't stabilize your weight either. Dieting is a very individual matter; you may react one way to a special regime, while your friend has a completely different result. There is no perfect diet that is good for everyone, nor is there any wonder food or formula that will do the trick. Losing weight and changing your shape is usually a matter of revising your eating habits rather than cutting down on food. If you are eating healthy foods you won't put on weight. It's the sweets, the snacks, the processed foods, the soft drinks, the white breads, that make you fat.

WHAT IS OVERWEIGHT

***You don't need to measure it or check with a chart –
a good honest look in the mirror will tell you***

You know if you are carrying around too much fat. You can see it, you can feel it. Actual pounds and inches are not always true indicators. What's your frame like? Do you have big bones, long limbs? Are your hands tiny, fingers slender? Bones make up about one sixth of your weight. Big-boned girls often need a fair amount of flesh covering otherwise they look gawky and awkward. Teenage bodies usually settle down at around sixteen years; before this time you should be concerned only with obvious fatness. You are going to get rounder and curvier simply because you are developing into a woman. So don't diet because of that. But do watch the type of food you eat. The rules remain the same whether you are on a diet or not; fattening foods are fattening foods no matter who's eating them and what size you are. So follow the guide-lines.

Weight can fluctuate each day – you usually weigh more in the evening. It also changes according to your menstrual cycle – you are usually heavier and inclined to be bloated just before you menstruate.

No to fattening snacks:
  sweets
  chocolates
  cakes
  biscuits
  ice-cream
  potato chips
  carbonated drinks

Yes to nourishing snacks:
  cheese
  raisins
  fruit
  fruit juice
  vegetable juice
  peanut butter

Why are you fat?

Excess food is stored as fat. If you are overweight it is because at some time or other you have eaten more food than you need. Overfeeding in childhood, family habits of eating the wrong foods, indulging children in treats such as cakes, sweets, chocolates and rich desserts, may all eventually produce a weight problem.

Glandular function also has some influence, as it controls the balance of food metabolism. The thyroid gland is particularly significant. It can produce too much hormone, thus causing cells to metabolize so fast that food is burnt up as fast as it goes in. Accordingly, high-thyroid girls are usually thin and nervous. On the other hand, too little thyroid production means slow metabolism; cells cannot keep up with the intake of food, energy output is low and the body stores food as fat.

Water and weight

You may be a little overweight because you retain more water than you need. There is a lot of water in the body and the balance is mainly controlled by salt. You need a precise amount in your body – no more, no less. If too much salt is taken, water accumulates, the tissues swell up and you weigh too much. You only need about one gramme of salt a day. Most of us eat ten to twenty times as much. So cut down on salt.

When on a diet it is necessary to understand the difference between loss of fat and loss of water. Usually the water goes first, resulting in a magical loss of weight overnight.

But if you drink a lot of water it doesn't mean you are going to retain it – actually it's quite the opposite. Water washes right through you, taking with it any toxic matter. When dieting, you should drink eight glasses a day – it's very good for your kidneys.

Food in – energy out = fat deposited
If you eat more than you expend in energy you will put on weight

This is the simple equation of overweight. The amount of energy released by burning up food is measured in units called calories. The principle of all diets is based on the balance of food intake with energy output. The three food groups – protein, carbohydrates, fat – react differently. Excess fat not burned off is stored as fat; excess carbohydrate is also stored as fat; protein makes the body burn its fuel more quickly.

How quickly can you change shape?

It takes six weeks for your new body to work out its final shape. When you diet you seem to lose fat from the head down. This means that when you start a diet you usually lose weight in your face, arms and breasts first, then in your waist, hips, stomach and legs. But once you have lost weight and kept it off, your body starts to move fat around and redistribute it. After six weeks you'll find your face getting fuller again, your hips slimming down. It's then that your new shape appears – keep it in form by sensible eating and an exercise programme.

Why are we the fatter sex?

There is no question that women are more prone to fat than men. This emerges even during teenage years. Female hormones are fat-producing and fat-hoarding – and have fluid-retaining properties. Also a woman is biologically constructed to bear babies, so there's always a layer of fat ready and waiting in case the foetus needs extra food, protection or warmth. In addition, women require fewer calories than men because more calories are needed for the large muscle mass in a male.

Watch your foods – know your foods

Check these lists and use as a basis for any diet. Some foods should be stopped, others taken every now and then. Altogether it means you'll be eating in a healthier way even if you sometimes eat too much.

THUMBS DOWN	PAY ATTENTION	THUMBS UP
Sugar carbohydrates **sugars:** all types, glucose, sweets, chocolate, spreads, sweet sauces, confectionery decoration **pastries:** biscuits, cakes, pies, tarts **preserves:** jams, marmalade, jellies **fruit:** tinned, candied or preserved in any way **Starch carbohydrates** **breads:** all white breads, rolls, buns, breadcrumbs **cereals:** white flour, refined grains and cereals, puddings, flour sauces **vegetables:** dried or tinned, cream soups **Fats** **sauces:** all cream ones like mayonnaise, unless freshly made with oil, bottled sauces and relishes **delicatessen foods:** processed meats, pâtés, sausages, processed cheese	**Starch carbohydrates** **bread:** wholewheat varieties, any made from unrefined grains **cereals:** natural oats, unprocessed rice and grains, whole-grain flour **Cellulose carbohydrates** **root vegetables:** potatoes, turnips, parsnips, white onions, beetroot **pod vegetables:** peas, beans **fruits:** some tropical varieties – bananas, water melons, avocado pears **Fats** **dairy produce:** butter, margarine, milk, cream **Protein** **meat:** ham, bacon, pork **dairy produce:** cheese made from cows' milk, eggs **poultry:** goose, duck **nuts:** all varieties	**Proteins** **fish:** fresh- and salt-water fish, shellfish **meat:** beef, veal, lamb, pork, liver, kidney, heart, brains, sweetbreads, tripe **poultry:** chicken, turkey **game:** venison, pheasant, quail, guinea fowl, rabbit **cheese:** made from goats' milk, mozzarella, feta, cottage cheese **Cellulose carbohydrates** **leaf vegetables:** artichokes, asparagus, broccoli, brussels sprouts, cabbage, cauliflower, celery, chicory, endive, kale, lettuce, all salad greens, spinach, watercress **root vegetables:** spring onions, radishes, carrots **fruit vegetables:** tomatoes, peppers, aubergines, courgettes, cucumbers, marrows **fruits:** citrus – lemons, oranges, grapefruit, tangerines; berry – raspberries, strawberries, blackberries, bilberries, cranberries, gooseberries, currants (black and red); orchard – apples, pears, plums, apricots, peaches, cherries, grapes; tropical – mangoes, papaya, pineapples, cantaloupes, figs **Fats** vegetable oils: olive, soya, unsaturated fats

SPECIAL TEENAGE DIET

1,500 calories a day; sugar is cut out, fats are cut down

If you are really overweight, try this special teenage diet. You should lose 2–7 lb (0.9–3.2 kg) a week, depending on how overweight you are and how much food you usually eat. Some of the initial weight loss is water. You will lose more the first week. A weekly weight loss of 2 lb (0.9 kg) means you are doing well. Stop when you reach your ideal weight.

Foods to include every day

1 pint (6 dl) skimmed milk
5 oz (140 g) lean, well-trimmed meat, poultry or fish
3 servings vegetables – at least one green or yellow

1 portion each of potato and pasta
3 servings of fruit – at least one citrus
4–6 slices of whole-grain bread or servings of cereal
6 teaspoons margarine or oil

Foods to have

Dairy products: skimmed milk, low-fat yogurt, three eggs or less a week, skimmed milk cheeses such as cottage cheese
Meats, fish, poultry: lean beef, veal, pork, lamb, ham; chicken or turkey; white non-fat fish
Grains: preferably whole-grain varieties of rice, pasta, bread

Vegetables: potatoes, green-leaf varieties, pods and seeds
Fruit: all fresh fruits, particularly citrus varieties, limited amount avocado
Nuts: all except cashew and macadamia nuts
Fats: margarine, vegetable oils
Beverages: tea, coffee, skimmed milk, fruit and vegetable juices

Foods to avoid

Dairy products: whole milk, cream, cream cheese, cheeses made with whole milk
Meats, fish, poultry: bacon, sausages, luncheon meats, poultry skin, frozen and packaged dinners, convenience foods
Grains: white breads, sweet biscuits,

cakes, pastry, commercial crackers
Fruits: tinned varieties
Fats: butter, lard, suet, dripping
Beverages: whole milk, sweetened carbonated drinks

Cooking rules

Don't fry anything. Grill, roast or poach meat, poultry, fish and eggs. Don't overcook vegetables, eat as many raw as

you can. If you don't use your margarine allowance on your bread you can use it in cooking.

Suggested meal plan

Breakfast
fruit or juice
whole-grain cereal or whole-grain bread or toast (1 or 2 slices), 2 teaspoons margarine, 1 teaspoon honey or preserves
coffee, tea, water, milk – honey for sweetening

Lunch
2 oz well-trimmed meat, poultry or fish
potato or pasta
vegetable and salad

fruit or yogurt
1 slice whole-grain bread
coffee, tea, water, milk

Dinner
3 oz well-trimmed meat, poultry or fish
potato or pasta
vegetable or salad
fruit
1 slice whole-grain bread
1 teaspoon oil for salad
coffee, tea, water, milk

MORE ABOUT DIETING

Don't try to lose weight too quickly – if you need to go on a diet, choose one that is well balanced

Drastic dieting can be harmful, particularly for teenagers who are still growing and developing. It is much better to lose weight gradually by changing your eating habits – and keeping them changed.

Avoid crash diets

They are not a good way to lose weight. Although you can shed a lot of pounds in a few days, they quickly go back on again and you often end up fatter than you were in the first place. Crash diets are usully undertaken as an emergency measure – a last desperate effort to look good for a holiday, a date or a special party. Your body is put under considerable stress and you are probably not getting the minerals, vitamins and proteins your body needs. It makes better sense to use a crash diet as an encouraging start to a long-tern dietary plan. For teenagers, a two-day banana drink diet is the one that can be safely undertaken. But don't continue with it for longer than two days (see box).

You can have this drink four times a day and, if you like, have one cup of tea or coffee as well.

Stay away from pills and diet foods
Such short cuts can be harmful

Obviously one way to eat less is to curb your appetite. There are pills that do this – called appetite suppressants. They act on your central nervous system and get to the centres of appetite control in the hypothalamus. They also stimulate mental and physical activity. The snag is that not only do you put on weight very quickly after stopping such drugs, but they can be addictive, which causes a withdrawal problem.

Slimming pills are widely available – their active ingredient is nearly always a laxative. Laxatives will get weight off temporarily due to loss of water and malabsorption of food, but the ensuing thirst usually puts back weight in the form of water desperately needed by the dehydrated body. Constant use of diuretics and purgatives can harm you.

Packaged diet foods – biscuits, liquid meals – are low calorie but contain large amounts of stomach filler. This is harmless cellulose but it expands and fills up the stomach, so that you feel you have had a reasonable meal. Protein and vitamins are added, but these foods often lack essential nutrients.

One of the best ways of dieting: Weight Watchers

For anyone who is very overweight and with minimum will-power to go it alone, there is the Weight Watchers organization. It's a long-term plan with

---

Banana drink: OK for two days:

1 banana
juice of 2 large oranges
1 teaspoon liquid honey
juice of 1 lemon

Mix well, then add 1 banana finely sliced. Mix together – put in a blender if you can.

You can have this drink four times a day and, if you like, have one cup of tea or coffee as well.

Diet with a friend

It's easier, it's a challenge

Going on a diet with someone else helps you to stick to it. Firstly you can eat together and not feel deprived looking at others. You can discuss your meals and work them out together. You are also less likely to cheat because you wouldn't like your friend to lose more weight than you, would you? Finally, you can exercise and do some sport together to help burn off extra calories. Dieting in twos or threes does work. Try it.

an average loss of 2 lb (0.9 kg) a week. What makes it work is the attendance at weekly meetings, where you are measured, weighed and encouraged to continue. Teenagers are welcome; don't be embarrassed, because everyone there has one thing in common – fat. It's very friendly and stories are exchanged about food and weight problems. You are given monthly food charts. Food is controlled by quantity, not calories, and has to be weighed exactly on a postage scale. All rules must be followed to a T. Off the list completely are the sugar carbohydrates; fats are at a minimum; cooking is steaming, boiling and grilling, absolutely no frying.

On the opposite page is a week's plan from the Weight Watchers programme and as you can see, it makes for substantial and varied fare. You must have 1 pint (6 dl) skimmed milk a day and you may add seasonings and a reasonable amount of low-calorie drinks.

There's such a thing as too much dieting. A wish to be too thin is a disease that can seriously affect health

To be too thin is as dangerous to your health as it is to be too fat. An obsession with being thin is a psychological problem leading to a condition known as *anorexia nervosa* – an extremely serious disease.

Slimness is often pursued for the wrong reasons. Excess weight is unhealthy, but so is extreme slimness. The lean and slender form has come to symbolize beauty and desirability, mainly because fashion magazines show clothes on very thin girls. But these girls only look good on the pages of a magazine – in real life, they look skinny and not nearly so attractive as you might think. You don't look good when you are too thin. Nor are you very attractive.

One out of a hundred teenage girls plunges into a diet so rigorous that it will seriously impair health – all with the intention of becoming ultra-slim. It starts off innocently enough with the desire to lose a little weight, but it then becomes compulsive and food is avoided at all costs. This is when the mind takes over – you are terrified of your body getting fat, you believe even a morsel of food will produce fat, you are happy that you can control your body in this way. In fact the feeling of control goes further, because once your mind is set on this course, you start to believe you can control many aspects of life because you have shown such control over your body.

No degree of thinness is thin enough; the next step is a refusal to eat almost any solid food and taking a minimum amount of fluids. There is a constant fear that just one bite of food can mean the start of an eating binge. If food is indulged in at this point, you'll force yourself to be sick.

Side-effects are bad. Periods can cease, hair can fall out, skin becomes dry to the extent of being almost too sore to wear clothes. At this point hospitalization is necessary to recoup the body and psychiatric help is necessary to readjust the mind. It can take months to cure and there's always a chance of a relapse. Some girls never recover and literally starve to death. So watch out for any feelings about wanting to be too thin.

BREAKFAST	LUNCH	DINNER
Monday		
4 fl oz (1.1 dl) orange juice 1 egg, poached 1 slice (1 oz, 30 g) bread 1 teaspoon margarine ½ pint (3 dl) skim milk	3–4 oz (85–115 g) chicken 3 oz (85 g) mixed salad 1 teaspoon mayonnaise 2 slices (2 oz, 55 g) bread 1 medium apple ½ pint (3 dl) skim milk	4–6 oz (115–170 g) white fish 3 oz (85 g) peas 1 slice (1 oz, 30 g) bread 1 teaspoon margarine 1 medium orange ½ pint (3 dl) skim milk
Tuesday		
4 oz (115 g) grapefruit segments 1 oz (30 g) uncooked cereal 1 slice (1 oz, 30 g) bread 1 teaspoon margarine ½ pint (3 dl) skim milk	3–4 oz (85–115 g) grilled liver 3 oz (85 g) cauliflower 2 slices (2 oz, 55 g) bread 1 teaspoon margarine 1 small pear 1 pint (3 dl) skim milk	4–6 oz (115–170 g) chicken 3 oz (85 g) carrots 3 oz (85 g) rice 1 teaspoon margarine 1 medium apple ½ pint (3 dl) skim milk
Wednesday		
1 medium orange 1 oz (30 g) hard cheese 1 slice (1 oz, 30 g) bread ½ pint (3 dl) skim milk	3–4 oz (85–115 g) beefburgers 3 oz (85 g) mixed salad 2 teaspoons mayonnaise 1 (2 oz, 55 g) bap 1 medium apple ½ pint (3 dl) skim milk	4–6 oz (115–170 g) tinned fish 3 oz (85 g) tomatoes 1 slice (1 oz, 30 g) bread 1 teaspoon margarine 1 small pear ½ pint (3 dl) skim milk
Thursday		
4 fl oz (1.1 dl) orange juice 1 oz (30 g) uncooked cereal 1 slice (1 oz, 30 g) bread 1 teaspoon margarine ½ pint (3 dl) skim milk	1 hard-boiled egg 1 oz (30 g) hard cheese 3 oz (85 g) mixed salad 2 slices (2 oz, 55 g) bread 1 teaspoon margarine 1 medium apple ½ pint (3 dl) skim milk	4–6 oz (115–170 g) white fish 3 oz (85 g) green beans 3 oz (85 g) potatoes 1 teaspoon margarine 2 small tangerines ½ pint (3 dl) skim milk
Friday		
½ medium grapefruit 1 egg, scrambled 1 slice (1 oz, 30 g) bread 1 teaspoon margarine ½ pint (3 dl) skim milk	3 oz (85 g) smoked fish 3 oz (85 g) mixed salad 1 teaspoon mayonnaise 2 slices (2 oz, 30 g) bread ½ teaspoon margarine 1 medium orange ½ pint (3 dl) skim milk	4–6 oz (115–170 g) lamb chops 3 oz (85 g) cabbage 1 slice (1 oz, 30 g) bread ½ teaspoon margarine 1 medium apple ½ pint (3 dl) skim milk
Saturday		
4 fl oz (1.1 dl) grapefruit juice 1 oz (30 g) uncooked cereal 1 slice (1 oz, 30 g) bread 1 teaspoon margarine ½ pint (3 dl) skim milk	5 oz (140 g) cottage cheese 3 oz (85 g) mixed salad 1 teaspoon mayonnaise 2 slices (2 oz, 55 g) bread ½ teaspoon margarine 1 small pear ½ pint (3 dl) skim milk	4–6 oz (115–170 g) beef sausages 3 oz (85 g) cauliflower 3 oz (85 g) sweetcorn ½ teaspoon margarine 1 medium orange ½ pint (3 dl) skim milk
Sunday		
4 fl oz (1.1 dl) grapefruit juice 1 egg, boiled 1 slice (1 oz, 30 g) bread 1 teaspoon margarine ½ pint (3 dl) skim milk	3–4 oz (85–115 g) chicken 3 oz (85 g) carrots 2 slices (2 oz, 55 g) bread 1 teaspoon margarine 1 medium apple ½ pint (3 dl) skim milk	4–6 oz (115–170 g) haddock 3 oz (85 g) tomato 1 slice (1 oz, 30 g) bread 1 teaspoon margarine 1 small pear ½ pint (3 dl) skim milk

LOOKING GOOD AND FEELING GREAT

GIORGIO E. VALERIO LARI

SKIN

The impression you give depends more on the look of your skin than you probably realize.

When you think about it, skin does literally cover every part of you, so the state and condition of it is of major importance. To have great-looking skin is an enviable asset. You are born with a certain type of skin and there's nothing you can do to alter the basics. Texture and colour are genetically determined, but the appearance and behaviour of the skin depends upon your individual metabolism and on the amount of care and attention you give it.

During adolescence, skin goes through a tricky stage, because at this time the hormones, generated by the sex glands, begin to make their presence felt. The look and condition of your skin depends entirely on the mix of these hormones. Both sexes have a combination of male and female hormones: androgen, the male hormone, which triggers the release of more oil, enlarging the pores and therefore making the skin look coarser, and oestrogen, the female hormone, which minimizes oil output and gives the skin a finer, less porous look. Between twelve and sixteen your skin is in transition while your body tries to work out the right hormone balance. At first there is usually too much of the male hormone, which means that the outpouring of oil leads to a constantly oily skin with its resultant blackheads, blocked pores and spots. The teenage years are not always happy ones for skin, but there's a lot you can do to control and counteract problems.

WHAT IS YOUR TYPE?

How you care for your skin depends on its texture, its colour and its condition

Examine your skin closely in strong light; if you can, use a magnifying glass to get a really good look. You have to determine whether it's oily or dry, whether you are fair or dark skinned, whether you have blemishes or not.

Texture: oily, dry or balanced?

Most teenagers have an *oily* skin, caused by over-production of sebum by the oil glands. Darker skins are often worse affected than light ones. An oily skin shines constantly and has enlarged pores. It is often plagued with blackheads, spots and acne.

Light skins are sometimes *dry*, but rarely during adolescence – it is when a fair skin is mature that dryness becomes a problem. Dry skin is generally of a fine texture but looks and feels tight; it chaps, flakes and peels easily.

A *balanced* texture is ideal but rare; it exists only when oil, moisture and the skin's acid mantle are all in harmony. Your skin simply looks perfect.

Colour: light, medium, dark?

The colour of your skin depends on the degree of pigmentation – and that depends on heredity. Light skin tones are graded from pale to pink, beige to rosy; dark skin tones go from olive to caramel, brown to black. The term 'black' covers a much wider range than 'white' – one skin specialist came up with thirty-five variations of black skin and only ten of white. There is no difference in structure and quality, and therefore no difference in how you take care of your skin, although black skin is inclined to be oilier and has more sweat glands.

Condition: sensitive or blemished?

If you have dry skin it is often sensitive and reacts quickly to climate extremes of heat, cold and wind, and you need to watch out for allergic reactions. Oily skin is often blemished – it is troubled with pimples and some degree of acne.

Some facts about skin

- It is the body's largest organ, weighing approximately 6 lb (2.7 kg).
- It acts as a thermostat, retaining heat or cooling the body with its sweat glands.
- It absorbs the shock of blows to the body.
- It is a protective covering, guarding the body against bacteria, chemicals and foreign objects.
- It breathes, contains blood vessels, sebaceous gland ducts, nerves and hair follicles.
- It is constantly growing and dead cells are shed, allowing the new ones to come to the surface.
- It varies in thickness over the body – the thinnest part is around the eyes where it's approximately one fiftieth of an inch (0.5 mm) thick, the thickest part is on palms and soles where it's nearer to a quarter of an inch (6 mm) thick.

TAKING CARE OF YOUR FACE

What count most are the simple basic things you do each day; skin needs to be kept clean and moist and there's nothing to equal soap and water

Body skin more or less takes care of itself through bathing and an occasional application of body lotion. Facial skin is more fragile and vulnerable, so its needs are special. The main thing about taking care of your skin is not to disturb its normal functioning any more than you have to. Keeping your skin in good condition often means doing less, not more. Many girls are lured by beauty preparations which claim to be essential for good skin. It's not so – certainly not during adolescence. Your skin should be kept free to develop on its own. Of course, spots and blemishes need special care, but basic everyday needs are minimal. Your skin should be washed with soap and water, freshened sometimes with a liquid toner and moisturized sometimes; you should also occasionally get rid of the dead surface cells. And that's it – so don't let anyone persuade you that you need a collection of preparations; you don't.

Step-by-step basic care

Now is the time to establish the good habits which will help your skin look its best, now and in the future.

Remove any eye make-up
If you use eye make-up you will have to remove this first with a little oil – put it either on a cotton wad or directly on the eye and then wipe off with cotton wool or a tissue. Don't buy a special eye make-up remover; ordinary baby oil is absolutely fine.

Now to the soap and water
Any ordinary soap does a very good job of cleansing the skin. Most soaps are mild, but particularly good are the non-alkaline soaps which are now made by many cosmetic houses and are called 'facial soaps' or 'soap bars'. They are really good, though they may seem terribly expensive. However, as you only use them on your face they last up to six months. Don't use too much of any soap. It's not likely that your face will be filthy. Work up a light lather.

Rinse and rinse and rinse
This is even more important than the soap. Soap can never harm your skin during the few minutes of washing, but it must be thoroughly rinsed away – a dried-up surface of soap is bad for your skin. Splash cool clear water on your face many times, until it squeaks.

Rose-water moisturizing lotion

5 tablespoons glycerine
3 tablespoons rose water

Pour into a bottle and shake very well each time you use it.

Rose-water and witch-hazel toner

1 cup rose water
½ cup witch hazel
Simply combine and shake in a bottle.

Cider-vinegar toner

1½ cups distilled water
1 teaspoon cider vinegar
Shake well in a bottle.

Dab dry with a towel

Never rub your face as though you were polishing silver. Remember your facial skin is delicate, so use a gentle touch whatever you're doing. Let the towel just soak up the water.

Special treatment 1: if your skin is oily

If you have spots or pimples, it's a good idea to wipe the skin with a 'toner'. This cleans away any last bit of dirt or soap and also restores what is known as the 'acid mantle' of the skin. This is a natural protective covering that helps fight bacteria. You can use simple toners without investing in special ones. One of the best is witch hazel, which is readily available at any chemist's. Soak a cotton wad and wipe all over the face. You'll see how fresh your face feels. There are two other toners you can make at home (incidentally, commercial toners are also known as fresheners or astringents).

Special treatment 2: if your skin is dry

You can also use these toners to cleanse the skin completely, and then apply just a little of any standard face cream. Do this only if your skin is particularly dry; otherwise just rub in a moisturizer.

Start to use a moisturizer

This is the only skin preparation you should use in your early teens. It is very important to keep your skin moist – that means retaining a certain amount of water in your skin cells, keeping skin supple, smooth and in its best working order. Look for a simple, inexpensive moisturizer. Actually the word 'moisturizer' is a misnomer, for the product doesn't give moisture to the skin, but puts a film on the surface that helps to seal in the skin's natural moisture. Moisturizers are invisible, so you don't look as though you have anything on your face. In general, the moisturizing lotions are lighter than the creams. Try the various products to see which one is best. A moisturizer is applied after washing and, if you do it, after using a toner. Just dab a little on chin, forehead, nose and cheeks, then gently rub in until it disappears. There's no need to use much. A moisturizer is not a must unless you have dry skin, but it helps to prevent dry skin and it can only do good to normal and oily skins. It is the first skin preparation you should try. You can make a very good one yourself:

Every two weeks get rid of 'dead' cells

Because your skin is constantly renewing itself, you sometimes get a collection of dry, dead cells on the surface. If you can get rid of these, there is less chance of surface blockage and therefore less chance of spots. There's a very simple way to do this – and it's a method used by many famous beauty salons. All you need is a face cloth and some ordinary kitchen salt. Soak the face cloth in warm water, sprinkle salt on it and gently rub over your entire face – your clean face, as this should be done directly after washing with soap and rinsing. You only need to rub a few times, then rinse all the salt away in clear water. Now feel your skin. Isn't it very smooth? It may look a little red, because the rubbing has increased your circulation. But you have completely cleared your skin of all debris – pores are clear, your skin is breathing. You'll be surprised how this salt-rubbing can help minor blemishes and make your skin look alive. If you have acne, don't rub hard, but a very gentle scrub with salt every now and then can do some good.

How often should you wash your face?

The answer is: whenever it's dirty. However, you may think your face is dirtier than it is. Two or three times a day is enough, but if you play sports, you'll need to clean and refresh your face more often. But don't overdo it; as far as your skin is concerned, there is no advantage in washing it very often – it's your personal standards that are in control. The less you upset the balance of your skin, the better.

PROBLEMS AND BLEMISHES

Treating them – going to a specialist

Do not despair – many skin blemishes will respond to treatment, either at home or by a specialist. A healthy diet is important for a glowing, healthy skin.

Food for good skin

Your skin reflects your eating patterns: if you eat certain foods they may turn up on the skin in the form of spots and rashes. Although your type of skin is determined by genes, you can improve or aggravate its condition by what you eat. A simple rule is: if your skin is oily eat a minimum of fatty and sugary foods; if your skin is dry, eat dairy products, nuts and natural vegetable oils (but not meat fat).

Fish, lean meat, poultry, eggs, fresh vegetables and fruits are all good for the skin. Avocado, cucumber and cabbage are particularly recommended. The vitamin the skin needs most is vitamin A, which is widely available in everyday foods.

There are two kinds of professional help for skin conditions

A skin specialist or aesthetician is a person who cleans and cares for the skin, usually in a salon. She will analyse your skin to determine its type and texture and suggest suitable skin-care products and cosmetics. In the salon your skin can be cleaned of surface debris, blackheads and whiteheads can be taken care of and you'll be given instructions for a home-care regime. A skin specialist will also advise if it's necessary to consult a dermatologist.

A dermatologist is a medical doctor who specializes in the diagnosis and treatment of skin problems. He is concerned not only with external correction but also with the internal workings of the body. A dermatologist is the only person qualified to correct severe skin disorders.

The facts about skin blemishes
What they are and what you can do about them

From time to time everyone's skin is subject to various growths and infections. Some need medical attention for removal if they become unsightly or irritating, but most skin troubles in adolescence are temporary. Indeed the skin has remarkably quick healing powers. Here are the main points about the most common problems.

Abscess

Also known as a boil, it is a point of inflammation in the skin with a collection of pus. It starts with a swelling that is red and tender. A core of pus will develop at the centre and finally burst through the skin's surface. It is nearly always started by bacteria. Boils are frequently caused when you squeeze a spot and expose an open area to infection, so try not to squeeze spots. To treat an abscess you need to apply hot poultices to bring it to a head. Sometimes the skin needs to be broken with a sharp, sterile instrument, but don't do it yourself, it's a job for an adult. If the abscess is large or you start getting several, consult a doctor.

Allergy

You've probably heard quite a lot about 'allergic reaction'. What it means is that the body produces antibodies to any substance it thinks would harm it. The result is inflammation of some kind or another. Such reactions vary from person to person. The most common allergy is hay-fever, due to contact with grass or flower pollen. Many girls find they are allergic to certain types of skin and make-up preparations, the result being a skin rash or streaming eyes. The main thing, of course, is to avoid what you are allergic to – the allergen. Treatment includes antihistamines, which you get from a doctor, and strong medicated creams for local application. It is possible to be desensitized – meaning making your body immune – but it can be a lengthy and very costly process. As regards skin preparations, there are many non-allergic products on the market. You just have to try and find the best ones for you.

Blackheads

These are oil plugs in the pores that blacken on exposure to air – the black has nothing to do with dirt, it's the result of oxidization. They are the most common form of blemish, particularly during puberty, and are due to hormone changes that give rise to increased output from the oil glands. There's little you can do to prevent them, but you can help to keep them under control by being fastidious about washing, by really working up a good lather, and by rinsing in clear water many many times. You can squeeze them yourself, but hygiene is imperative. First clean your face thoroughly, then warm the skin by putting a hot facecloth over it. Squeeze the blackhead by applying pressure around the opening with your fingertips – never with your nails. The tiny black plug should pop out. Dab the areas with a little alcohol and then wipe with witch hazel. If blackheads are firmly entrenched don't keep pushing and squeezing on your own, but go to a skin specialist. You really do have to be very careful with blackheads because if they become infected they can easily develop into acne.

What's bad for skin?

- too many fats and sugars
- over-exposure to the sun
- inadequate protection against wind and cold
- too much and too constant contact with water
- drastic weight fluctuations
- smoking, alcohol and drugs
- lack of sleep
- too little fresh air
- not enough exercise

Blisters

You've no doubt had many blisters in your life – the most common are those caused by friction or burns. A blister is an area of fluid under the skin; it can vary in size depending on the cause. The most important thing to note is that you should not burst the blister, as it's the body's way of protecting itself. If the blister does burst, it must be kept clean and covered with a gauze dressing. If the blister turns into a scab, don't meddle with it; let it fall off on its own accord.

Dermatitis

This is an overall term that covers inflammation of the skin – the causes may be physical or emotional. The most serious are eczema and psoriasis. This type of skin disease is usually hereditary and signs are apparent in infancy. The conditions come and go, but do not leave scars. Medical treatment is necessary – the various types of dermatitis can be controlled.

Freckles

These small brown flecks are more likely to appear on fair than dark skins and particularly on redheads. A freckle is a small collection of pigment cells. You may hate freckles as a teenager, but they can actually be very attractive. Exposure to sunlight encourages more to appear, so if freckles bother you always use a strong sunscreen lotion. There's no way of getting rid of freckles; all you can do is camouflage them.

Itching

All sorts of things can cause an itch and make you want to scratch; this is something you should never do because once the skin surface is broken bacteria can spread infection, but it's not easy to stop yourself. Calamine lotion cools and soothes; a home-made remedy is one of the best, however: dissolve 2 teaspoons bicarbonate of soda in a cup of warm water and wipe over the itchy area. If the entire body itches, you can put a cup of bicarbonate of soda in a warm bath and soak in it for a few minutes.

Moles

In the past these flat or raised brown patches were referred to as 'beauty spots'. They are large collections of pigment cells, often containing hairs, which are formed during the development of the skin and there's nothing you can do to prevent them. Whatever you do, don't pluck or pull hairs from a mole. If a mole gets larger, itchier, swollen or inflamed, you should see a doctor.

Pimples

Red pimples or spots are often found on the face and shoulders. They are simply inflammations of the skin and little can be done to prevent them, as they are either hereditary or caused by hormone changes. You must never squeeze them unless a blackhead or pus is obviously there – if you do, the spot will get bigger and harder. Wait until pus develops, which it will in time, and then gently let it out. Don't use any creams or lotions – the skin will heal itself very quickly.

Warts

Warts are a virus infection – you get them from contact with other warts. They are, in fact, very infectious, so if you have a wart, picking at it will very likely cause others to appear. Warts are more prevalent during childhood and teenage years. They can be flat or raised, single or in a clump, almost white, beige or dark. The average lifespan of a wart is two or three years, though some come and go within a few months. The body will gradually build up antibodies that will kill the virus. Warts cannot be prevented. Don't play around with commercial wart cures, but go to a doctor for specific treatment if warts really bother you, or if they are in uncomfortable or embarrassing places. Eighty per cent of warts are curable. They can be frozen off, chemically removed or electrically treated. Surgical removal is the last resort because of the possibility of scarring and infection.

ACNE: THE TEENAGE MENACE

*Everyone has acne; it's a matter of degree;
it can be an occasional blackhead
or it can be a constant mass of pimples and scars*

First of all acne is not contagious, nor does it have anything to do with oily hair or greasy foods. And it's not an infection. What exactly causes acne is not known, but it is believed that heredity plays an important role – if your parents had severe acne, you are more likely to develop it. Male hormones are a major culprit – during puberty their increased production (even in females) causes the oil glands to enlarge and somewhat overdo the release of oily sebum, to such an extent that the channels to the skin surface become clogged. Blockage alone produces a blackhead or a whitehead. It is when bacteria cause inflammation that a red spot develops, which starts as an ordinary pimple and, if irritated at all, can quickly develop into acne. Inflammation can spread and, if serious, can leave scars behind.

Which parts of the body are most affected by acne?

The sebaceous glands which are responsible for acne are concentrated in the face, upper back and upper chest so it is in these areas that you will be most affected.

Does diet play any role?

It has long been said that eating certain foods tends to make acne worse. Chocolate, sweets, milk products and fried foods have been blamed particularly. There is actually no very good evidence for this – though you should stay away from some of these foods anyway, in the interests of a diet for good health. There's no harm in cutting them out – try it, it may help.

Do emotions affect acne?

Yes, indeed. On the day of a party, an exam or some special event, there may be an obvious outbreak of acne. Anxiety often makes acne worse. The explanation is that stress increases the production of hormones which have an effect on the sebaceous glands.

Do cosmetics aggravate acne?

They are insignificant in the development of acne, provided you remove them carefully at the end of each day. Excessive washing, however, may actually precipitate acne. So if you have an oily skin or one that is inclined to be pimply, don't wash the face and affected areas more than twice a day.

Is it necessary to see a dermatologist?

Mild acne does respond to home care, but if it gets worse it must be professionally attended to. If you are not sure if you are beyond the mild stage, get advice anyway; there's nothing to lose and possibly lots to gain. If there's a sign of even one pimple becoming red, irritated or swollen, check with a doctor for guidance on what to do. It's not being vain, it's being sensible and cautious.

There is no one treatment which is good for everyone, so you cannot just go into a chemist's and ask for 'something for acne'. You will probably need a combination of products, and only a doctor can work that out properly.

Are creams and ointments any good?

There are a variety of ointments, creams, lotions and gels which help milder cases of acne. They work either by a peeling or an abrasive action which prevents blockage of the sebaceous gland, or by an antiseptic action on bacteria. Many contain more than one agent. They frequently cause some irritation of the skin, which can be minimized by restricting their use to the spots and taking care to avoid healthy skin. Creams may be too drying, ointments too greasy. Gels and lotions are the most acceptable. Follow the package instructions religiously. If there is an adverse reaction, stop. Check with a doctor.

What about cleanliness?

You do need to keep your skin clean, but too much rubbing and scrubbing can make things worse. Gently wash the face, rinsing it well and patting it dry. Try to do it only twice a day.

Today dermatologists can control 80 per cent of all acne cases and a future drug brings hope for all

The most significant development has been the use of antibiotics. They suppress the process rather than cure it and so they have to be continued for months and always under medical supervision. There are few side effects. Current and future hopes lie in a chemical derivative of vitamin A, which, after international research, has been found to be successful in even the most severe cases. The new drug works by reducing the body's production of the natural oil sebum. Research on methods of conquering the acne problem continues.

Acne is the most common of all skin conditions and affects almost half the number of teenagers. If you are afflicted, remember there are many others like you. You may be disgusted with your own appearance and you may be depressed. You probably think you are being rejected by your friends – but don't let it ruin your days. Cheer up. Today much can be done; don't mess around on your own – you'll only make matters worse – go and see a skin specialist and get a care programme specially worked out for you.

SUN AND SKIN

The right amount is great for health and looks, but too much harms the skin and causes burns. All skin needs some kind of protective cream

A perfect tan

- *Start slowly, building up from half an hour on the first day.*

- *Avoid the midday sun. Ultraviolet radiation is at its most intense at noon. To be on the safe side, avoid exposure between 11 a.m. and 2 p.m.*

- *Be aware of the extra strong reflection from water and snow.*

- *The combination of sun and wind can result in quicker – and more painful – burning.*

- *Don't wear perfume when sunbathing; some scents, particularly those that contain natural bergamot oils, cause nasty reactions in sunlight.*

- *Always use a sunscreen, applying it often to all parts of the body. Use more when on the beach or skiing.*

- *If the sun bothers your eyes, wear sunglasses. In any case you must never look directly into the sun.*

Being out in the sun is just great. You feel better, you look better – and there's nothing quite like a golden, glowing tan. But a word of caution: even during teenage years you must be aware that it's bad to over-expose your skin to the sun. It can burn and blister, at times to such an extent that it can no longer perform its normal functions. At the extreme it can cause sunstroke – yes, it does exist. In the first stage, excessive moisture is lost by sweating; eventually the body's heat-regulating mechanism may go out of control, which is a serious emergency. When running around, playing sports, going in and out of the water, you are not aware that the sun is beating down on you all the time, and its effect is intensified if you are near water, which reflects the sun's rays. You don't have to avoid the sun completely. What you do have to do is to protect your skin and to limit the time that you stay out in the sun according to your type of skin. See the chart opposite.

What exactly is a sun-tan?
Why does your skin darken?

A sun-tan is a defence mechanism. It works this way. It is the ultraviolet rays from the sun that are the trouble-makers. They affect the cells of the skin and cause an increase in the melanin pigment, which produces a sun-tan. This acts as a screen, filtering out the harmful rays of the sun and protecting the delicate layers of skin underneath from being burnt. Well, isn't that good, you may ask? What's the worry? So far so good, it's true, but unfortunately when you are hot the blood vessels in the skin expand to allow heat loss by radiation. This is why you go a lobster colour when you get burned – it's the extra blood rushing to the skin. A little later, the blood brings a serum to the tissues. This leads to swelling and pressure on nerve endings – hence the pain of sunburn. The skin is stretched and broken and finally peels off; sometimes you get blisters. Whatever happens, your tan goes and you are back with a fresh layer of pale skin, while underneath are some damaged cells which finally work their way to the surface and can make the skin hard and leathery. You are young, and your skin can take a lot of misuse and still renew itself. Nevertheless, having a serious sunburn is no joke, and it's better for you to learn the habits of safe sunning for your particular skin as soon as possible.

You need a cream for sun protection
This is how it works

The idea of a sun cream is to protect your skin, not to encourage a tan. There are many products on the market, usually referred to as sun-tan lotions, that claim to make you tan faster and deeper; if they don't have any protective elements in them, you can get a bad burn. Some are only moisturizers or oils which attract rays and merely prevent drying. Be cautious, and read the labels, particularly the small print.

A sunscreen is something else. It protects the skin by copying the function of your own natural screen, melanin. It scatters all the light rays that beam down on the skin, and also selectively absorbs the harmful wavelengths.

Sunscreens come in varying degrees of strength, which are indicated on the label by reference to the sunscreen index or 'sun protection factor'. A protection factor of 2, for example, means that if you use that product you should be able to stay in direct sun without burning for about twice as long as you would if you were unprotected. A protection of 6 lets you expose yourself with impunity for six times as long. Protection degrees usually lie between 2 and 9, but some go up to 15.

Whatever product you use, it should be applied liberally to all exposed parts, and re-applied every two or three hours. Your most vulnerable parts are face, nose, shoulders, upper chest, backs of knees.

Check on the sun protection factor you need for your skin-type

This chart is a guide to the length of time you can safely stay in the sun relative to your type of skin and the strength of the sunscreen you use. Remember to read labels. Choose products that clearly indicate the degree of protection. But remember that protection also varies according to the intensity of the light, the time of year, the time of day, and whether you are on land or near water.

Sun safety chart

| Skin type | Sun protection factor of product used | | | | | |
	2	4	6	8	9	15
	Safe exposure time					
Fair	–	–	30–60 mins	40–80 mins	45–90 mins	$1\frac{1}{4}$– $2\frac{1}{2}$hrs
Medium	30–40 mins	60–80 mins	$1\frac{1}{2}$–2 hrs	2–$2\frac{1}{2}$ hrs	$2\frac{1}{4}$–3 hrs	5–$5\frac{1}{2}$ hrs
Dark	50–60 mins	$1\frac{3}{4}$–2 hrs	$2\frac{1}{2}$–3 hrs	$3\frac{1}{4}$–4 hrs	$3\frac{3}{4}$–$4\frac{1}{2}$ hrs	all day
Black	2 hrs	4 hrs	6 hrs	all day	all day	all day

Fair skins burn faster than dark ones
How to work out your own sun system

Know your own skin. Everyone has an individual limit when it comes to sun-tanning. Any attempt to go beyond this limit is pointless. If you have fair skin you will burn after only a brief time in the sun; you will never go a deep brown, no matter how cautiously or how long you sunbathe. Even with dark skins, there comes a point when further exposure causes a burn. Check on your skin/sun type.

Which one are you?

Fair	Medium	Dark	Black
You have light hair, eyes, and/or skin, and have never achieved a tan easily	You are not sure of your skin type – it's somewhere in between – but you do tan most of the time without difficulty	You have dark hair, eyes, and/or skin, and probably you tan deeply and quickly, rarely burning	You don't burn easily, but you can be subject to skin damage from prolonged sun exposure

Even using a screen, you must follow basic sun rules

A reminder: anything you do under the sun counts as exposure – sunbathing, sports activities, even walking or gardening. You don't have to stop doing these things – just cover yourself up with T-shirts, etc., when you have reached your time limit.

How long does a sun-tan last?

As long as the 'browned' cells stay on the surface of the skin. You are constantly shedding skin cells as new ones work their way to the surface. Your tan disappears because the cells flake off. To preserve your tan involves controlling this natural shedding. It can't be stopped but it can be slowed down by using oil in your bath and body lotion afterwards. In this case cells tend to cling to the surface longer – dry cells will rub away quickly.

What about a fake tan?

There are products that contain chemicals which make the keratin cells on the surface of the skin gradually turn a browny orange. These products are not dangerous, but they are very difficult to apply evenly, as the tan takes several hours to develop and you therefore have no instant visual guide. You can all too easily come out streaky or one part of your body may emerge darker than another. Also, you can come out an odd shade of orange depending on your natural skin tone. The tan fades gradually over a few days as the dead cells are shed. Avoid sun-tan creams that claim to help you tan artificially while protecting you from the sun. It's better to keep the two separate. Another thing to avoid is an artificial tan by means of a sun lamp. In no way can you judge the exact timing necessary, and any extra second spent under the lamp can be highly dangerous. Professional sun-tan treatments are best left until you're older, when your skin condition has settled into maturity.

Did you know you can get a light tan by having a tea bath?

It's true. Make a strong pot of tea – four dessertspoons of tea to a quart of boiling water. Let it steep for 10 minutes. Then pour into a shallow warm bath, straining it first, of course. If you have fair or medium skin, you'll be surprised at the difference in the degree of colour. Not dramatic, but there's usually a tone or two change. Try it and see.

The big bonus: sun helps acne

One way of unblocking the oil-clogged glands is to make the skin peel slightly. So a slight sunburn is, in this case – and only in this case – a good thing. As the dead layer of skin peels from the surface, it takes the cells blocking the oil outlets with it. What happens in this natural exposure to sunlight is the basis of ultraviolet radiation therapy for acne treatment. So if you've got acne – face the sun as often as you can.

Opposite: OLIVIERO TOSCANI
Overleaf: PATRICK DEMARCHELIER

Remedies for sunburn

Sunburn can be terribly painful, apart from looking dreadful. Try these methods to bring relief.

Bicarbonate of soda
Mix 1 cup of soda with 2 cups of water. Pat on to the sunburn, leave on for half an hour, rinse off with tepid water.

Egg and oil
Beat the white of an egg with 1 teaspoon of castor oil, and smooth it over the skin. Leave on for half an hour; rinse off with tepid water.

Vinegar and water
Put 2 tablespoons of vinegar in 1 cup of water. Dab on the burn.

Ordinary tea
Make a fairly strong pot of tea, allow to cool and wipe over the sunburn; it is very soothing.

BATHING

The most basic beauty routine – it's the only way to keep fresh and clean; learn to enjoy it – make it a pleasure

It's the first act of health and beauty and without it all other efforts are useless. All you really need is water, a bar of soap and a towel. There you are, clean as can be and off to a fresh start. There's nothing wrong with leaving it simply like that – you've achieved your goal: cleanliness. But bathing can open up a whole new world of self-indulgence, where pampering is considered neither a vanity nor a sin, but constructive to your physical and mental well-being. How about that?

First of all, you can relax in the bath. That's good for your body. You can think and dream in the bath. That's good for your mind. You can have a nourishing, toning or lubricating bath. That's good for your skin. You can have a herbal bath. That's good for the spirits. And you can read in the bath. That's good for pleasure, but bad for the book.

So you see, there's more to a bath than you might have thought. Want to know more? Here are some of the things you can do.

A morning shower wakes you up

It's invigorating, it gets you going. Turn on the water full force and don't have it too warm. Make the final rinse as cold as you can stand it. It will stimulate the circulation and help tone your skin. Rub vigorously with a towel.

An evening bath is lulling

Laze in a scented bubble bath before going to bed. The water should be rather warm but not too hot. If you like exact figures, it should be 85–100°F (30–38°C). It's the best temperature for relaxation. Rinse yourself with water of the same temperature, using a shower attachment. Take a warm towel, wrap it around you and dab yourself dry gently. All these things help you relax and have a good night's sleep.

Bath basics

There's a lot of rubbing and scrubbing to be done – here is a checklist of the essentials which you should have by you.

Loofah

A dry, rough vegetable gourd that softens and swells when wet. It's ideal for rubbing off dead skin and giving a boost to your circulation. It makes the body tingle. Get a long one, so you can reach any part of your back.

Friction strap

Usually of hemp blended with horsehair. It looks like a rough, knitted string scarf with handles at each end. It's gentler than a loofah, but it does the same thing. The same material can be seen in a bath mit – you just slip in your hand and scour the body.

Sponge

Many are now made from synthetic materials, but did you know that a natural sponge is the skeleton of a marine animal? They come in all different shapes and sizes. Their porosity varies too. Sponges need to be rinsed of soap every time you use them, otherwise they get clogged and begin to smell awful. At this stage the best thing to do is soak the sponge overnight in vinegar, then rinse many times in clear water. A sponge is just a pleasant means to soaping.

Flannel or washcloth

Made of cotton towelling, it is used for rubbing in soap, rubbing away dead skin and rinsing off the soap. Flannels need to be laundered frequently; otherwise they get slimy and smelly.

Bath mit

Some are made of towelling and do exactly the same job as a flannel – they often contain soap granules. Others are made of rough, stringy material and are used to stimulate the skin surface.

Body brushes

You really need two. A long-handled one for your back, and a smaller one for hands and feet. Both are best when made of stiff, natural bristles.

Pumice stone

This is a piece of volcanic lava. It is used to soften and rub away hard skin on spots such as heels, soles of feet and elbows.

Bath-time specials

You'll find most of the things that you need for these baths around the house. If you cannot get the herbs at a chemist's, try a health shop.

To soften the skin and prevent dryness

Milk is the easiest. Remember Cleopatra always bathed in milk? Well you can do the same by simply emptying a cup of powdered skimmed milk into a bath of warm water. It feels lovely.

Oatmeal (1 lb, 0.45 kg) stirred into a warm bath thickens the water and makes it cloudy. It is much more pleasant to bath in than you would think – not at all porridgy.

To tone the skin and make it tingle

Sea salt or coarse salt rubbed all over the body – except the face – removes dead skin cells and really does make the skin feel softer. It is rather invigorating too, because the salt stings. Rinse the salt off with warm water, bath or shower as usual, and then moisturize the skin with a cream or lotion.

Seaweed can be put in a muslin bag in a warm bath, letting it soak for ten minutes before getting in. It smells like a whiff of sea air. (Buy the seaweed at a health-food shop.)

To help dried-out skin

Home-made bath oil can be made by adding 1 tablespoon of any liquid detergent shampoo to 1 cup of any kitchen oil – olive, corn, sesame, soya, etc.; to this add ½ teaspoon of any aromatic oil, which you can buy at a health-food shop or specialized chemist's. Pour the mixture into a bottle and shake well each time you use it. You'll need 2 tablespoons for each bath.

To perk up the spirits

A mint bath requires 1 cup peppermint leaves, ½ cup pine needles, and 2 drops of oil of rosemary. Mix and stir well. Keep in a sealed glass container. Put 2 tablespoons of the mixture in a muslin bag and soak in a warm bath. It is a good idea to tie the bag on to the tap so it hangs in the tub.

To cool the body on a hot day

A lemon bath is very refreshing. Mix 1 cup lemon verbena with 1 cup lemon balm and add 3 drops of oil of lemon. Mix well; keep in an airtight container. Put 2 tablespoons in a tepid bath.

To protect you from insect bites

A camomile bath can be made by pouring a pint of boiling water over a cupful of dried camomile flowers in a bowl. Cover and leave for half an hour. Strain and pour into a warm bath.

Bath luxuries: all the extras

These make a bath special, turning an essential routine into an experience that appeals to the senses. These bath preparations not only cleanse, but also help keep the skin in good condition.

In the bath

Bubbles are the most popular; apart from looking and feeling great, they also soften and scent water.

Crystals are coloured mineral salts that perfume and soften the water.

Essences don't alter the water, but they provide a refreshing aroma. Pine and lemon are the most popular for reviving the body and mind; rose, jasmine and geranium are the most relaxing.

Oils are good for your skin but not so good for the bath – they leave a greasy rim round it (which you should clean away, not your mother). They act as conditioners and moisturizers, as they cling to the skin. Oil in the bath is the best way by far to help dry skin, particularly in the summer when sea and sun take away the skin's natural oils.

Milks are powders that soften the water, and also smooth your skin.

Remember: you only need a little of these products. Using a lot is a waste – and they are quite expensive.

After the bath

Body toners are colognes and toilet waters that you splash on your body to make it feel fresh. They are less concentrated than regular colognes and are also known as 'splash' and 'friction' waters.

Body lotion is a fragrant cream that moisturizes the body and keeps skin supple. It is best to apply it when you are still a little damp. Use sparingly and smooth into the skin until all has been absorbed.

Talcum powder absorbs moisture, cools and smoothes the skin and is pleasantly perfumed. It can be sprayed or patted on with a large puff. Don't get carried away with powder, it can be very drying – use just a dab here and there, under the arms, on the soles of the feet. It is very refreshing in hot weather.

You can make an after-bath rose water yourself. Get hold of some red roses – best if gathered straight from a garden early in the morning. You'll also need a ceramic jar and a piece of gauze to cover the top. Pull the petals off the flowers, weigh out $3\frac{1}{2}$ oz (100 g) of them, put them in the jar and pour over 2 pints (1.1 l) of white vinegar; cover with the gauze. Leave for fifteen days, strain and put in an airtight bottle – a glass-topped vinegar bottle is perfect. You can use the same method to make scented water from lavender or orange blossom.

Bath essences
If you need to relax

try one of the following:
5 drops of lavender
2 drops of camomile
2 drops of orange blossom or
2 drops of rose

If you need stimulation

use
5 drops of rosemary *or*
3 drops of peppermint

If you need refreshing

there's a choice of
4 drops of lemon
4 drops of rose geranium *or*
3 drops of bergamot

PERSPIRATION

Embarrassing, but also necessary and healthy; it controls body heat

Sweating is a particularly human activity. Whether energetically playing a sport or simply lying in the sun, if you did not sweat your body temperature would rise after just a few minutes. When the temperature of your blood rises, the hypothalamus (your brain's signal box) sends a message to your sweat glands to start work. Would you believe that you have between two and three million sweat glands that respond in seconds to the body's need for temperature control?

The whole point of sweating is to put water on your skin where it cools the body through evaporation. We are capable of sweating a great deal – as you have no doubt observed during sports sessions. If you sweat a lot you need to replace the lost water by drinking more.

Sweating begins on the arms and legs; if the body is not cooling down fast enough, the sweat glands on your torso then start to work. And there's an odd thing to note: you usually sweat more on one side than the other and usually on the side opposite the dominant hand. Check it some time.

Not all sweating is for cooling. Have you noticed that you often have a film of perspiration on the palms of your hands and soles of your feet? This is there to improve your sense of touch to enable you to make the most precise movements. Then there's nervous sweating which happens when you are emotionally or physically under stress – before an exam, at the start of a match.

Sweat itself does not smell; odour is caused by bacteria
Only certain areas are affected

You have two types of sweat gland. The largest group is evenly distributed all over the body and secretes almost pure water for temperature control; these you are born with. However, during adolescence you develop additional glands concentrated in specific areas: underarms, groin, buttocks and nipples. Their activity is triggered mainly by nervous and emotional reactions and they secrete water containing some protein and fatty substances. This liquid attracts bacteria (normal, essential inhabitants of the skin) and supports their growth, and in the process they produce compounds with a pungent smell. It is most obvious under the arms.

Bathing deals with general sweating
Deodorants combat underarm odour

If you bath or shower regularly, general body perspiration is no problem. It's another matter under your arms. This is made worse by the presence of hair which traps the sweat and provides a congenial environment for bacteria. It is helpful to remove the hair by shaving under your arms. You can control odour by using a deodorant.

A deodorant is a chemical compound which impedes the bacterial action, which means there'll be no smelly by-products. Deodorants come in cream and·liquid form and allergic reactions are rare. One application a day is usually sufficient. You must apply a deodorant to a thoroughly clean area. Apply when the body is cool – not directly after a bath, but fifteen minutes later. How well a deodorant works depends on many things – whether you naturally perspire lightly or heavily, exertion, stress, temperature, clothes.

Apart from commercial products there are some effective natural deodorants you can make at home.

Apple cider vinegar

Put $\frac{1}{2}$ cup of vinegar in 1 cup of distilled water. Keep in an airtight bottle. Apply to underarm area with cotton pads. The aroma of vinegar disappears in about fifteen minutes.

Lavender oil

Mix together 3 drops lavender oil, 1 tablespoon white sugar and 1 pint distilled water. Put in an airtight bottle and leave for two weeks. Always shake before use; apply with cotton pads.

What is an anti-perspirant?
How does it differ from a deodorant?

An anti-perspirant has an additional asset: it limits wetness by reducing the volume of perspiration, as well as reducing odour by fighting bacteria. Anti-perspirants contain more chemicals and some girls find these irritating, but if you perspire heavily and are embarrassed by constant wetness obvious on your clothing, the only way to control it is by using an anti-perspirant. However, most girls find a deodorant sufficient.

HAIR REMOVAL

**Skin can be hairy. If you don't like the hairs
you can easily get rid of them.
Here are all the alternatives . . .
the pros and cons**

It is perfectly normal and healthy to have a certain amount of body hair. Just about every part of your body – except palms and soles – grows some degree of hair. The question is: is it visible enough to bother or embarrass you? Hair patterns are usually established during adolescence, and dermatologists still do not know why some girls grow hairs and others do not; they simply come up with 'heredity and hormone balance' – neither of which you can do much about. There are, however, several efficient methods of getting rid of unwanted hair. Here they are.

Bleaching

It goes without saying that fair hair shows less than dark hair, so merely bleaching your hair might be the answer. In fact, at your age it should be your first choice for hair other than that in the underarm area, because your hair growth patterns are still in the process of adjustment. It's a good camouflage tactic and lasts from three to six weeks. There are several commercial products; be sure to follow instructions carefully – it is best to get some adult guidance the first time. Play safe and do a patch test first – a small area on your arm or leg. Wait twenty-four hours and if there is no reaction – meaning no inflammation – you are clear to go ahead. Bleaching is the best method for facial hair, particularly the upper lip, when you're a teenager. On the body it can be tedious if you have a lot of hair to deal with.

Shaving

Most girls deal with unwanted hair by shaving it off. The reason is obvious – it's fast and easy. You can shave legs, underarms, around the bikini line; but never shave arms or upper lips or hairs on your breasts. If you shave carefully and properly you can do so ad infinitum without worry of skin irritation. However, hair returns more quickly after shaving than after any other method. It does *not* grow in thicker and darker – don't believe this old myth. It does grow in rough, though, not smooth. The best time to shave is after a hot bath or shower when the pores are more open and the hair shafts are swollen. Safety razors are best – forget the electric ones. Always use soap and water, working up a light lather. Work in the opposite direction to hair growth. Finish with a cold rinse and splash with a body toner.

How do you shave under your arms?

There are special razors for women, but the plastic disposable ones are perfectly adequate. Always be sure you have a clean sharp blade. Wet the underarm areas and with a little soap (any ordinary soap will do, there's no need to get a special shaving soap) work up a slight lather. Work from your arm towards your body, holding your arm high to make the skin under the arm as taut as possible. With short but firm strokes shave the entire area. Be gentle, don't hack away; remember the skin here is particularly sensitive. You'll find you'll have to go over the area several times before all the hairs are removed. Should you nick yourself, don't worry and don't put anything on it – it will soon stop bleeding. It is better not to use a deodorant or anti-perspirant for twenty-four hours after shaving but if the skin is a bit raw, soothe it by dabbing on a little powder. Should you get any inflammation from shaving don't use a deodorant until it clears up, otherwise you may cause an infection. If inflammation shows signs of spreading or becoming infected, you must see a doctor right away because if not checked it could be very serious.

Depilation

This means using a chemical formula – a cream, gel, spray or foam – which softens and dissolves the hair shaft but doesn't disturb the root. Depilatories

---

Body zones for hair removal

Face
Tweezing for the odd, stray hair and eyebrows; bleaching, waxing or depilatories for upper lip. Electrolysis only when older

Underarms
Shaving is standard because it's fast and easy. Depilatories are OK and sometimes last longer

Arms and breasts
Bleach or waxing for arms is best; depilatories next. You may pluck the odd hair from the breast, but never from the nipple (snip these with scissors) – no shaving, waxing or depilatories for breasts

Bikini line
Waxing is by far superior to other methods – you can use depilatories or shave, but beware of irritation

Legs
Shaving is ideal; waxing is good, depilatories also work well. If you don't have many hairs, bleach first

don't prevent hair growth; they take an average of ten to fifteen minutes to work; they leave the skin slightly smoother than shaving, for slightly longer. The chemicals can be harsh enough to irritate the skin, so patch-test for sensitivity first, following package instructions.

You can use depilatories almost anywhere – arms, legs, underarms, the bikini line. If you're going to use one on your face, make sure the label says it's safe for facial use. The only way to get rid of hair around ears, forehead, nape of neck and hairline is with a depilatory. If you need to remove hair because of a small bikini, wear a pair of old briefs while doing it to gauge what needs removing and to prevent the depilatory getting too close to your vaginal area. NEVER use depilatories on your breasts or eyebrows.

Waxing

This is not permanent either, but it gets at the hair lower down in the follicle and leaves your skin particularly smooth – and it lasts longer, up to eight weeks. Waxing is painful, but less so when done by an expert. You must go to a salon first to get the hang of it, and even then you have to be pretty adept to do it yourself. It is one method that is always better done by a professional.

Tweezing

Easy and efficient for the odd stray hairs and eyebrows. NEVER pluck hairs on the breasts or hairs growing out from a mole – only a doctor should remove the latter. Apply a hot, wet washcloth to help open the pores, then with tweezers firmly grasp the hair at its base and with a jerk pull it out in the direction it's growing. If tweezing eyebrow hairs hurts, try desensitizing skin with an ice-cube. Afterwards rub with alcohol or an astringent.

Electrolysis

The only permanent hair removal method – the hair root bulb is destroyed. Electrolysis has to be done by a qualified technician as it is a very skilled job. Hair can be removed from anywhere, but it is a method used mostly for the face; it is time-consuming – the hairs are treated one by one and you might need to go for treatment week after week – and it is also expensive. Electrolysis is not recommended for teenage girls until they have been menstruating regularly for at least a year. This is because hormone changes can drastically alter hair patterns – you might very well get less hairy anyway.

HAIR

All the facts about basic care.
All your questions answered.
All the ways to make it healthy.

If your hair isn't healthy, shining and manageable then you are not taking advantage of all the knowledge at your fingertips. There is no reason why your hair shouldn't shine and bounce, have a look of vitality about it and yet be under perfect control. Natural-looking hair is best – happily a thing that young people appreciate today. This doesn't mean letting hair go without any attempt at styling, but getting the best look for the temperament of your hair without any artificiality. First you have to know about basic hair care, the ways to make it healthy and lustrous and the ways to cope with all its problems. Do you actually wash your hair properly? Maybe you think you do but check and see if you are doing everything right. In the eighties hair care is less trouble than ever before because hair-care products have become more specialized and more effective. Get to know your hair, learn how to control its condition – and finally with your perfect head of hair you can step into the fun area of finding the best possible style to suit your looks and personality. But that's at the end of the line. Right now, it's down to the basics.

ABOUT HAIR

Why is everyone's different?
Structure and form largely depend on your family genes and the environment

Before you can appreciate the best way to take care of your hair, you need to understand its basic structure. Each strand, regardless of how fine it may look, consists of three layers. There's an outer layer called the cuticle which protects the interior of the hair shaft. The secret to super hair is to keep the cuticle in good condition so it provides a smooth surface that reflects light and gives hair shine. The next layer (the cortex) contains the pigment, which gives your hair its colour, and cells that give hair its elastic resilience. The inner-most layer is mainly spongy tissue.

The part of the hair you see is called the shaft and the small part that lies under the skin is the root. Around the root is a nourishing bed of cells where a new hair is born and fed and pushes its way to the outside world – and at the same time it pushes out the old hair. Hairs are constantly replacing them-selves and this is where your hair has a very positive advantage over your skin – any damage will simply grow out. At the base of the root there are also glands which give out oil, which lubricates the hair and gives it gloss and suppleness. The condition of your hair is really the condition of your scalp; if it's oily, so is your hair, at least near your head, though the ends may be dry – a common teenage problem.

Each strand of hair grows out straight or curly. What determines that? It depends on the structure of the root. If it is even, the hair comes out perfectly straight, while if it's uneven or distorted in any way the hair emerges wavy or curled. The contours of the roots depend entirely on heredity – you are always going to get the same type of hair as your parents, either one or the other or a combination of the two.

How about colour? Is it always inherited?

Yes, it is, though there are many possible combinations going back several generations. You could, for example, get the exact same red shade of hair as your great-grandmother – a colour no one else in the family has had since.

You may be surprised to learn that all hair colours derive from three colour pigments – black, red and yellow. These three are present in varying numbers in the hair and can combine to give thousands of different shades. Just try mixing paints using these three basic colours and you'll get some idea of the vast variety of hues that are possible. Black and dark brown hair are concen-trations of black with touches of the other two. Red begins to become more prevalent in brown hair. Light brown hair contains more yellow. Red hair is mostly red pigment with black or yellow shadings. Blond hair is yellow with traces of red. Hair can become darker as you mature. Babies often have beautiful blond hair which gradually changes at puberty; this is due to the metabolic change of hormone balance.

What's bad for hair?

- Incorrect washing
- Harsh combing and brushing
- All chemical treatments such as perming, bleaching, tinting
- Direct heat from a too-hot dryer
- Extremes of weather, particularly the sun; heat from the sun can scorch the hair's outer layer – the lighter your hair the more you need to protect it
- Wind; it destroys the smoothness of the cuticle and causes tangles
- Hair-styles that pull the hair too tightly – ponytails, pigtails, tight plaiting

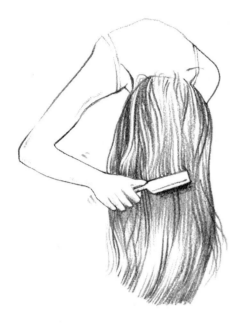

How fast does hair grow?
Is there anything that will make it grow faster?

Hair grows, on the average, half an inch (1 cm) a month or about 6 in (15 cm) a year. It grows faster during warm weather. Around the ages of fourteen and fifteen hair growth may accelerate for these and the next ten years. After hair reaches a length of about 10 in (25 cm), it slows down to half its normal growth rate. The growing phase can last from two to six years before an individual hair falls out. The reason why some girls can grow hair to their waists is because they have the combination of a quick growth rate and a long life-span for each hair. There is nothing you can do to make your hair grow faster and it's not true that cutting hair makes it grow like a weed – it carries on growing at exactly the same rate.

Do you know that you lose fifty to a hundred hairs a day?

This may seem like a lot, but when you consider that you have between 90,000 and 140,000 hairs on your head, it is like a few straws from a haystack. Normally about 90 per cent of your hairs are growing and 10 per cent are resting. The resting hairs stay put for two or three months, while a new hair is being formed below – and as it grows upward, the old one is pushed up and out. Every hair that falls out is replaced by a new one – at least when you are young. When you pull a hair out 'by the roots' you leave behind the breeding 'nest' which will eventually manufacture and nourish a new hair. Because of this, plucking is never a permanent way to get rid of the odd unwanted hair – and hair loss through breakage will eventually be replaced.

Ten steps to perfect hair care

No matter what condition your hair is in, no matter what its length or style, these rules will bring out the best in your hair and also respect its structure.

1 Treat your hair gently; attacking it roughly will cause breakage.

2 Brush and comb with a light hand and only often enough to keep it tidy. Don't overdo, especially the brushing.

3 Use the correct brush and comb (see page 128) and keep them scrupulously clean.

4 Get to know your hair type and treat it accordingly.

5 Take a lot of trouble to select the right shampoo and then use it sparingly.

6 Wash your hair as often as necessary; there's no such thing as too much washing. Remember dirty hair ruins your whole appearance.

7 Learn about conditioners and use them after every shampoo.

8 Hair is best dried naturally, running fingers through the strands.

9 As a teenager, you should avoid *all* chemical treatments such as perming, bleaching, colouring and straightening.

10 Protect hair from over-exposure to the sun – a little is healthy, a lot is not. Cover up your hair or rub in a conditioner or sunscreen lotion.

LOOKING AFTER YOUR HAIR

Healthy hair is part of a healthy body

The texture of your hair is inherited but its strength and condition are influenced by what it is fed. A high-protein diet with lots of fresh fruit and vegetables is good for hair. Foods containing all the B vitamins are essential. Important too are vitamins A and C. In the mineral group iron and iodine contribute a lot to hair health – in fact *lack* of iodine can be the cause of really bad hair conditions.

Is your hair oily or dry?
Here's a quick test to determine your type

Shampoo your hair as you normally do. After two days check on its condition. Does it look greasy, with separated strands that seem to stick to your head? If so, you have oily hair. Does it tangle easily, fly out of control and is it brittle to touch? Then your hair is dry. It is possible to have normal hair which falls midway between oily and dry, but at your age it is rare – it is more common to have oily roots and dry ends. Teenage hair is almost always oily because the hormonal changes that take place during adolescence stimulate the oil glands around the roots of each hair to produce much more oil than usual. Once you know your hair type, you must follow a care routine based on it. Whatever sort of hair you have, you always need to use some conditioning treatment after you have shampooed and rinsed well.

Oily hair: rules on care

You must shampoo your hair as frequently as is necessary even if that means every day.

Use a mild shampoo; many commercial shampoos are too strong and often provoke the oil glands into producing even more oil. The best is home-made green soap shampoo.

Use very little shampoo – your hair cannot possibly be dirty with so many washings; you only need enough shampoo to get rid of the oil.

Don't use a cream conditioner over all your hair; if you have dry split ends, apply conditioner to the tips only with a cotton ball, but use it sparingly.

After rinsing thoroughly you should apply a scalp lotion that you can mix yourself.

Dry hair: rules on care

Shampoo your hair every three or four days.

Use a mild shampoo; it is not necessary to have a rich, creamy shampoo as often suggested for dry hair. Your shampoo gets rinsed off anyway; it's the conditioning that counts.

Home-made green soap shampoo

8 oz (225 g) old-fashioned green soap
2 pints (1.1 l) water (preferably distilled)

You can buy both of these ingredients at a good chemist. Using an aluminium pan on a moderate heat, melt the soap in the water, stirring all the time with a wooden spoon. When the soap has dissolved completely move from the stove and let it cool. When cold you'll find there's clear liquid on the top and sediment underneath. Pour only the clear liquid in a bottle – and that's your shampoo.

Always use a cream conditioner after every shampoo, combing it thoroughly through the hair and leaving it on a few minutes.

Never brush your hair when wet, always comb, and gently.

Give yourself a special home treatment once a week – admittedly messy, but so valuable. See below.

Always protect your hair from the sun. If you can't be bothered with a hat or scarf, use a haircream on your hair – or you can use some of your sunscreen lotion. Apply at the roots and massage into the whole head until all hair is covered with a film of cream. Comb through your hair gently to eliminate tangling.

Home treatments for dry hair

Hot oil treatment

You can use any vegetable oil (soya, saffron, corn, sunflower) but olive oil is the best, though more expensive and difficult to wash out. Warm 4 tablespoons of oil in a sturdy pan. Part hair down the middle going from forehead to the back of the neck. Pour some of the oil into the palm of your hand and apply to the entire length of the parting. Part your hair again an inch (2.5 cm) either side of the centre line, apply oil; repeat until entire scalp is covered. Now massage the oil into your hair so every strand is soaked and all the oil is used up. Massage gently, using your fingers – this takes about five minutes. Take a towel, wring it out in hot water and wind it around the head like a turban. Leave on for at least half an hour. Afterwards shampoo your hair, rinse well and apply a commercial conditioner.

Coconut oil treatment

Melt 2 tablespoons coconut oil in a pan, add 1 beaten egg and stir it in (with a wooden spoon) and then blend in 1 tablespoon vinegar. Massage into the scalp as explained above, cover with a steaming towel. Leave on for at least half an hour. Afterwards shampoo, rinse and condition.

Avocado conditioning

Simply mash a whole avocado, and massage into the scalp and hair. Cover with a plastic bag as it's particularly messy, then with a steaming towel. Leave on for an hour before shampooing.

What is a trichologist?

This is a professional for hair condition and problems. He or she is not medically trained, but is knowledgeable about all hair matters – the causes and cures. So if you really have problems with your hair, it is wise to go and consult a trichologist early on in the game. Special treatments and advice on diet are given, and formulas for shampoos and conditioners are made to suit your individual problem.

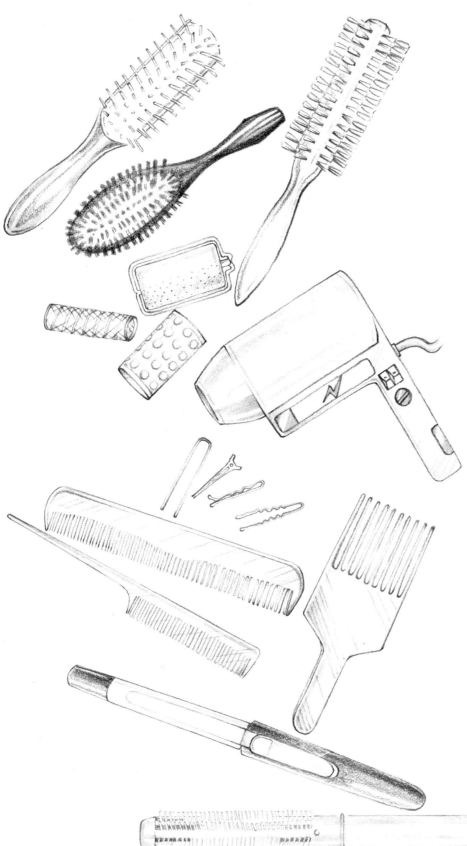

Hair Tools

Brushes
Wide-spaces between bristles give the best results – flat brushes for getting out tangles and giving shine; circular brushes for creating flips and a curly look, and for use with a hand-dryer to get the shape you want.

Combs
It's ideal to have three, but all with wide-spaced teeth and rounded tips. The comb with fine and stronger teeth combined is for regular combing; the long-handled comb is for styling; the spatula big-tooth comb is for lifting hair into place and separating strands when styling.

Rollers
The best three are – mesh for fine hair, sponge rollers for delicate hair, perforated plastic ones for strong and also curly hair. Remember, the bigger the roller, the less curl you get.

Hairpins
Straight big pins are for securing rollers or for putting up long hair; steel clips for holding rollers and for setting waves and curls – never for use on the finished product; grips are for securing hair in setting and can be discretely used in public – though decorated clips are much better; pins with a concertina section firmly hold complicated hair in place and don't show.

Dryers
A regular blow-dryer will dry hair quickly and you can style your hair very effectively by using circular brushes; for special effects there's a brush dryer which is circular and narrow and does two jobs at the same time; then there is a styling wand, a heated steel tube that's good for straightening hair or getting waves exactly where you want them – it should, however, be used with great care because your hair can get burnt so easily. In fact, all electrical drying or styling equipment should be used with restraint.

All you need for styling hair see p. 185

BRUSH AND COMB

The right tools – the right technique

Incorrect combing and brushing can cause a lot of damage. Forget the 'hundred strokes a day' – it's too stressful for your hair. The modern thinking is that you should only brush and comb your hair enough to style and groom it, but no more. Excessive brushing can cause your hair to break and split, and wet hair is more prone to breaking from brushing than dry hair. Also, if you brush too much you can aggravate an oily scalp condition – and teenagers have enough trouble with that as it is.

How to care for your brush

Always keep your brush spotlessly clean, otherwise you'll brush dirt and grease back into the hair. First loosen dirt and hair by running a wide-toothed comb through the bristles. Swirl the bristles thoroughly in warm, soapy water; never immerse rubber cushion or wood-frame brushes in water – you'll loosen the bristles or rot the wood. A quick dip in a mild solution of ammonia and water will quickly lift the grime. Remember to rinse a couple of times in clean water. Shake away water and dry, bristle side down, on a towel. Never dry your brush on a radiator or with a hair dryer; it will dry quick enough at room temperature.

The best way to brush

Hair responds better to gentle treatment than to an attack. Start by brushing in smooth strokes from the forehead through the entire length. Now throw your hair over your head so that your hair is hanging in front of your face. Gently brush from the nape of the neck out to the ends of your hair. Make long, lifting strokes away from the head. If the hair is tangled, divide into sections and work your way piece by piece towards the forehead. Throw your head back, and when hair has settled down, use your brush to smooth it lightly. Brush just enough so that you've covered every strand.

What about combs? Is there a perfect one?

Yes, there is. It is one that is saw cut, which means that each individual tooth is cut into the comb, leaving no rough or sharp edges. Teeth should have rounded tips (not squared off or pointed) that are wide-spaced so that the comb can get through the hair without any pulling. The best type is made of vulcanite (hard rubber) and, if you can afford it, there's the luxury of a comb of horn, tortoiseshell or ivory. You can get saw-cut combs made of plastic – but check the tips carefully before buying, as the majority of plastic combs are moulded and have very sharp pointed teeth that are very destructive to the scalp. Never use a metal comb.

A better way to wash your comb than just swilling it in soapy water is to dissolve one tablespoon of soda in a bowl of hot water and add a teaspoon of antiseptic. Let the comb soak for a few minutes, swish around until it is really clean and rinse in clean water.

Picking a brush

What you should look for

- Natural bristles are best, but if you choose a nylon brush, be sure the ends are rounded

- Wide spacing between bristles is important as this makes it easier to get through the hair without causing damage

- Watch the texture of your brush to your hair; thick bristles are for thick hair, a soft brush for fine hair

- Rubber cushion brushes are good as they prevent bristles from tugging at hair.

WASHING YOUR HAIR

It seems so simple but the chances are that you are doing it wrong – there are four steps to follow: shampooing, rinsing, conditioning, drying

The most common mistakes are: rubbing too hard, too much shampoo, not enough rinsing, ignorance about conditioning and too tough a towelling. Are you sure you know what you are doing? Check all the points below.

Rule number one

Be gentle. Hair washing is a much finer skill than you think. If you do it wrong, you not only damage your hair but you will probably aggravate problems rather than help them.

Rule number two

Settle on the best place for washing. This is usually under a shower, but if you don't have one, wash your hair by bending over the bath tub. And because lots of rinsing is essential, have either a shower attachment or a basin or bucket handy.

The right way to shampoo

First a word on water – the temperature doesn't matter, so long as it is comfortable. A pre-rinse is essential before you shampoo. Really soak your hair in water for a few minutes, otherwise you'll never get a good lather from the shampoo. As you wet your hair, don't let it get knotted up, but draw your fingers gently through your hair, front to back.

You'll need only a little shampoo, about a tablespoon altogether. Never pour it directly on to your hair, but pour a small amount on to the palm of your hand, rub your hands together and smooth the shampoo all over your hair. Be gentle. As the shampoo starts to lather, massage your scalp with the tips of your fingers – but not with your fingernails. Do this for two to three minutes. A warning – don't pile hair on top and rub it around – this is the way to get it in a real tangle. It's better to run your fingers through your hair following the way it grows – front to back.

If you wash your hair very frequently it will only need one shampooing. If it's dirty it will require two, but the first one must be rinsed away before starting again. If the shampoo doesn't lather the first time, don't add more – rinse off and apply another. And remember, use only a little.

The right way to rinse

Hair that is not properly rinsed might just as well not have been washed at all. Always rinse your hair for a much longer time than you think is necessary. Rinse, rinse and rinse again with clean running water. If you are under a shower throw your head back and let the force of the water stream through your hair. If you are rinsing over the tub, use a shower attachment or pour over buckets of water, letting your hair fall forward and rinsing from the back. The slightest remains of soap will leave your hair dull and sticky, attracting dirt immediately. Try to make the last rinse of cool water, in fact as cold as you can stand it. This is particularly beneficial if you have an oily head as it helps to close the pores. When you think your hair is completely rinsed, take a swatch of hair and run it between your fingers. It should squeak – check to see there is no trace of lather when you squeeze it.

There is a final rinse you can add which is good for all types of hair as it provides an acid mantle, but it is particularly good for oily hair:

For dark hair – 1 tablespoon of wine or cider vinegar in 2 pints (1.1 l) of water;

For light hair – 1 tablespoon of lemon juice in 2 pints (1.1 l) of water.

The right way to condition

Conditioning is a protective measure. It is essential for any dry hair, whether it's your entire head or just the ends. If your hair is in good condition, it is very beneficial for the look of your hair and helps prevent problems. Conditioners are creamy lotions that coat the hair shaft. Their advantages are:
- hair becomes much softer and less brittle
- hair can be combed through when wet with much less force, thus reducing damage
- tangles and snarls are more easily manageable
- hair looks shinier, more alive, has more lustre
- flyaway hair can be controlled.

If you look at commercial products, you'll notice various descriptive names: cream rinse, conditioner, re-conditioner. What's the difference? There isn't any. They are just different terms for the same thing. Conditioners are designed to be used after a shampoo, so it's advisable to stay clear of products that claim to clean and condition at the same time. Shampoos and conditioners require separate application to be truly beneficial.

Once your hair is squeaky clean, you are ready to put on your conditioner. Remember to keep your hair type in mind. Only apply conditioner to your entire head if you have dry or normally healthy hair. Never cream-condition a head of oily hair. Do condition the ends if they are dry or damaged.

Apply the conditioner to the palms of your hands, rub together and then gently apply it to the hair shafts. Don't massage it in – you are conditioning your hair, not your scalp. Drag your fingers through your hair, working from front to back in the direction of hair growth. If you are only conditioning the ends, soak a cotton ball with conditioner and rub over the tips.

You only need to leave the conditioner on for a minute as, contrary to what you may hear, it is fully effective in that time. Gently comb the hair whilst the conditioner is in it, starting at the ends. Don't tug on any knots, ease them free slowly and calmly. Rinse all the conditioner out – two or three times as you would after shampooing.

How do you choose the right conditioner? It's trial and error only; you will need to try a number until you find the one that works best for you.

The right way to dry

Until recently nearly everyone let their hair dry naturally. It's still the best way, particularly for teenagers, because dryers can cause unnecessary damage to the hair. In any case, what could be easier? There are some snags to watch for, though.

First – before combing – pat the hair gently with a towel. Pat it from front to back, don't rub it wildly at random. Just pat enough to absorb all the drips. Then wrap the towel around your head and leave it there for about ten minutes. Unwrap the towel and comb your hair. Use a very wide-toothed comb with rounded edges. Never brush wet hair. You must start combing at the ends and only when they are smooth work your way upwards. Don't start at the scalp – your hair will almost always snarl and you'll end up with a bird's nest on the crown. And do it slowly and gently; if you hack away you'll break strands and tear some out by the roots. After combing, wrap again with a towel and press out excess moisture. Remove the towel and give your hair another combing; then leave to dry naturally.

What about shampoo?
How do you know which is good?

Finding the perfect shampoo for you is a matter of experiment, but if you have natural hair (no perm, no bleach, no tint) you can immediately eliminate all those that say they are specially for tinted or treated hair. The basic things you require from a shampoo are that it should:
- be easy to apply and distribute
- be quick and effective as a cleanser
- produce a moderate amount of lather only
- be easy to rinse out
- not irritate the scalp
- have a fresh, pleasing odour
- leave hair soft and manageable.

There are three types of shampoo: soap, soapless and dry. Of course, you must never wash your hair with any odd bar of soap. The *soap shampoos* are excellent for natural hair; they are the old-fashioned types that were always used before the introduction of synthetics. Soap shampoos are made from natural vegetable oils – watch the labels. A particularly good shampoo for teenage hair is one you can make yourself from ordinary green soap (see recipe on page 126).

Soapless shampoos are also called detergent shampoos – these include most of the over-the-counter commercial ones. Most are well-formulated and as non-allergenic as possible. Many different substances are added to the basic cleansing matter – oils, creams, conditioners, thickeners, colours, perfumes, foam boosters, protein, etc. These additions are all very nice, but it is the cleansing agent that matters and the benefit from all the rest is minimal. Read the labels well – they provide all the information as to whether the shampoo is for dry, oily or normal hair. Many products make reference to pH; this is a measure of the acidity or alkalinity of the product. This is relevant only if hair has been treated and its acid mantle has been altered. It is not likely to affect you.

Is your hair dull no matter how much you wash it?

The chances are you are over-shampooing – not washing your hair too often, but using too much shampoo. You only need a little shampoo; too much strips the oil off the hair. You may also not be rinsing thoroughly – any shampoo residue dulls the hair. Then there's another factor, over which you have no control – hard water. If your tap water is hard, the minerals it contains will combine with the soap to form a dull film. The only way around this is to add a water softener (available at most chemists) to your rinsing water. There is, however, one remedy – a final rinse of diluted vinegar: put one tablespoon of vinegar in two cups of water, preferably distilled.

Dry shampoos are not recommended for teenage hair, unless you have been ill for some time and have been unable to wash your hair. Continual use of a dry shampoo will clog your pores and attract more dirt. They are based on talc or corn starch and work by absorbing the oiliness from hair strands and scalp. You brush the powder through your hair, using a gauze-covered brush that absorbs the dirt and oil. A common error is to use too much shampoo.

Does lather matter?

It has nothing to do with the efficiency of a shampoo. If your hair is dirty it won't lather so quickly. However, some shampoos have foam additives, put there to make you believe your hair is getting a thorough cleansing.

Is baby shampoo milder?

Not necessarily. The main thing about it is that it doesn't sting the eyes — which babies wouldn't like. Some of the good cleansing agents in adult shampoos have to be omitted for this reason — so you might be missing out.

PROBLEMS

Which treatments are effective?

The most difficult problem to deal with is dandruff – if it does not respond to home treatment, you may find that a specialist can help.

Is there any way to eliminate split ends?

The only solution is to cut off the ends that are affected. If you don't, the split may spread up the hair shaft. Preventing splits in the first place is the best way. Everyone gets some splits and they usually come from too aggressive brushing and combing, hair dryers being used too near the hair or at too high a temperature, or pulling hair around curlers. Split ends cannot be repaired – off they go!

What about lice or nits?
Clean heads of hair can get lice too – they are very contagious; but treatments are effective

Lice can spread through a school very fast. It only needs one head to be the breeding ground and a whole chain reaction starts. The head louse is specific to human beings and it itches like mad. The adult lays her eggs at the root of the hair and cements them to the scalp with a special excretion, so they are very difficult to remove. Lice should be treated promptly – not only the head where they are breeding, but also anyone who has been in close contact. There are several effective preparations on the market. These kill the eggs, which should then be removed with a fine comb. If itching continues, repeat the treatment after seven days.

Dandruff: a common teenage problem
What it is – what you can do about it
It's not contagious; its cause is vague

It is in adolescence that dandruff usually begins. It is the single most common scalp complaint and if you don't keep control of it, dandruff will continue into your adult years and cause a lot of stress. It is not a disease, nor is it contagious. It is simply a build-up of dead skin cells that refuse to go away through normal brushing and washing. Your scalp is likely to feel itchy as well, and if you scratch it, dandruff will easily come off. You will often notice it on your hair or on your shoulders.

What causes dandruff? No one really knows. Bad hair hygiene is suggested, but it's not necessarily so. Then there's the possibility of fatigue, stress, normal adolescent hormone changes, a too-fat diet, hereditary factors and climatic conditions – if you live in a cold climate you are more likely to get dandruff than if you live in the tropics. As you see, there are many possibilities, but as yet no one has come up with a definite, positive answer. Oily hair and dandruff often go together.

The skin all over your body is constantly being shed – it is washed off in the bath or carried away by clothing. Usually in the case of the head, more brushing and more frequent washings will take care of the build-up of flakes. Daily washings may be necessary. If dandruff persists use the following routine.

First: treat with a mild shampoo plus an antiseptic lotion
Your scalp is delicate so you should not resort immediately to anti-dandruff and medicated shampoos. They can be quite strong. It's much more sensible to cope with the matter step by step.

Shampoo with your normal mild product – preferably your home-made green soap shampoo. Rinse very well. Do your usual conditioning procedure for your hair type. Rinse and rinse and rinse.

Make an antiseptic lotion by taking any good mouthwash (like Listerine) and putting ½ cup in 1 cup of distilled (please note, *distilled*) water. Apply the lotion with a cotton ball, dividing your hair front to back and in parallel 1-inch (2.5-cm) sections. You dab all the roots so that the entire scalp gets treated. Leave the solution on your scalp for thirty minutes. Rinse your hair thoroughly several times with clear water.

Second: cautiously use an anti–dandruff shampoo and lotion
If, after a period of time, the mild shampoo and antiseptic lotion treatment is not doing much good, you should turn to something stronger. These are medicated and you might be sensitive to the components, so keep track of scalp reaction and if you find you have either irritation or redness, don't use any more. It is important that you follow the instructions on the label.

Third: seek professional help if dandruff shows signs of worsening
If neither of the above two steps brings relief, you must go and see a qualified trichologist or dermatologist. It may be more serious than 'common' dandruff, in which case it should be dealt with by a specialist.

TEETH

A healthy set of sparkling teeth is an invaluable asset both to your general well-being and your looks.

Teeth are one of your most noticeable features, not just when you smile but all the time you are talking. Dentistry is constantly improving and a trip to the dentist need no longer be frightening. Today a far stronger emphasis is being laid on prevention of decay and gum disease. Nearly all teenagers have some degree of gingivitis, inflammation of the gums – our diet of over-refined foods and high sugar content is responsible. You must learn to clean your teeth properly, not merely brush them. You may have to go to the dentist more than twice a year. Don't wait until a tooth aches, go for check-ups and professional cleaning. Almost anything can be done to improve the look of your teeth; they can be respaced, straightened or capped if necessary. There's nothing quite like a dazzling smile – get to work on having one.

Some facts on teeth

- *You should have twenty-eight teeth (or thirty-two if your wisdom teeth have come already).*
- *Size and shape are inherited from your parents.*
- *Quality depends on your diet, and the health and diet of your mother when she was pregnant.*
- *You have three types of teeth:*
  incisors at the front for cutting
  canines come next, pointed for gripping and tearing
  premolars and molars at the sides and back of the mouth –
  flat and square for grinding.

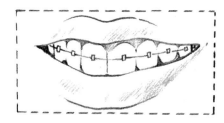

AT THE DENTIST'S

When to go and what to expect

Everyone should have a clean and a check-up at least every six months – three or four visits a year is still better than the customary two. Cavities need to be filled as early as possible, but usually you cannot see or feel early cavities on your own. Modern equipment and methods now mean that drilling and filling shouldn't hurt at all. Emphasis is on pain-free treatment using high-speed drills. Most dentists apply a local anaesthetic to the gum area and then inject a novacain-like liquid. For front teeth that show there are filling preparations that are so natural looking you can't see them. Silver amalgams are used for back teeth as they are more resistant to pressure – actually gold is even better, but more expensive.

Your regular dentist does the repair work, any cosmetic alterations and cleaning. But if cavities are allowed to get too bad, they often need work on the root canal. A specialist, called an *endodontist*, is then required. The infection is cleaned out and the area sterilized; it is then filled with silver or rubber-like materials. The work of the endodontist is very important because once a root canal becomes infected it can pass destructive bacteria into the bloodstream and affect your general health.

Teeth straightening

This is often required in your teens. In fact it should be done between the ages of twelve and sixteen when it is relatively easy to shift teeth around. If you leave it until you are an adult it is a much more complicated and lengthy process. An orthodontist is then needed, a specialist who deals solely with correcting developmental problems of teeth and jaw. Taking steps now to correct faults avoids future functional and cosmetic problems.

Teeth can be too overcrowded or too spaced out, they can be growing sideways, they can often be growing to very uneven lengths. Jaws can be unbalanced, resulting in buck teeth, an incorrect bite or protruding lower jaw. Treatment varies according to the fault – and the purpose of the treatment is not just to improve your appearance, but also to prevent gum disease and tooth decay. The successfully treated teeth not only look better but are easier to clean. No longer are you stuck with cumbersome metal braces – there are now nearly invisible plastic braces as well as plastic removable appliances that have barely visible wire springs. Initially you may have plastic brackets bonded to the teeth (practically invisible) to secure the retaining wires. You will need regular check-ups and on the average it takes between one and two years to complete treatment. It's well worth it.

Arabella says:

'I had unevenly spaced teeth *and* an incorrect bite. My top front teeth had a gap between them and the teeth either side were growing in sideways. At first I had a removable brace to wear at night and as often during the day as I could. It didn't take long to get used to it and I quickly got over the initial embarrassment.

What's in a tooth?

- It's covered in **enamel**, which coats and protects the outer surface. The colour can be deceptive – very white teeth are not always the healthiest. Whiteness may mean soft, porous enamel. Hard enamel is thin and clear, showing the yellowish-white dentine underneath.

- **Dentine** forms the bulk of the tooth covering; it's a thin, hard layer.

- Inside is the **pulp**, the soft tissue which contains the nerves and blood vessels. These have their outlet to the root – and to the rest of the body – through a narrow canal, quite logically called the root canal.

- The **root** accounts for two thirds of the tooth and it is firmly embedded in the bone of the jaw.

'After two months I had little plastic squares cemented on my top teeth and wires running through them with sort of springs at each end. This really did hurt and my teeth were sore, particularly when the wires were tightened – a bit frightening when it was being done too, as the dentist used pliers for the wires and odd-looking instruments to fit and adjust them.

'Eating and talking was difficult at first – I could only cope with soft foods. But then I gradually got so used to the brackets and the wires that I never noticed they were there, though after each check-up and adjustments my teeth hurt for a few days. After nine months they were taken off – just clipped off in fact – and there were my teeth straight and even. I couldn't believe it. I had to have a removable retainer base which I'll need for a few years, but only for wearing at night and periodically during the day.'

Tooth decay starts with the formation of plaque

The greatest cause of tooth loss is decay and the resulting cavities. What causes decay in the first place? It is a substance called plaque, a mixture of bacteria, saliva and food residue which adheres to the teeth. It is colourless and transparent, and therefore invisible to the naked eye. It settles in the spaces between teeth and along the gum line. After twenty-four hours it produces acids which attack the tooth enamel, starting decay. Plaque can harden and build up into tartar – a rough, hard substance which can only be removed by the dentist's instruments. Your diet influences how readily plaque forms in your mouth. Plaque bacteria use sugar – so sweet foods and carbohydrates like white bread and cakes should be avoided. Fibrous foods, however, have a natural cleansing action.

Gum disease

Unless plaque is removed daily through brushing and flossing it can cause inflammation of the gum tissues. This is called periodontal disease – and four out of five teenagers already have it in its early stages. It can be prevented or stopped at this point, but if it's not cleared up it will gradually eat away at the bony structures that support your teeth, so that the teeth eventually become loose and fall out. Periodontal disease is almost entirely preventable; it means taking the time and trouble to clean your mouth and teeth properly every day and twice-yearly visits to your dentist for professional cleaning. Mouth and gums give clear warnings of the disease – red, swollen gums that often bleed, and bad breath.

What is scaling?

It's a thorough cleansing done at the dentist's. It involves scraping away all the plaque deposits on the teeth and then polishing them. Your mouth really feels immaculately clean as well as looking it. Scaling should be done two to four times a year depending on the state of your teeth.

What sort of toothbrush?

It should always be medium. Hard brushes don't remove plaque any more efficiently, but make a very good job of damaging teeth and gums. Children's

---

Five points for good teeth

- Cut out sugar.
- Finish each meal with a glass of water or something raw and chewy – a carrot, apple, celery – to encourage the flow of saliva, your body's cleansing agent.
- Twice a day brush and floss teeth in order to prevent plaque build-up and decay.
- Visit the dentist at least three times a year, not only for check-ups but for professional cleaning.
- Correction of crooked or badly spaced teeth is best done during teenage years.

brushes are actually the best, because the bristles are small enough to reach every crevice. Bristles should have soft rounded ends – current opinion favours nylon brushes. Electric toothbrushes may appear very efficient, but they don't do a better job – and they are harder to handle. You should replace your toothbrush every three months.

Dental floss: it is essential for thorough cleansing

To brush your teeth with a brush is really not enough. In order to clean your teeth properly and get rid of plaque you need dental floss, which goes between the teeth and under the gums where a toothbrush cannot reach. Floss is a thread of nylon filaments which fan out when they are pulled between the teeth and rub away the plaque. Unwaxed floss is best. You need to use floss at least once a day. For the health of your teeth it is more important than your toothbrush.

Fluoride: an important aid to teeth

Fluoride is a chemical compound that builds up a resistance to the acid in plaque – and it's the acid that causes decay and eventually leads to gum disease. During teenage years, fluoride is essential. Some tap waters contain it, but not all, because although fluoride may be good for teeth, many scientists believe it is not good for general health. So be sure to buy a toothpaste which contains fluoride – it will help cut down decay. There are also fluoride products in the form of gels and fluids which can be applied to the surfaces of the teeth, left on for several minutes and then rinsed off. This can be done at home or at the dentist's.

How do you know you have plaque?

For a sight of the enemy, you can use a disclosing tablet which can be bought in any pharmacy. After you have brushed your teeth pop one in your mouth and wait until it has dissolved – then look closely in the mirror – the areas where plaque and food debris still remain will show up red or purple. The stain will show how careless you have been. Don't worry about the stain – it will disappear within a few hours – but the plaque won't go away until you start brushing and flossing properly. Begin today.

A simple five-minute routine keeps teeth healthy and clean

Cleaning is more than brushing. Most cavities start between your teeth and in order to remove plaque you need to use dental floss as well. This is the procedure to be followed twice a day, morning and evening.

Place the toothbrush against the outside surface at a 45° angle. Move to and fro with short strokes, sliding the bristles so that they spray along the gum line. Brush all the surfaces in this way.

Keeping the brush at 45°, brush top teeth on both inside and outside surfaces from the gum vertically down to the biting edge, paying particular attention to the gum line.

Now brush bottom teeth from the gum line upwards; the brush must be at 45°. Wriggle the brush around the gum line using a circular motion. Don't forget the back teeth, scrubbing well along the flat biting surfaces.

Now comes the dental floss. Take about 18 inches (45 cm) and wrap the ends around your middle fingers, leaving a free section of about 1 inch (2.5 cm) in the middle. With a slow sawing motion, coax the floss between teeth and rub in a direction away from the gum. You'll be surprised how far into the gum the floss can go. Rub gently, don't hurt the gums – though they may bleed at first due to the presence of some gum disease. Take the floss between each tooth – this is the only way to remove plaque and bacteria thoroughly. At first it is tricky and awkward using floss – but practice makes perfect and soon you'll be able to whizz proficiently through the whole procedure.

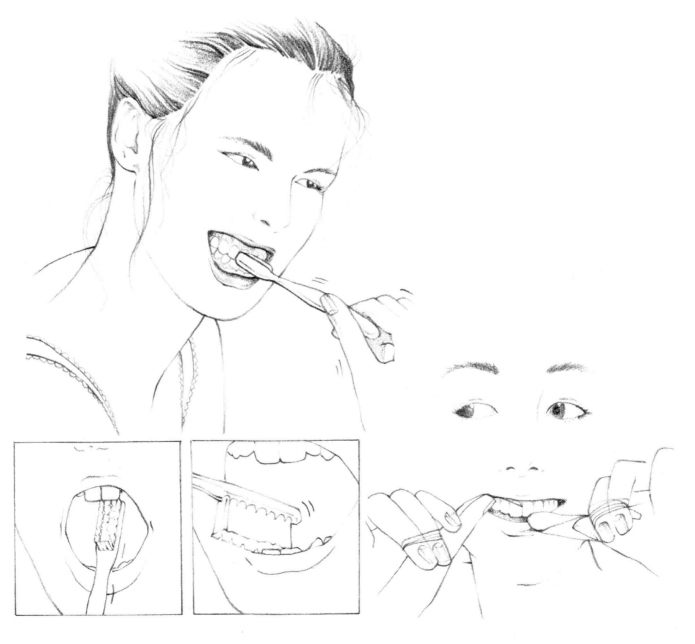

Food for teeth

It is widely known that teeth need calcium to build up their strength. But you also must be sure of adequate vitamin D as well, otherwise the calcium cannot be used. Vitamin C is important to strengthen the connective tissue. Vitamin A is also essential.

Vitamin A	Vitamin C	Vitamin D	Calcium
eggs	cabbage	eggs	milk
carrots	orange	cheese	cheese
liver	grapefruit	sunshine	olives
broccoli	tomatoes		broccoli

What is a cap? Is it the only solution for a broken tooth?

A cap is a permanent covering which looks like a natural tooth – it even has the slight imperfections and variations of colour. It can be made of plastic or porcelain, which is more natural-looking, fused on to a strengthening metal.

If you have a broken or chipped tooth, or one where decay is advanced, you don't need to lose that tooth. It can be treated and capped, even if there is only a stub left. The tooth is first ground to a pointed peg (sometimes the root canal is treated) and a temporary plastic jacket is cemented over it. There is a lot of drilling involved, but this is painless due to the use of numbing injections and high-speed equipment. A permanent cap, or crown, is cemented into place on a subsequent visit. If teeth are missing, a fixed bridge can be made to hold new ones; it is attached to neighbouring teeth, which are usually capped to support the bridge.

An alternative to capping a chipped, cracked or broken tooth is to apply a special resin that fills in the area and blends in with the colour and texture of the natural tooth. But whatever the method, it is always better to save what small amount of tooth there is. Extraction should be the last resort.

LIPS AND MOUTH

How to look after them

You may suffer from chapped lips, cold sores, ulcers or bad breath – all of these are problems which can be treated or prevented.

Protect lips from cold and sun

Lips chap in the cold; lips burn in the sun. They need protection, a little care and attention – and the same rules apply to both extremes. Lips need to be kept moist – this prevents adverse effects in both cold and hot environments. You can use a greasy lip block, you can simply smear oil over your lips, you can actually use butter, margarine or lard – it all has the same effect. If you have dry, cracked lips, this home-made preparation will help.

Lip salve you can make

1½ oz (40 g) beeswax
1 oz (30 g) honey
2 oz (55 g) sesame oil

Melt the beeswax in a double boiler; blend in the honey and then the oil, whisking to a smooth consistency.

Cold sores – what are they?

They are also known as fever blisters and usually appear on the lips. They are caused by a virus infection called *herpes simplex*. You'll know you're getting one if your lips begin to feel sore or itchy, or burn. Doctors are not sure how you catch the virus, but once in the system you have it for life. The bacteria live and reproduce in the nerve roots without necessarily producing blisters. Blisters form when the virus is activated by such stimuli as colds, fever, sun, emotional disturbance and sometimes menstruation. Tiny bumps will appear filled with a yellowish fluid – often they enlarge into one large sore. They are unsightly but eventually they dry up and disappear. Fortunately they don't leave scars. You can get rid of them more quickly by applying compresses soaked in alcohol – leave on for five minutes and repeat several times a day. There are also antibacterial ointments that speed up the healing process.

A mouth ulcer – grin and bear it

These are inflamed sores, caused by irritation or a scratch becoming infected. They gradually disappear of their own accord but take care not to irritate them with hot liquids or spicy food. Gels give some relief as they deaden the pain, but are constantly washed off by saliva. There's really not much you can do – just be patient.

Bad breath – what causes it and what to do about it

This is something that, supposedly, even your best friend won't tell you about. It's not easy to be aware of your own bad breath as it's going away from you and in the direction of others. Medically it is called halitosis – from the Latin word 'halitus' meaning breath and the Greek 'osis' meaning condition. Now doesn't breath condition sound better than bad breath?

It is usually caused by something decomposing in the mouth. Particles of food stay around, sticking between teeth and then literally start to rot. Decayed teeth can produce an unpleasant odour; so can gum infections. Bad breath can also be the result of an incorrect diet – too few carbohydrates and too many proteins. There are also temporary changes – early in the morning your breath can be unpleasant because the flow of saliva has diminished during the night and the automatic cleansing processes of the tongue and mouth don't function as in the daytime when you are talking and swallowing.

Many causes of bad breath can be prevented by good oral hygiene. If diet is the problem, make sure you eat plenty of whole grains and carbohydrates. The juice of any green vegetable is a natural antidote – and try munching parsley.

Mouthwashes – a warning

Don't over-use commercial ones, particularly those that claim to freshen breath. They can disturb the mouth's natural flora and upset the health balance. Hydrogen peroxide can be used regularly – it kills bacteria and strengthens gums. A good natural mouthwash is peppermint tea or a mixture of equal proportions of rosemary and mint steeped in hot water for half an hour; strain before use.

EYES

Your eyes are your windows on the world.
We see more than we hear, touch or smell.

Eyes are also your most significant communicators to others — by looking straight into your eyes, someone can tell quite a lot about your character, feelings and reactions. Something of your inner self comes through. It's true, isn't it? Beauty today is an open and honest look, it's a glow that comes from good health.

Vibrant, sparkling eyes are essential if your face is to look healthy. They need care and attention; they need first and foremost plenty of sleep. If your eyes look tired, you look tired and no amount of clever make-up will help. In fact eyes set the mood of your face, the impression of your thoughts, the expectations of the moment. Eyes need to be regularly checked for any vision faults. Should they ever get infected they should instantly be treated by a specialist. Eyesight is a very precious thing and not to be played around with. To retain perfect eyesight or immediately correct any impairment during adolescence will pay off for the rest of your life. Eyes need protection — from sun, from pollution, from the dangers of sport. Are you aware of the pitfalls? Do you know what to do about them?

HOW THE EYE WORKS

An eye is functionally mature at ten years of age and as a young adult you should be able to focus easily close up as well as adjusting to distance

An optician classifies normal sight as 20/20 (or 6/6) – which simply means that you can see at 20 feet (6 m) what has been precisely gauged to be visible at that distance. If your eyesight is say 20/40 (6/8) that means you only see clearly at 20 feet (6 m) what you should be able to see clearly at 40 feet (8 m). The letter charts that are read to test eyesight are precisely worked out to monitor your vision range.

Your eyeball is circular, but only about a twelfth shows. The part you see through is the black pupil, where light passes through to the back of the eye. The cornea is a transparent layer on the surface which acts like a lens and helps the eye to focus – further back (and invisible) is a lens that takes care of the fine focusing. Eventually an image reaches the retina at the back of the eye, which passes it to the brain. All of this takes place in a split second. Focusing power depends on the relationship of the cornea and the lens.

Bad eyesight is hereditary and not caused by strain

Vision defects usually occur because the lens is the wrong proportion in relation to the eyeball; this is invariably inherited from your parents. No permanent damage can come from eye strain, incorrect glasses or too much television viewing. Eye movement is controlled by six muscles and eye strain is caused by the contraction of these muscles.

Conserve your eyesight
Use the right light

Watch for fatigue and if you are constantly tired see a specialist. Eye strain commonly occurs after you have worked too long in bad light or when eyes are trying to make up for a vision defect – a shortsighted student straining to see the blackboard from the back of the class, for instance.

Writing, reading or close work need not necessarily strain the eyes so long as it is done under the right conditions. Correct lighting is very important: a reasonable amount of overhead or natural light, plus a table light for close work. Daylight should come from behind and above rather than in front.

Can you really be colour blind?

Yes, but it's not actual blindness – it's inability to recognize or distinguish between a few colours only, usually red and green.

WHAT ARE THE MOST COMMON EYE DEFECTS?

Perfect vision is uncommon

Most people who are sure they have normal vision probably have eyes that are slightly out of kilter, but they have the ability to compensate for imperfections with unconscious ease. Adolescents have strong eyes that can cope with minor faults.

There are three common forms of defective vision:

Long sight
Vision is fuzzy close up, clear at a distance

The problem is that the light rays entering the eye through the pupil focus behind the retina instead of precisely at it. It is corrected by putting a convex lens in front of the eye; this makes the rays converge at the right point. If you are far-sighted you usually need glasses for close work.

Short sight
Things are clear close up, far away is foggy

In this case the light rays focus in front of the retina instead of at it. Concave lenses are needed to correct it, but very thick glasses are often required. These are not only unsightly and cumbersome but may strain the eyes. For severe cases of short sight (also known as myopia) contact lenses are preferable, as they give you a wider field of vision – and you need no longer peer through those thick spectacles.

Astigmatism
At any distance things look blurred

This happens when the cornea is uneven, so vision projection is also uneven because the eye's lens cannot focus on vertical and horizontal objects at the same time. Corrective lenses affect the light rays. Glasses need to be worn all the time; but the good news is that scientists recently have been able to develop special contact lenses to counteract this problem.

What is a squint?

A squint occurs because eye muscles aren't holding the eye in place or lack pulling power. It's often called a lazy eye – and while one eye works perfectly well, the other will stay where it is or go in the opposite direction. Squints show up early in childhood and they should have been corrected by the time you are twelve. You'll require exercises and lenses to strengthen the lazy eye; the strong eye is often covered with a patch to make the weak one work. If correction is left too late, an operation may be required to get results.

When should you go to an eye specialist?

If you damage your eyes in any way, you should seek medical attention. Small foreign bodies such as pieces of dust or grit, an eyelash or a bit of make-up can often be removed by pulling the upper lid out and down over the lower lid – or by lifting it out with a tissue or cotton bud, but be very gentle. If it refuses to budge, or if the eye is sore or it waters, go and have it seen to in case of possible infection. It is advisable to have your eyes checked once a year during your teenage years, but you should see an eye specialist immediately if you experience any of the following: constant blinking, headaches, frowning, screwing up the eyes, blurred vision or dizziness after visual concentration.

EYE INFECTIONS AND SORES

These look a lot worse than they actually are; when there's something wrong with your eyes, you and everybody else know about it – they are unsightly and you feel awful

Don't panic about eye ailments; they usually heal and go away quickly, but while they are around they make you look terrible – from itchy, bulging styes to swollen lids and weeping pink eye. But don't fool around with home remedies – these things will usually clear up of their own accord in a few days, but if any aggravation persists, see a doctor. Your eyes are valuable, so look after them. Here are the facts about the most common infections.

Bloodshot eyes

They can look bad, but this is really an insignificant and purely temporary state. When you're tired your eyes become bloodshot – also, if you are over-exposed to the elements, such as wind, cold, seawater. Don't over-use eye drops – they are not a good idea over a long period. Use natural remedies instead.

Inflammation of the cornea

The cornea is the transparent protective coating of the eye. It can easily become scratched by fingernails, paper, make-up brush, etc. – a common accident among young women. Once there's a break in this covering, bacteria can invade the area, causing an infection. You need treatment from an eye specialist, particularly as breaks have a tendency to recur if they are not properly taken care of in the first place.

Inflammation at the roots of the eyelashes

If you have dry skin, dandruff or acne, this might trigger off an infection at the roots of the eyelashes; sometimes it occurs if you are allergic to a certain eye make-up. It is easily treated, but check with a doctor.

Help!
Bloodshot eyes

Use camomile – steep two tea-bags in hot water for three minutes, cool, then place a bag on each eye, leaving on for ten minutes. You'll need to lie down – and close your eyes.

Pink eye (conjunctivitis)

This is inflammation of the thin protective layer over the eye. It can be caused by allergies, irritation, chemicals or as a symptom of nervous diseases. The problem about pink eye is that it is contagious and can be passed on from one person to another. It is actually a very common eye ailment; the first signs are red, watery eyes, then your eyelids burn and itch and there's a secretion of pus which usually causes the lids to stick together during sleep. The eyelids also become puffy. There are various lotions and ointments which soothe the sore areas, but the only quick cure is the use of antibiotics which will clear it up in a few days. Great care must be taken to avoid transmitting it to your other eye or to other people. All your washing equipment – washcloths, towels, soap – must be used only by you.

Stye

This often occurs during adolescence; it's an infection in one of the glands that line your lids near the lashes; it is not contagious. It begins with a small red spot on the rim of the eye and slowly swells into a lump; as it does so the pain increases. It will come to a head and develop a yellow pus centre, which empties within a few days. Hot compresses can often speed up the bursting process. There are ointments to curb the infection and keep it from spreading. There's no need to worry about styes – they may look unsightly but they are not serious.

Swollen lids

Lids often puff up when you are tired, have a cold, or have been crying; in such instances they gradually return to normal. However, if you find a red swollen lump on your lid this is an infection of a gland deep in the lid. It usually resolves itself spontaneously, leaving a tiny lump. If this irritates the lid or looks unsightly, it can be removed by a simple surgical procedure done under local anaesthetic.

Food for eyes

Diet is important for healthy, attractive, shining eyes. You should eat plenty of food rich in vitamin A, lack of which can cause diminished sight at night – it is readily available in vegetables, particularly carrots, celery and tomatoes. Vitamin B-2, vitamin C and vitamin D are also necessary. When there is a deficiency of B-2 eyes often become bloodshot, itchy and watery.

Vitamin A	Vitamin B-2	Vitamin C	Vitamin D
carrots	milk	cabbage	oily fish
tomatoes	cheese	green peppers	cheese
celery	brewer's yeast	tomatoes	eggs
eggs	chicken	orange	sunshine
broccoli	wheatgerm	lemon	
watercress		grapefruit	
		strawberries	

EYES NEED REST AND EXERCISE

If you give them both you'll help prevent eye strain and also strengthen your eye muscles

You probably don't realize how much you use your eyes, particularly during the hours at school when you are concentrating on books. It's a good idea to give your eyes a break every now and then.

Ways to rest eyes

Simply blink and blink as fast as you can for a couple of minutes.

Close your eyes and cover them with the palms of your hands, leaning on your elbows. Cut out the light for two to three minutes.

GLASSES

The optician decides on the lenses but you must decide on the frames

Choosing glasses is not easy; take your time, and don't let anyone rush you. If you're going to have to wear glasses you may as well find those that are the most attractive and the most comfortable. Here are some guidelines.

Stand in front of a full-length mirror when trying on frames. Glasses must be seen in proportion to your whole body, not just your face.

Glasses must fit well. Do they sit securely on your nose? Do they cling to your head without clamping it?

Watch the tops of the frames; they should line up with your eyebrows, otherwise you get two sets of lines.

It's better to keep to neutral tones of beige, brown, and grey, or light steel rims.

Shape is very important — try on as many different designs as you can. Square faces look good in rounded or oval glasses; round faces are balanced by square or angular frames. Long faces need long, deep frames that cover a lot of the face. Short faces are helped by rectangular frames or enormous round ones.

The current trend is for big glasses, simple and classic, with no fancy shapes at all. They make a definite statement. Narrow steel rims and rimless glasses are also favourites with teenagers.

Help!
Tired eyes
- Use witch hazel – first make it very cold in the refrigerator; soak cotton wool pads thoroughly, leave on closed eyes for fifteen minutes.
- Use cucumber – place a fresh slice over each closed eye, leave on for fifteen minutes.

Sun and fun glasses

Do you really need them? Or are they just for effect? A bit of both actually. The glare on a bright day means eyes have to work harder and they tend to tire easily. However, a little bit of sun is good for them, as it forces the muscles of the eyes to work when they adjust from bright to shady spots. There's no doubt that sunglasses can look rather snazzy – particularly if well chosen. Grey, green and brown are your best bets as glare-fighters. Lenses of paler colours such as pink, yellow or blue are fun to wear, but forget them for sun protection.

Will wearing glasses all the time weaken your vision?

No, not at all, though many people will tell you that it will, in the belief that you can get used to glasses of a certain strength and in time will need more powerful ones. Don't believe a word of it. Glasses don't alter the optics of the eye – they are external aids to help you see better and be more comfortable.

Sports glasses

They look dashing, active and give necessary protection. All ball games, racket games and skiing have elements that could potentially harm eyes. Play safe and wear protective eye gear – you can hardly call them glasses as they are really goggles, made of malleable plastic materials. They wrap round your head, often clipping on, and have cushioned bands for extra protection in case you fall. Look for comfort, for complete covering above and below the eyes, for secure fastenings.

Reading in dim light will <u>not</u> ruin your eyesight

Your eyes will, however, become tired more quickly and will be strained temporarily – but they will not be permanently damaged.

Contact lenses or glasses?

There's a saying that men never make passes at girls who wear glasses. Of course, that's not strictly true, but a lot of girls have a real complex about wearing them. The joy of contact lenses is, of course, that they are invisible. You don't have the nuisance of something extra on your face. Glasses can get in the way, particularly during sports; glasses can fall off, get smashed, get lost. Contact lenses are more or less permanently in place – but contact lenses can also get lost, and once lost, they often vanish completely. When one has dropped on the ground you need very good eyesight to spot it – the very thing contact lens wearers don't usually have. And because they are usually inserted in front of a mirror over a sink, they can literally go down the drain. They are more expensive than regular spectacles – both the initial consultation cost and any subsequent replacement. Lenses are more difficult to get used to than glasses; more time is needed to look after them. Which do you think you'd prefer?

> **One eye myth that's wrong: sitting close to a TV or cinema screen is bad for your eyes**
>
> It won't hurt your eyes, but most of us aren't comfortable in the front row or an inch away from the TV. It is important, though, not to watch TV in a dark room; the glare is too strong as the light comes from behind the screen. (In the cinema light comes from behind the audience, so you are not looking directly at it.)

> ## Some safety rules for eyes
>
> - Don't self-medicate; it's so easy to overdose even with mild eye drops. Any problems need professional attention.
> - Take care when playing sports – watch out for those fast balls. Protective eye shields are a good idea.
> - If you use hairspray close your eyes when you apply it. Tiny ulcers can form when hairspray gets into the eye.
> - Be careful when applying eye make-up – careless rubbing with sharp pencils and brushes can scratch the cornea and start up an infection.
> - Don't use anyone else's make up – it's a common cause of infection – and don't lend yours.

CONTACT LENSES

The way to perfect eyesight without glasses
What are they? How do they work?

Do you know that . . .

. . . contact lenses were first thought of by the famous Italian inventor, Leonardo da Vinci, five hundred years ago? But it was not until the middle of the 1930s that his ideas could finally be put into practice – made possible at last by the development of pliable synthetic plastics that wouldn't hurt the delicate surface of the eye.

They are exactly what the word implies: corrective lenses that are in direct contact with the surface of the eye. They are not miniature spectacle lenses as you may imagine; firstly, they correct the vision by a different optical principle and secondly they are made from malleable plastic materials. They move with the movements of the eye, floating on a cushion of eye fluid. They are considered perfectly suitable for adolescents. One thing may put you off – the idea of actually putting something in your eye. In fact you put something 'on' it and once you've learned how to do it – and got over the initial horror – it's very simple.

Different sizes and textures

The largest type dates back to the early designs and is shaped to fit the whole of the visible part of the eye. They are used today only by dedicated swimmers.

Then there are the small, clear discs, called corneal lenses, which may be hard or soft. The hard lenses have the longest lifespan (six years and over), are the most popular and also the least expensive. They are about the size of the flat end of a pencil and work well for all purposes, including active sports. However, hard lenses are difficult to get used to at first. Your eyes will stream and the lenses feel like saucers in your eyes. Initially you can only tolerate them for a short while, but with perseverance they'll soon stay comfortably in place all day. They must be taken out at night. There's a plus with hard lenses: they come in several colours and can make your eyes look green, blue or violet. But remember the lenses aren't opaque – they can enhance but not mask the natural colour of your eyes. You need to experiment.

The soft lenses are really flexible flakes of plastic. They are slightly larger than the hard ones, but they are easier to get used to and they are more comfortable right from the beginning. You can wear them for several hours immediately and finally sleep in them.

Examination and fitting of contact lenses

Lenses have to be expertly prescribed and fitted. After a detailed examination, the curvature of the eye is measured by special instruments. The various stock lenses are inserted to assess individual requirements. You will blink and your eyes will water like mad. Don't panic, it's normal. You may need more than one visit. The practitioner takes great care to ensure you know how to put in and take out the lenses properly – he won't let you leave until you can. It's very awkward at first, but adeptness does come with practice. You also have to learn how to take care of them – hygiene has to be fastidious, otherwise your eye becomes infected. Check-ups are required every six months.

HANDS

***What is the most nimble part of your body?
Your hands. The dexterity of your hands
enables you to perform the most delicate tasks.***

Hands are on the go with hardly a pause all through the day and they receive more rough treatment than any other part of the body. They are on show all the time and you are frequently judged by the state and expression of your hands. The shape and size are genetically determined; it is up to you to keep them in good condition and to learn to use them to enhance your personality and your image. Supple hands are more graceful and expressive than neglected ones. Clean, neat, manicured nails are a vast improvement on bitten stubs. So many of us are ashamed of our hands – we hide them, we sit on them, we clench our fists. How much nicer to be proud of them and put them on show. Hands need exercise for stimulation and flexibility, exercises also make you conscious of how you can move them for expressive articulation. They need regular daily care, and, in particular, constant checking for cleanliness and smoothness. So take a good look at your hands. If you don't like the look of them, no one else will. Do something about them.

HAND CARE

Do you wash them enough?
Do you cream them enough?

Water is fatal to hands: but make no mistake – this doesn't mean cutting down on washing. It means making sure that hands are properly dried with a towel after every contact with water. Hands dry out all too easily, even on exposure to the elements – sun, cold, rain, sea, etc. There is one simple rule for keeping hands in good condition: lots of cream. This will hold in the moisture and prevent chapping, rough skin and cracks. Any heavy cream will do – you can actually use something as ordinary as vaseline. Don't skimp, use the cream liberally – you'll notice how hands literally soak it up. Any excess can be wiped off with a tissue.

How to make your own hand cream

6 oz (170 g) lanolin, 3 oz (85 g) honey, 3 oz (85 g) almond oil

Melt the lanolin in a double boiler, cool slightly then add the honey and whisk until thoroughly blended – by hand or in a blender. Finally, stir in the almond oil, drop by drop, and beat until smooth. Put in an airtight container.

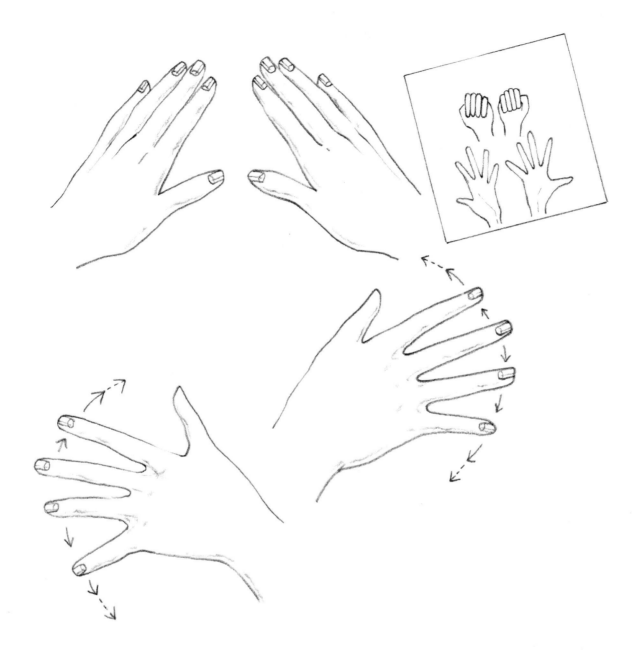

***Exercises to make hands more flexible and graceful . . .
they're great for circulation . . .
for keeping tips warm and preventing chilblains***

Clench the fist tightly, your thumb buried under the fingers. Then open the hand, throwing the fingers forward and spreading wide; hold rigid for a minute. Exercise both hands together – clench and open six times.

Put your hands in front of you, palms down, with the fingers held tightly against each other. Suddenly pull the fingers apart, separating them as widely as possible; hold for a minute. Go back to closed position. Repeat six times.

Always wear rubber gloves when using detergents, to protect hands and nails

ALL ABOUT NAILS

What they are ... how to get them in the best condition ... tips for growth ... details on professional know-how

Nails are actually horny extensions of the skin. The visible nail is only half of the structure; the rest is buried under the skin and you can see just the uppermost tip, which emerges as the half-moon section at the base of the nail. Your nail starts forming around the first finger joint and is composed of horizontal layers of keratin. Nails grow at the rate of about a quarter of an inch a month, so a new nail takes about four months to reach the tip from the cuticle. How strong or brittle your nails are is mostly a matter of inheritance, but nutrition is important. A high-protein diet, rich in iron, vitamin B, iodine and calcium, will keep nails healthy. Foods such as fish, eggs, yogurt and celery are particularly good. Nails will get a few ridges, ruts and bumps from time to time. Horizontal ridges are usually caused by rough treatment around the cuticles; vertical ridges tend to be hereditary and there's little you can do to prevent them. Nails grow quicker in youth, so if you start helping your nails now, you will soon see the results.

What's bad for nails?

Too much exposure to sun or extreme cold; chlorine or salt water can dry out nails and make them brittle.

Cutting with scissors or clippers often causes splits and fractures.

Metal nail files are too harsh and encourage splitting.

Nails will become soft if you use too much soap and water.

Neat acetone weakens nails; always use an oily remover but even this should be used sparingly – just once a week when you manicure.

What's good for nails?

Proper care and attention will improve nails.

Colourless nail polish or a liquid nail strengthener applied to the tip of the nail provides a protective shield and helps prevent flaking.

Apple cider vinegar applied straight to nails can help strengthen them.

Keep nails reasonably short – they are easier to look after and you will have fewer breakage problems – especially if you play a lot of sports.

Shape the nail by filing with an emery board; file with long strokes to an oval shape – filing to a point is asking for breakage – and don't file too deeply down the sides.

Avoid all metal manicure instruments – it's true that they're always part of a manicure case or set, but they are actually bad for your nails unless you can

handle them in a professional way. Use emery boards for filing, and orange sticks for lifting cuticles and cleaning under the nails.

Keep cuticles soft by keeping them well moisturized; use hand lotion liberally and push back softened cuticles with a tissue. Use a cuticle cream at night; get it to the base of the nail by taking an orange stick to lift the cuticle and putting the cream underneath.

If your nails are very dry, try to soak them once a week in warm olive oil – just five minutes is a great help.

Nails look healthy and at their best when they are buffed to a high shine; a buffer or a chamois leather will stimulate circulation and help strengthen nails.

If a nail splits or breaks, there's no reason to give up on it and it's often not even necessary to file it down – it can be temporarily patched until it grows out. There are many patching kits on the market consisting of thin tissue paper that is glued to the nail with a special adhesive – each brand has specific instructions – but you must polish over the patch.

Nail polish actually protects nails as it gives them an extra strengthening layer.

Do you bite your nails?

Yes? You, and many, many others.
It's a very common habit – so don't feel too guilty; but try to do something positive about it, as it makes it very difficult to have attractive hands. There's really only one way to cure nail-biting – willpower. There is a bitter tasting solution you can paint on to your nails, and this helps some biters. Or you might paint them a bright colour, which makes it even more obvious how awful those nibbled stubs look.

Be strong: make a big effort to stop.

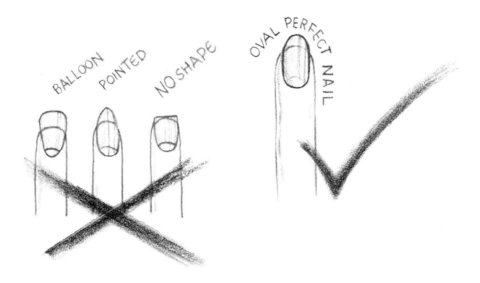

HOW TO GIVE YOURSELF A MANICURE

An easy step-by-step guide that takes about thirty minutes

A manicure isn't just a cosmetic treatment for nails. It conditions both hands and nails, and protects them from daily wear and tear. Also, if you take time and trouble with your nails, paying attention to how they look, how they grow and how they react, you'll quickly notice the effects of good and bad habits. Constant use of nail colour is not advisable for teenagers. Your nails need to breathe, so use it very rarely if at all.

Basic tools to have on hand

Without these things you cannot do a first-rate manicure – half the trick is in the tools.

Basket a good idea is to keep all your manicure equipment in a small bag or basket – a sewing basket is ideal

Towel for protecting your lap and for drying

Absorbent cotton to remove polish. Put on tips of orange sticks.

Nail brush made of bristle, for scrubbing nails and hands

Dish of soapy water; don't use a detergent; do use bath gels or a mild shampoo; warm water

Emery board for filing nails; use the long cardboard variety, never steel ones

Orange sticks for gently pushing back the cuticles, cleaning under the nails and getting rid of any smudges of polish

Nail buffer; the best thing for polishing nails to make them glow

Cuticle cream; this helps keep cuticles smooth and soft, helps avoid hang nail

Cuticle oil for a final attack on stubborn cuticles

Hand cream to keep hands in good condition and to prevent dryness and chapping

Polish remover for dissolving old polish; use an oily type

White nail pencil; this lightens tips and is wonderful for covering stains under the nail

Basecoat and nail enamel; if you don't use a clear foundation, the polish will discolour the nails

1 If you wear polish remove it with a cotton ball moistened with oily remover. A quick drag over the nail is not enough – you must press the cotton against the nail to dissolve the polish and then wipe it off slowly. Only in this way will all polish be removed; you may need to use more than one cotton ball.

2 Using the emery board shape nails into a neat, reasonably short, oval. You should work the board with long strokes from side to centre. Don't saw in one spot. Don't file too low at the corners, as this weakens the nail. If your nail is very short, leave the tip and sides straight – the nail will grow out stronger in this shape and it can always be rounded later.

3 Take the cuticle cream and with the tip of your index finger massage a little cream into the base of each nail. This helps soften and loosen the dry skin.

4 Soak nails in warm soapy water for three to five minutes. Scrub away any dirt or stains with a bristle nail brush. After soaking, dry each nail individually with a soft towel.

5 Apply cuticle remover or oil around the cuticle. This usually comes with a brush applicator; if not, wrap cotton wool around an orange stick and dip into the oil.

6 Wrap cotton wool around an orange stick, dip into the soapy water to moisten and, using the tip, gently lift the cuticle away from the nail and ease it towards the base of the nail in a smooth curve.

7 Apply hand lotion, a liberal amount, and massage into hands and fingers – and to help keep fingers supple, give each a good pull from the joint.

8 Dip finger tips into the water and scrub the nails gently with a bristle brush, stroking away from the base towards the tips. This removes bits of cuticle skin and all traces of grease from the nail.

9 Using the white nail pencil, run the point under each tip. This gives the nails a most attractive look if you are not going to use coloured enamel.

10 Buffing is a splendid treatment for nails as it stirs up the blood circulation. Buff gently in one direction only with a

Go and have a professional manicure

If you watch a professional do your nails, you'll see all the more easily how to give yourself a manicure. Don't be shy about nails in bad condition or badly bitten – the manicurist is there to improve them and during the course of her working day she sees many nails in battered shape. She will follow the procedure as outlined in the step-by-step guide, though she might cut your cuticles with a special instrument – this is something that takes skill, and at home it's one thing you mustn't try as it is so easy to nick the skin and cause an infection. A professional manicure is the best way to get yourself going on a home-care plan. You'll see the difference in your nails immediately.

nail buffer or a soft chamois cloth. Take about half a minute for each nail. You can buy a buffing paste, which comes colourless or tinted and gives a specially good shine. This is the perfect way to have good-looking nails if you are not using nail enamel. But if you are going to use it, don't apply the paste.

11 Apply varnish – do so with three straight strokes for each nail: one down the middle, one either side. First apply a base coat – this prevents varnish from discolouring the nail and also insures a smoother surface. Now the enamel – and incidentally this helps strengthen nails as well as providing the appeal of colour. Polish the entire nail – it looks neater. Pale shades look best on short nails; dark shades are best left until you're older. Fresh shades of apricot, peach and pink are good young colours – and they flatter a tan.

12 You may find you've smudged the polish in places – gone over the nail edges on to the skin. To get rid of it, run an orange stick, tipped with cotton and dampened with polish remover, along the edge of the cuticle and finger tip.

1–4   **5–8**   **9–12**

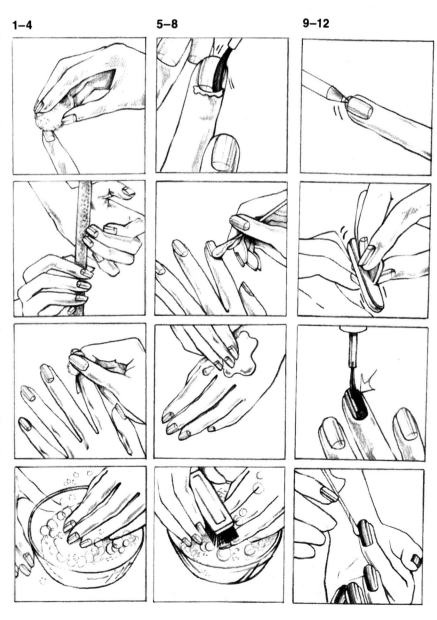

FEET

Your feet have a lot to do with good looks and a confident appearance.

If your feet hurt it shows on your face. On the other hand if your feet are at ease, you'll walk with a step that's sprightly and this affects your posture and your whole air. The average pair of feet walks some twelve hundred miles a year – and spends at least eight hours a day encased in shoes. Most babies are born with perfect feet but four out of five adults finally have foot trouble. The two causes of foot problems are badly fitting shoes or tights and neglect of basic and proper footcare. As a teenager you should start taking care of your feet now, as this is the time when the seeds of trouble are sown. Have you ever really looked at your feet, let alone begun to give them some attention? No? Well, then have a rethink because if they are going to stand you in good stead for life, you need to get into the habit of helping them along each day. It is easier to prevent a foot problem than it is to cure it, or learn to live with it.

The first step is to be sure your feet are clean and free from rough skin and cracks. Daily scrubbing with a pumice stone goes a long way to help prevent a build-up of hard skin. Feet need to breathe, so walk barefoot as often as possible. You'll feel freer – and it will do your feet a lot of good.

FACTS ON FEET

They are built to bear the weight of the body yet are intricately constructed

Without our feet we wouldn't be able to stand up. Much of the strength is in the big toe, which is attached to a leg muscle, while weight is absorbed by the arch. The joint of the big toe is particularly vulnerable to everyday stresses.

The structure of the foot is very similar to that of the hand, but it doesn't have the same mobility. There are many ligaments and muscles which bind the bones into place and give spring and elasticity to the foot. The arch gives grace and lightness.

The way you place your feet and balance your body decides your posture. If you stand with your feet about 8 inches (20 cm) apart and sway gently, you'll be aware of one point that is the best pivot for your stance. Memorize it and try to use it when you are standing, walking, running.

Feet also have to be exercised; if they are not, muscles slacken and they have trouble taking the body weight and supporting the bones. This means that your bones have to take too much wear and tear – friction causes hard skin areas and painful lumps, and arches drop. Even wriggling your toes from time to time gives the foot some movement, but here are some more ideas.

Foot cream

3 tablespoons lanolin
1½ tablespoons almond oil
1½ tablespoons glycerine
2 drops oil of rose geranium

Melt the lanolin in a double boiler add the almond oil, glycerine and rose geranium oil; beat well.

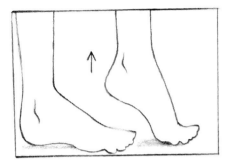

Walking barefoot is the best way to exercise feet

The best way of all is to walk barefoot on sand or grass, but walk around the house barefoot whenever you can. Wearing wooden-soled exercise sandals is the next best thing and is very good for feet as they are carefully shaped and balanced to give the muscles in the feet and legs the right kind of stimulus. You are forced to use your toes to grip and relax the foot. Get a pair to wear inside and outside the house – they're better than slippers.

Daily foot exercises can help prevent many problems

Feet get little opportunity to exercise freely, so try to do these three daily – they only take a few minutes. (Do them with bare feet, naturally.)

Toe raising
Stand straight, feet pointing ahead, then raise yourself up on to your toes, hold to the count of five, lower. Repeat five times.

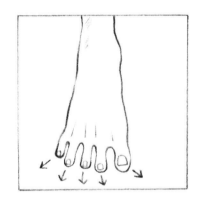

Toe control
Sit with your legs in front of you and try to spread your toes out as you would your fingers – then try to work each toe up and down individually. Repeat five times. You'll find it practically impossible at first, because although you can make your fingers do anything at will, it's quite a different matter with toes. But with practice you can achieve a certain degree of agility.

Foot circles
Sit with your legs stretched out in front. Arch the foot and make wide circles outward. Repeat ten times. Now make inward circles – ten times.

Treats for feet

They deserve tender loving care; some ways to help them at home

Scrub feet daily with a firm bristle brush; use a pumice stone on hard areas.

After your bath or shower massage feet with a hand or body lotion.

Relieve feet by lying with feet higher than your head for ten minutes; this is great after you've had an active day and are going dancing in the evening.

After sports, help feet by giving them an old-fashioned foot bath – throw a handful of Epsom salts in a bowl of hot water and soak for ten minutes.

Hot, swollen feet and ankles can be smoothed and returned to normal by rubbing ice cubes over them.

A few drops of lavender oil in a warm foot bath helps sore feet.

To warm up cold or wet feet, put a pinch of mustard in a bowl of hot water; soak for ten minutes.

Blisters are helped by dabbing on cornflour.

Powder feet – this helps absorb moisture.

For special dates, pamper feet by splashing on cologne before putting on shoes and stockings.

HOW TO GIVE YOURSELF A PEDICURE

It will be awkward at first; skill comes with practice. It should take about thirty minutes

You don't need a pedicure as often as you need a manicure – about every two or three weeks is sufficient. There are many people who never pay any attention to their feet at all, except for cutting the nails occasionally – and then they wonder why they have corns, misshapen toes, ugly nails, hard and rough skin patches. Feet respond very quickly to attention, and it's possible for them to look pretty. If you wear open sandals a lot, you must put your best foot forward. Here's how.

The tools you'll need

Be sure to have all your equipment lined up beforehand – you can't go running around with wet soapy feet to get something you've forgotten. It's usually more convenient to do it in the bathroom.

Basket; you use basically the same equipment as for a manicure, with just a few extra items – keep everything neatly in a basket

Towel; put on a low stool or bathmat and do your pedicure on it, as well as using it for drying

Absorbent cotton to remove polish, to put between toes to divide them when applying polish

Bristle nail brush; be sure it's firm; for scrubbing

Pumice stone for rubbing away hard and rough skin, for thorough cleaning of dirty cracks

Large bowl of soapy water deep enough to immerse feet to the ankles; use bath foam for soapiness

Emery board; the long ones are better; never use steel

Nail clippers; only for toes, never for fingernails

Orange sticks for cleaning under nails and down the sides, and pushing back cuticles

Nail buffer to shine nails if you're not using polish

Cuticle cream and oil for softening hard skin at cuticle

Hand cream – or alternatively use a body lotion – to prevent dryness

Nail polish remover (use only oily varieties); takes away polish

Basecoat and nail enamel; toenails look prettiest painted – use a base coat first.

1 Soak cotton in oily remover, press wad against nail, hold a few seconds, wipe off.

2 If your big toenail is tough, use clippers to cut a straight line across; never use scissors. Toenails should be kept straight – not oval or pointed even if they are long – as this prevents the nail cutting into the flesh and also prevents an ingrowing nail.

3 File nails to a smooth edge, but not down the sides.

4 Soak feet in warm sudsy water for five minutes or more (read a book while you're doing it); then scrub the feet all over – don't forget the heel and the underside of the foot.

5 On the rough and dry spots use a pumice stone (or a friction pad). This gets rid of dry flaky skin and if you do it regularly will reduce any hard lumps. Feet often become cracked when they are dry and dirt is lodged in the crevices. Only a pumice stone will get rid of it. Put feet back in the water and brush away any shreds of skin and loosened dirt.

6 Using a cotton-wrapped orange stick dipped in the water, clean under nails and down the sides.

7 Apply cuticle cream or oil all around the cuticle area; massage gently with a cotton-wrapped orange stick, easing the cuticle back.

8 Put foot back in the water to rinse for a second, and towel dry, being sure to dry in between the toes.

9 Massage in hand or body lotion over the foot and lower leg with firm upward strokes. Massage each toe individually, and then pull each one with a quick jerk.

10 Buff nails to aid circulation, but do this in one direction only. If you are not going to use polish you can put on a tinted buffing paste.

11 Before you apply polish, separate toes with a strip of cotton wool (or a folded tissue), weaving over and under toes. This prevents smudging of polish.

12 Apply a base coat and two top layers – cover the entire nail, it's prettier. Clean away any smudge marks with a cotton-tipped orange stick dipped in polish remover. Leave for at least ten minutes to dry before removing the dividing cotton.

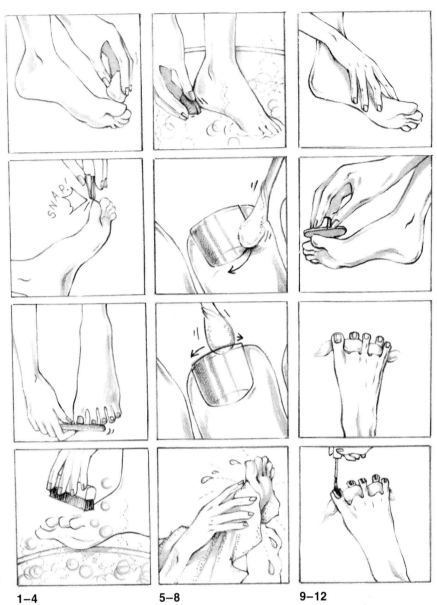

1–4   5–8   9–12

Is there any real point in having a professional pedicure?

Most people find it very difficult to take care of their feet properly. It is well nigh impossible to do it as well as a professional. It is worth investing in a pedicure early on because, firstly, you will learn many tricks by watching and, secondly, you will immediately realize how good your feet feel and look – and you will be more inclined to keep up the good work. One thing to watch out for: in some countries there are rules about how much can be done in a beauty salon if the pedicure is not done by a qualified chiropodist – you could end up by just getting your nails clipped, filed and polished, with no attention being given to hard-skin areas or other problems. In this case a pedicure is not worthwhile, as you can do all these things yourself.

SHOES

Ninety per cent of foot trouble is caused by wearing a shoe that is too small, too narrow, too pointed or too high

Everyone is guilty of buying shoes because they are fashionable rather than a good fit. You *can* have both, but it means shopping around and having the nerve to stand up to aggressive sales assistants – and that's not easy, even for an adult. But it really isn't worth investing in the wrong shoes – they can cause corns and callouses that will take months to get rid of. Do throw out any shoes that hurt your feet.

What is a good fit?

When you put the shoe on, there should be half an inch between the tip of your big toe and the end of the shoe. The toes should be able to move freely. The back of the shoe should fit snugly at the heel so that you don't have to grip the shoes with your toes to keep the heel in position. You must try on both shoes – one foot is invariably slightly different from the other. You must stand and walk around the shop in them. Shoes may feel fine when you sit down, but uncomfortable once you are standing on your feet. Never buy shoes with the idea of breaking them in: it's your feet that will be broken in, not the shoes.

What about heel heights?

The lower the heel, the better the legs are exercised and the less strain there is on the foot, as the body weight is evenly distributed over the foot. When heels

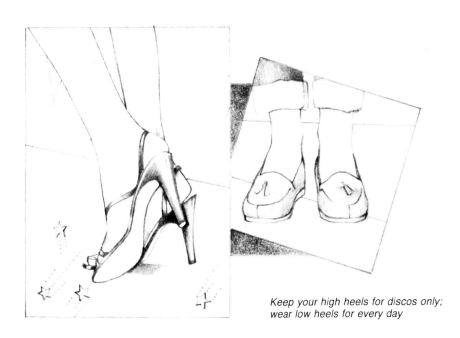

Keep your high heels for discos only; wear low heels for every day

These shoes are noisy but good for your feet

are over $1\frac{1}{2}$ inches (4 cm), the weight of your body shifts to the ball of your foot as the foot is thrust forward and the strain on that area will eventually cause callouses. This doesn't mean you should never wear high heels – you can so long as they fit well, but not for a long period of time and not for walking long distances. It's a good idea to alternate heel heights – low ones for everyday activity, high heels for a special occasion.

Leather shoes are better than plastic

Leather allows your foot to breathe; your feet will become sweaty in shoes made out of synthetics. Leather also shapes itself comfortably to your foot. Cotton and linen are fine for summer. Sandals are great for hot weather as they free the feet, particularly the toes, and allow them to straighten out, but they should have low heels as they give little support.

Do you have sweaty feet?

It's quite natural for feet to sweat, but some do more than others, particularly during adolescence. The problem can be helped by washing them twice a day and changing your socks or stockings twice a day. Always put on fresh socks and shoes after any sporting activity – and wear clean socks for sports. Powder can help, both to keep the sweat in check and to help offset the smell that often accompanies it.

Do you know that nylon tights can cause foot problems?

If they are not big enough, they can encase your feet rigidly, restricting movement and causing swelling. In warm weather, nylon tights also trap moisture, causing feet to be hot and sticky – perfect for virus infections.

WHAT CAN GO WRONG WITH FEET?

Feet that hurt should be taken to a chiropodist for expert care – watch for early signs

Many foot problems have to do with a build-up of skin that finally forms bumps and outgrowths which press on nerves or bones and cause pain. They are caused by ill-fitting shoes or incorrect foot balance and movement of feet. Professional care is very important; go at once for attention before the problem becomes exaggerated. Most foot ailments don't cure themselves, but get worse – and you have to stand on your own two feet for the rest of your life! Here's what to look out for.

Athlete's foot

This is a fungus infection contacted, like verrucas, in gyms and swimming pools when you are barefoot. It likes warm, damp skin and is very infectious.

It appears between toes and on the soles of the feet. Watch for itchy, flaky skin between the toes – you'll see it when you are drying your feet. It is hard to prevent, but it can be treated with medicated liquids and powders. Ask your pharmacist to suggest a remedy, but if the infection is still there after two weeks, go to a chiropodist.

Bunions

A bunion is a painful lump at the side of the big toe; it is basically bone growth and is caused by tight or pointed shoes and tight stockings. At the first sign of a bunion (rare in teenagers) do foot and toe exercises, wear a pad of cotton-wool for protection and see a specialist quickly because if the toe becomes really angled, surgery is the only answer.

Callouses

These are areas of hard, flattened skin caused by badly fitting shoes. They don't have any root and are therefore less painful than corns, but they often burn like mad. If you do a lot of sports and don't wear proper footgear you will get callouses on the soles of your feet. The hard skin can be rubbed down with daily use of a pumice stone. If this is not successful, see a chiropodist.

Corns

Corns are a build-up of hard, dead skin that appears on the joints and on soles of feet. They are cone shaped with a point facing inwards and when this presses on a nerve it can be terribly painful. They are really the body's way of building a protective pad on areas that are taking a lot of friction and pressure. They are almost always caused by badly fitting shoes. The way to get rid of corns is by having them removed professionally – and the sooner the better. Don't ever attempt to cut them down yourself – you may have seen an adult doing this with a razor blade, but it's no solution and you could easily cut your toe rather badly. Wearing a corn plaster may ease the pressure.

Ingrowing toenail

Sometimes a toenail will curl over and dig into the flesh at the side of the toe. It can be very painful. This could happen as a result of wearing tight shoes or socks. Preventive measures are to check on footwear and never to cut the nails away at the sides or cut them too short. An ingrowing toenail often has to be removed.

Nail infections

Your big toenail is more likely to pick up an infection than the others. The most common one is caused by a fungus that discolours the nail and thickens it. It can be treated with medicated liquid that is painted on the soft skin under the nail, and applied at the base under the cuticle. Sometimes the whole nail has to grow out before it is completely healthy again. You may even lose your nail, but don't worry – a new one will grow in its place.

Verrucas

These are caused by a virus infection picked up by bare feet, more often than not in changing rooms. They grow inward and can be very painful. They should be treated by a foot specialist.

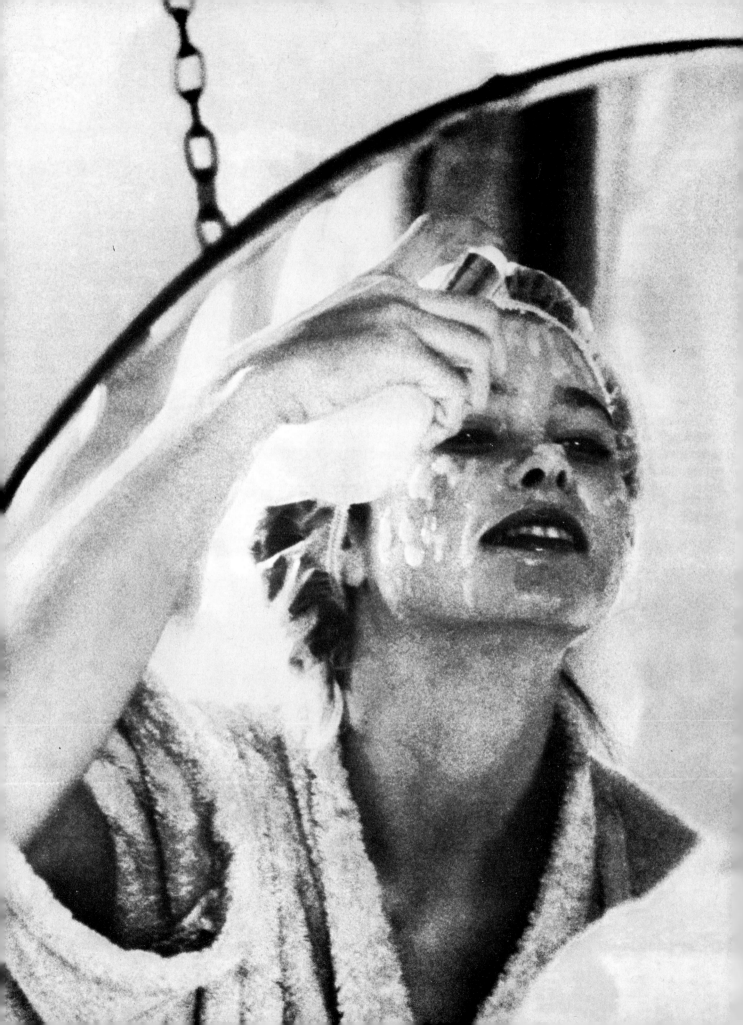

LEARNING THE BEAUTY TRICKS

TIM GEANEY

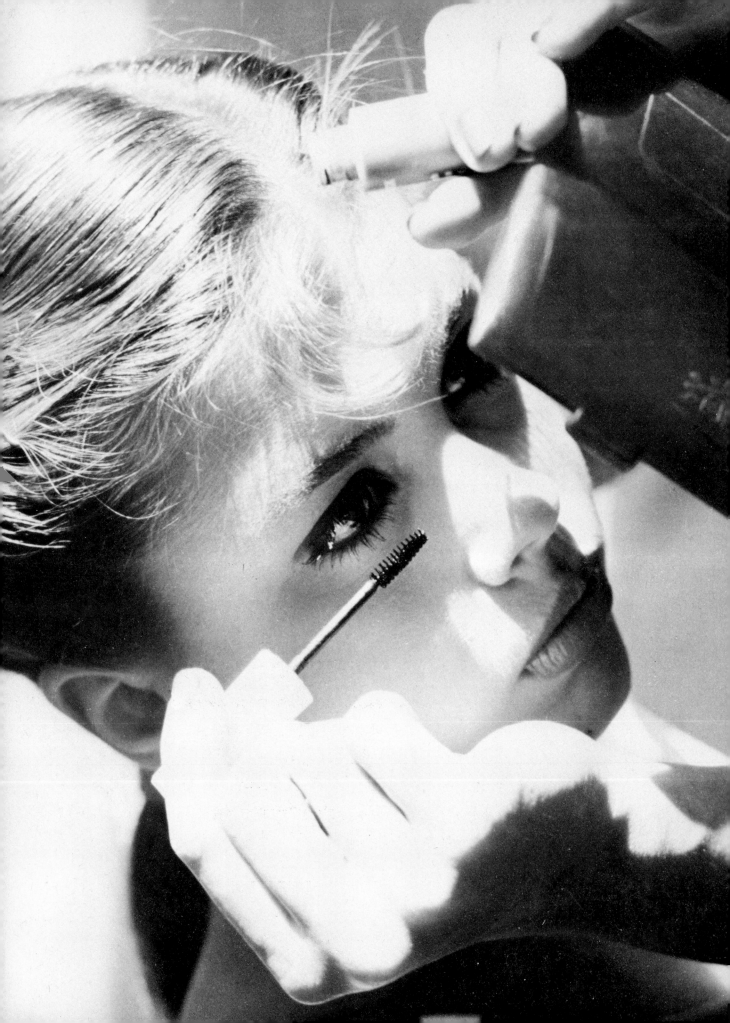

MAKE-UP

Make-up creates illusions.
The trick is to learn to use it so skilfully
that you give the illusion of wearing
hardly any make-up at all.

It should be a see-through glaze, not a solid covering. When you are young it's important that you look as natural as possible. You should glow – and your beauty should be a reflection of your health and vitality and your positive attitude to life. But make-up is fun. Dipping into pots of various textures and colours is a real pleasure; so is the challenge of seeing what you can actually do with your face. It is possible to make quite drastic changes. You can create the impression of more perfect features, higher cheekbones, larger eyes, brighter colouring. Colour is the key to it all, not the use of strong colour, but the subtle blending of tones that bring new dimensions to your face. Too much contrast shouts 'over made-up' and looks false. The focus of any make-up look should be the eyes, and eye colour is the one thing that you will need to experiment with a lot before you find the right shades and textures. There is no need to buy a wide range of expensive products. What counts is skill – it's very important to learn how to apply them correctly. A successful make-up depends on three things – cosmetics that suit your colouring and personality, the right equipment and a confident hand. Here's how you get them.

ERIC BOMAN

175

MAKE-UP

Make-up creates illusions.
The trick is to learn to use it so skilfully
that you give the illusion of wearing
hardly any make-up at all.

It should be a see-through glaze, not a solid covering. When you are young it's important that you look as natural as possible. You should glow – and your beauty should be a reflection of your health and vitality and your positive attitude to life. But make-up is fun. Dipping into pots of various textures and colours is a real pleasure; so is the challenge of seeing what you can actually do with your face. It is possible to make quite drastic changes. You can create the impression of more perfect features, higher cheekbones, larger eyes, brighter colouring. Colour is the key to it all, not the use of strong colour, but the subtle blending of tones that bring new dimensions to your face. Too much contrast shouts 'over made-up' and looks false. The focus of any make-up look should be the eyes, and eye colour is the one thing that you will need to experiment with a lot before you find the right shades and textures. There is no need to buy a wide range of expensive products. What counts is skill – it's very important to learn how to apply them correctly. A successful make-up depends on three things – cosmetics that suit your colouring and personality, the right equipment and a confident hand. Here's how you get them.

FOUNDATION

The first step in making up is to apply a coloured liquid or cream, called a foundation

"TOO DARK!"

Check the colour of make-up foundation in daylight

As a teenager, it is best to do without a foundation except for special occasions – a tinted moisturizer can double as a base. Nevertheless you need to know what to look for and what to practise with for the future.

The right foundation provides an ideal surface for other cosmetics – it's rather like the canvas of a painting. Foundations come in a wide variety of types, textures and colours. Colour is the most important – it must tone in with your skin. There is no point in picking a colour because you like the look of it in the bottle. You have to be realistic about the shade of your skin, and match it.

Take a friend with you when you buy a foundation and don't be intimidated. All cosmetic counters have sample pots, so use them. Don't wear any make-up. Apply the foundation to a small area on your face and go into the daylight to check it. If it is obviously not the right shade for you, try another. And don't let the assistant talk you into putting the colour on the back of your hand – or hers – to judge the shade. Neither will resemble your facial colouring. It's a question of trial and error, so persevere. There are many types of foundation and young skins can wear most of them; it's just a matter of using the one that looks and feels best. Colours range from white to the deepest mahogany. The consistency varies according to the type.

Most foundations are best applied with a damp sponge – not wet, just damp – and then blended with the fingertips. Use sparingly; a thin layer well blended is much more effective than a thick layer slapped on. If you prefer you can first dot the foundation over the main areas of your face and then blend it in with the fingers or a sponge or both. You can use either a cosmetic sponge or a small bath sponge.

Liquids come in bottles and give a very light coverage. They can be creamy for normal or dry skins or oil-free for greasy skins. They don't always provide an adequate cover and, because they tend to be runny, are best applied with a sponge.

Creams are available in bottles and tubes and are the most popular type as they suit most skins. They give a glossy look and are easy to apply with the fingertips or with a sponge.

Gels are usually packed in tubes. They squirt out like a runnier petroleum jelly. They are perfect for summer use, but for even application it's best to use a sponge. They provide a coloured sheen to match your body tan.

Solid cream sticks come in cases rather like a chunky lipstick container. The consistency is thick; they are used to cover up blemishes or uneven coloured skin.

Dot the foundation on the main areas of your face with your finger-tips or a damp sponge.

Opposite: ARTHUR ELGORT
Overleaf: ERIC BOMAN,
TERENCE DONOVAN

HAIRSTYLES

Finding the perfect style for you doesn't happen by accident.

If you were to ask a roomful of girls what they thought was the single most important aspect of looking special the chances are that all would answer: marvellous hair. And it's true. If your hair doesn't please you the rest of you looks wrong. The right hairdo can transform an attractive girl into a beauty and hair can be very sexy. Hairstyles today are uncomplicated, allowing hair to move freely, and there are literally hundreds of ways of doing your hair – you have to work at it, you have to experiment, try this and that. The key to success is natural simplicity – and you need to find a style that suits your hair as well as your personality. It should also take your total body proportions into consideration, not just your face. On the following pages are masses of ideas to start you thinking about what can be done. Your hair can be short, long, straight, curly, frizzed, fringed, knotted, plaited, tied, rolled, etc. Remember hair is the great confidence-giver – and there is no reason why yours can't be!

WHAT KIND OF HAIR DO YOU HAVE?

The first step to successful hair:
be sure of its type – be aware of its limits

There are three things to check on – texture, body and pattern. The texture can be fine or coarse, and it's very easy to tell which you have. Fine hair is usually thin and apt to be limp. Anglo-Saxons and Nordic people often have this sort of hair. Coarse hair is strong and is frequently wiry. If it's curly it can be hard to manage. You can also have hair that's between fine and coarse and this is usually the easiest to manage.

The next point to consider – is it thick or thin? Thick hair means there's a lot of it, whether it's fine or coarse. If you live in a warm or hot climate you are more likely to have thick hair – it seems to thrive under the sun.

Now think about the actual pattern of your hair – is it curly, wavy or straight? The more you go along with the natural tendencies of your hair, the easier it is to take care of it. No matter what you do with it, curly or wavy hair will always revert to its natural pattern – and amazingly quickly. Straight hair can be manipulated to curl, wave, or turn up or down, but it too will soon return to its natural line. Although you may lament having straight hair, it is actually easier to control and has many more possibilities of style – even if they are only temporary.

The most highly textured hair with a particularly difficult curling pattern is black African hair. It is also the most fragile and any manipulation, from excess combing to straightening, is potentially very damaging. On the other hand, hair of Latin or Oriental origin is usually straight, coarse and strong and can withstand a lot of messing around because this type of hair is very resilient.

Test the texture of your hair

If you answer yes to two or three questions in one group, your hair is that type.

Fine hair
Does your hair naturally fly away with no control at the ends?
Does your hair droop in the heat and whenever the air is damp?
Does your hair curl easily, looking marvellous for a few hours, and then flop?

Medium hair
Do you have fairly good control over your hair?
If you set or style your hair, does it stay in reasonable order for a few days?
Even when the air is humid, does the set remain?

Coarse hair
Is your hair on the wild side?
Do the ends tend to be bushy?
Do you feel your hair is practically impossible to manipulate?
Do you find you and the equipment you have seem inadequate to bring your hair under control?

CHANGING YOUR HAIR?

Is your hair too straight or too curly?
Do you think your hair would look better another colour?

These are serious issues, because if you want to change the pattern of your hair or the colour, it involves a process that drastically alters the natural construction of your hair. So if you perm, straighten or colour your hair, and if you hate it – you have to wait for it to grow out. If you have short hair, this

Gently blend in the foundation, using upward and outward strokes, to the very edge of your hairline.

Cakes and blocks are dehydrated and are applied with a damp sponge. They are fine for oily skins and great for covering spots temporarily.

Cover-ups are very dense creams used here and there on the face to camouflage unsightly blemishes.

POWDER

You may consider powder old-fashioned and ageing
This is because it is often incorrectly applied

Powder can look very natural; it sets make-up – not only the foundation but eye colourings as well – and stops the face from looking shiny, while preserving its natural glow. Of course you don't need powder if you don't wear any foundation or when you use a bronzing gel. Although powders come in many colours, it is best to use one that is transparent or colourless. All powders are based on talc, and baby talcum can be an effective alternative – its initial whiteness disappears when all the surplus is removed from the skin. Powder comes in two forms, loose and compressed.

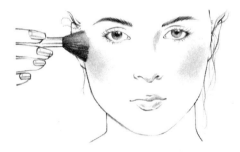

Powder blusher is applied with a wide brush; start high on the cheek-bones going in an upward and outward direction

Loose powder is good for most purposes. Apply with a clean puff or cotton-wool, with a press-and-turn action. Then, with the other side of the puff or with a wide brush, brush away all excess. Powder should be an invisible film and the most common mistake is to leave too much on. Powder should be used before you use any other powder cosmetics for eyes or cheeks, but after you have used any cream ones. The central zones of your face need more powder; the cheeks and the area around the eyes require very little.

Pressed powder is powder mixed with a little oil or wax and then compressed. It gives a denser coverage but is easier to carry around for touching up. Don't apply layer upon layer – it will cake and look awful.

BLUSHER

Also known as shader, contourer or highlighter

A blusher is a most valuable cosmetic – providing you use it correctly. It can add colour, shape and glow to the skin. It should never be obvious, so blend it in very carefully. The colours can look strong in the container; only a little is needed to give a natural look – any excess colour can be blended, brushed or wiped away. When using a blusher, a basic principle to remember is that colours paler than your skin tone will highlight features, making them more

Cream blusher is blended with a sponge; colour should merge with the foundation and go right into the hairline.

prominent, while darker shades will make areas recede. There are many different types on the market, but they fall into three categories.

Creams come in compacts or sticks; you apply them over foundation (if used) but under powder. Blend them in with your fingertips. They are particularly suited to young skin that doesn't need a foundation as they give a natural sheen.

Gels give a glossy look, so they look good on a tanned skin. Don't cover with powder.

Powders are by far the most popular and are usually presented in a compact, complete with a brush applicator. They are brushed on the face after powdering.

Blusher is applied high on your cheeks and worked upwards and outwards to the hairline. You will need lots of experimenting to find the right spot. It is most important that you do not cover your whole cheek. Blend it in so thoroughly that the blusher literally runs into your hairline and has no sharp edges anywhere – you can use your fingers, a puff or a brush for this.

EYE MAKE-UP

Eye make-up can be a very simple thing, such as a brushing of mascara, or a splendid artistic creation

With a little practice it is possible to change the appearance of your eyes quite dramatically. But at first just choosing the right kind and colour of eye make-up seems a hurdle. Here are the different types of products.

Eyeshadow

This gives colour and dimension to the eyes; it comes in a vast range of colours.

Powders have the consistency of pressed powder, with a moisturizer added to give greater cling. They have good staying power and should be applied with a brush or sponge applicator. By far the best for beginners; best for a natural look, too.

Creams are oil-based and blend easily into the skin. They need to be set with transparent powder or talc to prevent 'creases'. Apply with a brush or with the fingertips.

Sticks are more solid than creams – the consistency is similar to a lipstick. Unfortunately they often go runny in hot weather and become hard in the

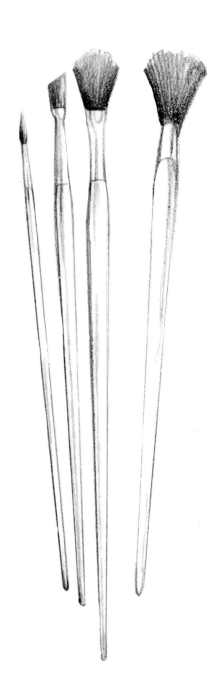

*Basic make-up kit:
lips, eyes, powder, blusher*

Tips for applying eye make-up

- A little moisturizer on the lid will make shadow go on more smoothly.
- Blend shadow so well with the fingertips that the colour never looks obvious, too dark or too muddy.
- Don't leave a gap between the lashes and the shadow – start applying colour at the lash line.
- Try using an eyelash curler; this really opens up the eyes and makes the lashes look longer.
- When applying mascara brush the upper lashes downwards from the top first and allow to dry; then brush up from below. Brush the lower lashes up first, then down.
- To make the lashes glisten, put a little petroleum jelly on a clean mascara brush and brush on.

cold, both hampering application. The stick is applied directly to the eyelid, blended with the fingertips and set with powder.

Liquids contain more water than the creams. They come in bottles with a brush and the colour is painted on. When dry, they are long-lasting, but the colour often looks harsh and it's difficult to get a natural look.

Watercolours are cake-like and are applied with a wet brush. The trouble is that when you blend them in with your fingers, the colour is apt to rub away.

Crayons and pencils are waxy and wide for smooth application. Colour is drawn on with strokes and curves and then blended in with the fingertips. Easy to use and effective, but it's important to do the blending well otherwise the lines are too harsh.

Eyebrow colourings

Eyebrow shadings give definition and importance to the brows; stick to greys and browns; harsh colours are unattractive.

Pencils have waxy, narrow leads that have to be sharp to be effective. Use short feathery strokes, to give a natural line to the brows; never draw a continuous line.

Powders come in compacts, usually with a slant-edged brush. Apply in short diagonal strokes.

Eyeliners

These are used to define the outline of the eye by colouring all or part of the rim. Painted-on lines are too harsh – use eyeshadow crayons or eyebrow pencils; kohl pencils are also very effective – try the blues and greys inside the lower rim.

Mascara

Mascara gives colour and thickness to lashes. It can be worn by itself or with other eye shading. It does more for the eyes than any other product. Browns and blacks are the most popular.

Cake mascara consists of a block of colour that is rubbed on to a wet brush and then applied to the lashes. It has to be built up slowly, coat by coat.

Creams are thicker and oil-based; they are applied with a dry brush but it's difficult to control the quantity.

Wands contain creams that can be rolled on to the lashes with a spiral brush or a screw-like rod. Several brands contain, in addition, fibres to build up lash length and thickness. This is the most efficient and least messy way of applying mascara.

How to make the most of your eyes

Your eyes can be shaded in such a way that your good points are emphasized and your bad ones are camouflaged so that they are hardly noticeable. Every eye shape is unique – no one has eyes quite like you – but there are certain basic shapes that cause problems. Here's what you can do about them:

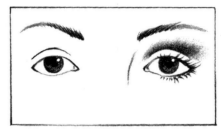

Deep set eyes can be brought forward if you apply pale eyeshadow on the lid, continuing it just over the hollow. Between lid and brow use brown, taupe or grey shading, blended so it hardly shows.

Close set eyes need to have the emphasis shifted to the outer part of the eyes. Using a deep smoky shadow, apply it from centre of lid to the outside corner and extend it outwards with your fingertips. Pluck the eyebrows in the centre if they are too close.

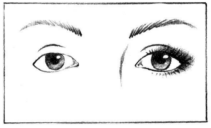

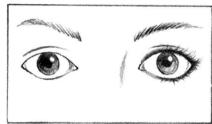

Narrow eyes can look bigger and more oval if you put neutral smoky shadow all around the outer corner and blend towards the centre both above and below the eye.

Eyes that are too round can be balanced by using shadow from the centre of the lid and bringing it out from the corner in a half circle; do not emphasize the shadow under the eye.

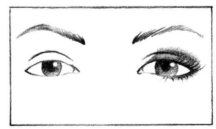

Protruding eyes appear less prominent if you blend a narrow band of smoky colour all round the eye; also, using a crayon, smudge an arc of dark shadow to define a socket crease.

Droopy lids will liven up if shading is used to lift them at the outer edge. Blend the colour up and out, widening gradually to the outer corner and continuing the colour under the eye.

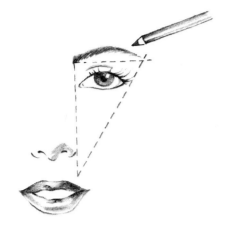

Eyebrow shaping

Eyebrows balance a face and open up the eyes. They need grooming and definition, but you shouldn't alter their basic form. The ideal eyebrow proportions are shown in the sketch – the brow starts at a point above the inside corner of the eye, curves to its maximum height above the outer rim of the iris and extends gradually downward. Check the shape by brushing, first upwards and then across. Pluck out straggly hairs with a quick, firm tug from underneath – slant-edge tweezers are easier to work with. The idea is to neaten the brows while keeping them natural. If you have scanty brows, they can be filled in with a pencil, using short feathery strokes, and then smudged with your finger. You can mascara your brows for more definition, add gloss to make them shine or smear with a little moustache wax to give them more body.

LIP MAKE-UP

For hundreds of years women have coloured and reshaped their lips

Lip colour was one of the very earliest cosmetics. Today it's a matter of fashion – sometimes it's trendy to wear lipstick, at other times it isn't. Nevertheless, lipstick is the final touch and it can really make your face come alive. Moreover, it's fun and a great lifter of the morale. When you are young, you should stay away from strong shades – the subtle pinks and corals are usually more complimentary and you may very well find that a light lip gloss suits you best. Whatever colour you choose, lips need shine; dry, made-up lips are not attractive. All today's products are formulated to give a moist, shiny look. They are a blend of oils, waxes and glycerides, plus colour, perfume and flavour. Do you realize that lipstick is the only cosmetic that has to be pleasant to the palate as well as pleasing to the eye? Lip colour comes in four forms.

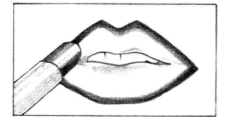

Lipsticks are the conventional form and remain the most popular. The texture is usually creamy and lustrous. Application can be direct or with a brush.

Creams are available in compacts or pots. They vary in density and they must be applied with a brush.

Lip gloss comes in tubes or pots and gives shine but not much colour. Clear gloss can be used over conventional lipsticks. Apply with a brush or the fingertips.

Lip pencils are soft, wax-based crayons that come in two thicknesses – thin for outlining the lips and thick for filling in.

To apply lipstick, it is best to outline your lips first and then fill in. Outlining can be done with a pencil or lip brush. If you use a pencil make sure it tones with your lipstick. Outline the bottom lip first, from the centre to the right-hand corner and then from the centre to the left-hand corner. Outline the upper lip in the same way. Fill in with colour, using either a brush or the lipstick. Be careful not to run over the outline. For extra shine use gloss over lipstick, but don't take it right to the edges as this might make the lipstick run.

Camouflaging faults

Important rule: don't attempt to reshape your lips – alterations can be very obvious. Faults can often be helped by just playing around with colour tones.

For big lips, outline just inside the natural line with a light colour and fill in with a slightly deeper tone.

For thin lips, outline just outside the natural lip line, stopping a little short of the corners; fill in with a deeper colour.

For unbalanced lips (if your top lip is much narrower than the bottom, or vice versa), the trick is to use two different shades, a darker one for the thicker lip, a lighter one for the other – but be sure that the tones match.

How to avoid the most common make-up mistakes

Never choose a foundation to brighten your skin – do this with a blusher.

Don't put on too much foundation, otherwise it will look like a plastic mask; apply lightly and blend in well.

Don't overdo the blusher – the idea is to give you a healthy glow, not a feverish look.

Don't cover the entire cheek with blusher; apply it high on the cheek-bone and blend it into the hairline.

Use powder sparingly and brush away all excess.

Eyeshadow should draw attention to your eyes, not to the colour of the shadow; so use low-key colours.

Don't match eyeshadow to your clothes – stick to neutral shades.

Don't feel that the colour of your face has to outshine that of your clothes – a brightly coloured dress looks better with a naturally coloured face.

Avoid harsh eyebrow lines – pick a colour lighter than your brows and make short feathery strokes to fill in.

Don't put on so much mascara that your lashes look glued together and almost knitted – the lashes should look long and fluttery.

Avoid strong lip colour – a natural gloss is much more effective.

Don't bother about lip colour matching clothes – it's too contrived; use soft shades that go with and flatter your skin.

To keep make-up tidy

If you have all your make-up products in order and at hand, it is easier to think of creative possibilities with colour and to try out different ideas. It is not necessary to buy special boxes – a simple tray for holding cutlery makes a good make-up box. It has compartments to keep the various products separate for easy use; the wicker ones are particularly attractive. Or you might like to consider the trays fishermen use for their equipment, or tool-boxes for handymen – this is how professional make-up artists keep their wide array of products in perfect order.

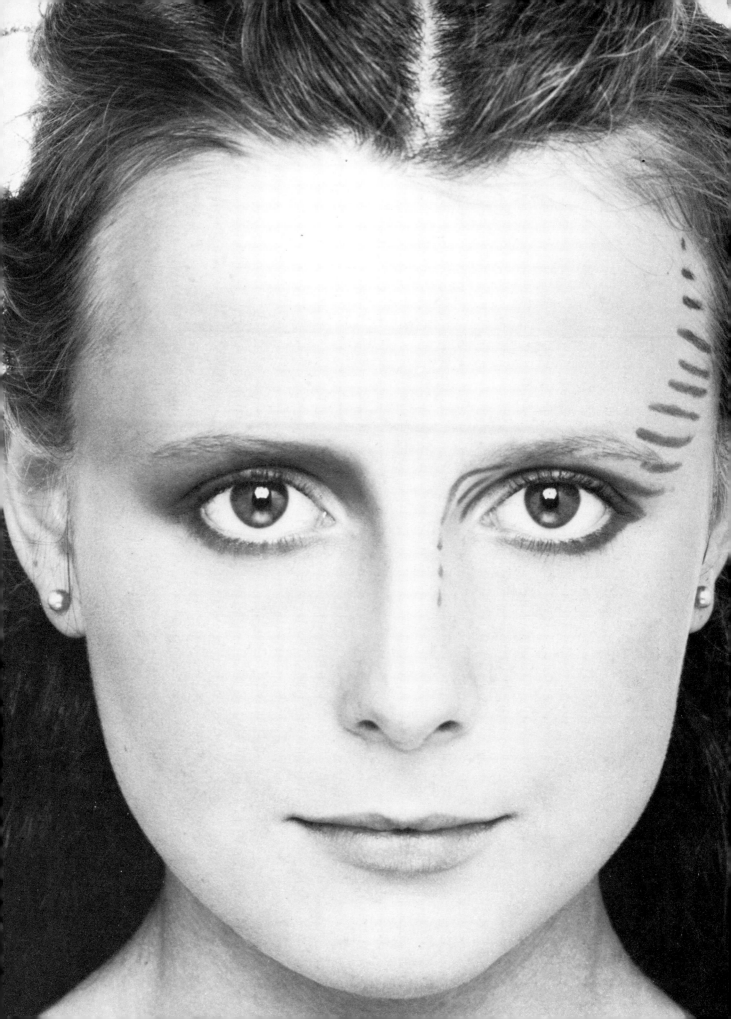

is only a few months, but if your hair is long it can be a year. And it can be a year of agony. So remember this when you consider any radical change. Remember, too, that no one is ever absolutely satisfied with her hair. It's one of those things – but it's true. Ask your mother. She probably still hasn't decided what is best. Bear that in mind and don't go out on a limb for extraordinary change at first. You have many years for experimenting.

What chemical treatments can do to hair

Whenever you put a chemical product on your hair, you alter all of its three basic qualities to some degree. A change of colour will also alter the hair's texture and body, a change of pattern will do the same; when you interfere with one, you are interfering with the others as well. Not everyone realizes this, but in relation to hair looks and health it's very important.

It really is best to keep your hair natural. There are so many possibilities of cut and style that drastic structural change should be unnecessary. However, if change you must, here are the alternatives.

Permanent wave

The idea of a permanent is not to provide waves and curls as such, but to give texture and body in order to make styling easier. You can do it at home as it's a relatively simple procedure, but you must be sure to follow the directions faithfully. You have to concentrate on what you're doing as the process involves using strong chemicals on your hair.

Each product has its own directions, but there are some general rules to follow. Your hair must be washed first, as dirt and grease can affect the action of the chemicals. Do a test curl – this will show you how your hair takes to the perm. Try one section on a narrow rod, the other on a roller; then decide which type of curl you want – the bigger the rollers, the looser the curl. Long hair is easier to handle on big rollers as you must not put too much hair on each roller. Use rollers the same way as for setting (illustration on page 190).

Home perms come in three strengths, for fine, medium and coarse hair. Check the labels and match your type. Most are two-step procedures, using a waving solution first and then a neutralizer to stop the chemical reaction and stabilize the wave. One-step home perms are also available. Be prepared for the smell – many use chemicals with an unpleasant odour.

Straightening

Hair straightening is a permanent wave in reverse. It is potentially the most dangerous hair process and should never be attempted at home. In a salon, it takes about two hours, and it shouldn't be done more than once a year. Very few hairdressers recommend straightening because so often it results in extreme breakage and hair loss.

Colouring

There are three kinds of hair colouring – temporary, semi-permanent and permanent. Temporary rinses last only until the next shampoo – they coat the outside of the hair shaft and, because they contain no bleaching agent, they

What about lotions and hair-sprays?

Setting agents are a definite plus as they help control hair and also give a certain degree of protection. Hair-sprays used in moderation will cause no harm, but remember that they shouldn't be inhaled. If used excessively they make the hair look stiff and artificial. Hair looks best when swinging naturally, not held primly in place.

Watch out for weather

Climatic conditions can radically affect your hair. On a rainy or humid day hair will absorb moisture, and may become frizzy and unmanageable. Heat from the sun can dry it out and also change its colour; it may even scorch the cuticle. The lighter your hair, the more it needs to be protected from the sun. Wind causes tangles and can make you look dishevelled in an instant.

cannot lighten hair. You can only make subtle changes, adding highlights within the same colour range as your own; for example, on light or mousy hair, you can add darker or red tones. Temporary rinses have less affect on dark hair, but will sometimes give highlights.

Semi-permanent tints

These work on the same principle as temporary rinses but they are stronger and last longer. They have no bleaching agent and cannot lighten the hair, but they do contain a chemical that diffuses the hair shaft with some colour. They add highlights within the same shade range – nothing startling. With each shampoo a little colour is washed away – after four or five it's gone.

Permanent colourings

These contain bleaching and colour-penetration agents. Any colour change is possible, but the results depend on what colour hair you have to start with. Looking at the colours on a package is only a rough guide, as these indicate how the tint would take on colourless hair. Darkening hair is much simpler than lightening. To lighten hair by more than a few shades requires pre-bleaching. Cream formulas are brushed or swabbed on the dry hair section by section. If you are doing it at home you must make two tests before doing your whole head. First a patch test for allergic reactions: make up a small amount of colouring, wash the skin just behind the ear, swab on some of the mixture and leave for twenty-four hours. If there's no sign of irritation, go ahead. If there is a reaction, try another product. At the same time do a strand test to check on the colour: cut off a few strands near the scalp and use the rest of the trial mixture on them, following the instructions on the packet. You'll quickly see the colour reaction; but always check the results in a strong light.

Bleaching

A bleach strips your hair of colour – it attacks the melanin in the hair shaft. The most commonly used bleach is hydrogen peroxide. It comes in different strengths, from 10 volume up to 100 volume – the stronger the solution the faster the bleaching action. A warning: when you use peroxide always be extremely careful; never use peroxide stronger than 20 volume – it can be very dangerous. The longer the peroxide stays on the hair, the lighter the hair will become. After bleaching, you usually need to colour-rinse your hair to tone it down – otherwise you will get a brassy or red look. It is not advisable to play around on your own with bleach; if you must have lighter hair, go to a professional hairdresser.

Henna

This is a natural vegetable colouring with no synthetic chemicals at all. It gives a red tint and, although harmless, should be used with caution because you can end up with very strange shades of red – the colour is very unpredictable. Never do your whole head without first doing a strand test. Hair must be shampooed before using henna. Wear gloves because it stains fingers and nails. Follow the instructions – each product varies in density – and keep checking the colour.

STYLING

Are you happy about the look of your hair?

Perhaps up to now your hair has been ordinary hair – hanging down, tied back or simply cut short to get it out of the way. Now is the time to change, to think about your hair as the most terrific asset. The first move is to have it really well cut. Then you can try out different styles, either setting your hair on rollers or blow-drying it. Either way there are many possibilities – why don't you see what you can do?

The best strategy: well-cut hair

Only a professional can cut your hair really well. Decide on the type of style you want and then discuss it with a hairdresser. Don't be shy. You may have made up your mind, but the hairdresser knows what is possible and what can or cannot be done with your type of hair. It may take much trial and error before you get exactly what you want. Hair should be cut wet, after it has been shampooed. It is cut in sections and usually cutting starts at the neckline. Today the trend is to cut hair bluntly, which means that the hair is clipped straight across even when the style is layered. This helps prevent split ends and encourages hair to move with a healthy swing. No matter what length your hair is, it should be cut about every six weeks, otherwise the ends become straggly.

How to set your hair in rollers

Sometimes it is better to set hair on rollers for greater control: the bigger the roller, the looser the set. If you have curly hair it is best to use large rollers. Avoid rollers with brushes inside as these can split the hair. Setting lotion makes hair easier to handle. Don't put too much hair on the roller and work in sections of $1\frac{1}{2}$–2 in. (3.5–5 cm). The hair should be wrapped smoothly, but not tightly, round the roller, first stretching it straight in the opposite direction from which it is to be rolled. Use strong metal clips to hold hair and rollers in place. It can be dried naturally or with a dryer, but before taking out the rollers let your hair cool down to room temperature. This helps you control the set for a longer time. Take out the lower rollers first. In brushing out, brush straight back to the tip of the curl. Then put your head forward and brush from the nape upwards. Finally, fling back your hair and adjust it with a brush and a comb. Don't fiddle around too much; don't be too contrived. A natural look is best – both for your looks and for your hair.

How to blow-dry your hair

This is the way to achieve a really polished smooth look without the bother of using rollers. You can persuade your hair into many shapes by using a brush or comb and any type of hand-dryer.

If your hair is straight, dry it first with a towel. If it is curly and you want to get it as straight as possible, start blow-drying when the hair is soaking wet.

Style: four major points

Individuality – this matters more than fashion. Your hairstyle expresses your character and makes you stand out in a crowd.

Compatibility – does your hair go easily in the style you want? Hair has a will of its own and will always return to its natural ways no matter how much you try to force it in another direction. This is particularly so with wavy or curly hair.

Flattery – the shape of your hair can dramatically change your looks, emphasizing your best features, distracting from others. Move your hair around to see what works best for you; a good time is during a shampoo, when the hair is full of suds and can be pushed into almost any shape.

Versatility – how many ways can you do your hair? Much of the fun of hairstyling is in change. You can easily become bored with the same look; each day and each mood can bring a need for a different look. Also if your hair is versatile it will work with all sorts of clothes and all kinds of necklines.
(See the wide choice of styles on pages 192–7

How to set your hair in rollers

Set for style with no parting or centre division

Comb your hair back from the face; start with the centre area and wind the hair back on six rollers from forehead to nape. Use four rollers on either side, winding down. Make clip curls around the ears – or use another roller. Soft bangs can be rolled back in the rollers and, when dry, brushed forward for a casual, light effect.

Set for side-parting style

For the front hair use five rollers to wind the hair down on one side, two on the other. Hair from the crown is rolled back and down. At the nape and the sides near the ears use either clip curls or rollers.

Set for a flat, straight fringe

Comb the fringe forward while wet and hold in place with a tissue secured with clips or scotch tape. Rollers are then placed as for the no-parting set.

Set to control long, wavy hair

To get unruly long hair as straight as possible, you can set it like this: put two big rollers on the crown, and then, with a brush, wind your hair round your head, keeping it smooth and securing all stray ends. It needs to be clipped into place. When it is almost dry, take it down and wrap it in the opposite direction.

How to blow-dry your hair

First divide your hair into four sections, secured with clips.

Always begin by drying the back. Dry the roots first, then the centre strands and then the ends. When you have done the back do the sides and dry the crown last.

Points to watch

● Never have the dryer so hot or so near the scalp that it scorches your hair, and never concentrate too much heat on too small an area.

● Do not pull hair too taut – this will cause a lot of damage.

● Wrap the hair round the brush to control its direction, under or over.

● A fringe should be brushed backwards first and then brought forward twirling it round the brush.

● Brush short hair away from your scalp.

AT THE HAIRDRESSER'S

What goes on at the salon? How does it work?

Fact number one: hairdressers are intimidating and even adult women are often afraid to speak up and say what they want done. You have to be strong and, believe me, it's not easy. Hairdressers do not like to be dictated to and they often see your hair in a way you'd never see it – which may or may not be an advantage. Trusting your hair to a new hairdresser, or going to one for the first time, can be very nerve-racking and mistakes take a long time to rectify.

It is best to choose your hairdresser by personal recommendation. Your mother probably knows of one, or a friend may be able to help. If you are starting out cold, the look of the salon will tell you a lot: is it clean, is it busy, what about the photographs in the window?

If you are thinking of going to a hairdresser for a drastic change – a cut, a complete new style – don't have it done the first time. Go for a wash and a set first to give the hairdresser a chance to get to know your hair and to give yourself confidence.

Study photographs and sketches before deciding on your new style. Play around with your hair at home. Take pictures to show the hairdresser, as this will be a much better indication of what you want than a mumbled 'short here, curly there' suggestion. If you desperately want a certain look don't let the hairdresser talk you out of it. It's your hair after all, and if your idea doesn't work then at least you know it's your fault and you can try something else. But do listen to professional advice – between you, you might very well hit upon something that's exactly right.

Salon procedure

Usually an appointment is necessary and you should specify what you want done – wash and set, cut, perm, etc. On entering the salon you check with the receptionist, who will show you where to put your clothes and get a wrap. You will be directed or taken to the wash-basins where a young assistant washes your hair – she will ask whether you want a normal or special shampoo, and whether you want a conditioner. Your hair will be combed through at the basin.

The stylist is in the main part of the salon, where your hair is cut and styled in full view of everyone else. This is when you need courage to speak up and put forward your ideas. At first you may not really know what you want, so you more or less have to leave it in the hairdresser's hands. Should your hair be set in rollers or blow-dried? Should it be straight or curled? Should it be short or long? Only experience can answer these questions.

Hairdressers expect a tip; it is usual to give 10 per cent of the bill. The person who shampoos your hair expects a small tip too. You can either give it direct to the person concerned or leave it with the receptionist.

Prices vary and it is wise to check first. Most salons have a printed list.

1

SHORT HAIR

By far the easiest to take care of. Short hair gives you freedom. It is essential to have it cut well and planned by a professional; to keep it in shape you need to have it trimmed every four to six weeks. Finding the best style takes trials and time, and it depends primarily on the type of hair you have – fine, thick, curly, straight, etc. Here are some ideas.

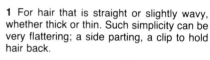
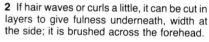

2

3

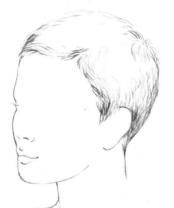

4

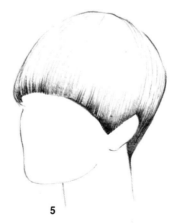

5

1 For hair that is straight or slightly wavy, whether thick or thin. Such simplicity can be very flattering; a side parting, a clip to hold hair back.

2 If hair waves or curls a little, it can be cut in layers to give fulness underneath, width at the side; it is brushed across the forehead.

3 The classic French look and only possible with straight hair. Bangs are long, the rest cut evenly and drawn back to show the ears.

4 Just like a boy – a look that can be very appealing on a young girl. Almost any hair can be cut like this – it will curl, spring or lie flat according to its natural texture.

5 This cap effect can only be achieved with straight hair and if your hair is thick so much the better. It is one of the most favoured geometric cuts.

6 To get a side flick like this, hair has to be cut in layers and trained to go back with a brush. The idea is to let it swing across the forehead so the whole effect is one of bounce.

7 A variation on the cap cut, where uneven geometric shaping is emphasized. It can be used to great advantage to camouflage any facial problems such as large ears, low forehead, close-set eyes.

6

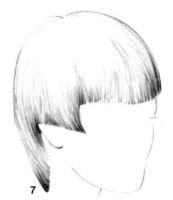

7

MEDIUM HAIR

This length is, as it sounds, neither long nor short but hovering somewhere around the neck. It is, however one of the most difficult lengths to cope with, which is very irritating because it is invariably the most flattering. You are one-up on short hair though and you can vary your style from one cut.

1 Straight thick hair looks good in a simple blunt cut where hair is an even length all round. It swings from a centre parting or can be held by clips up and away from the face.

2 For wavy hair of any texture, a simple wind-blown, natural style. Hair is cut and trained to turn under, and there's a flattering dent of a wave at the side.

3 A look young girls like – eyebrow bangs and hair evenly cut to hang at neck-line. Again it is a matter of using clips to put hair back or up, thus varying styles. Many types of hair – except curly – will give this look.

4 Wavy hair cut in layers so that it flicks up at the sides and can either go up or over at the back. It is better when the top layer is not too short.

5 Curly or crinkly hair left to do as it pleases, falling from a side parting. Even if your hair is straight you can achieve this look by plaiting hair into many strands, leaving it overnight and then brushing it free in the morning.

6 Curly or wavy thick hair when cut evenly gives an impressive mane of waves. It's easier to control from a centre parting and it looks more balanced.

7 The long bob – simple and neat, turning under on the shoulders. To achieve this, hair must have some body and be practically straight. Thin fly-away hair cut this way would look messy.

LONG HAIR

The great thing about long hair, of course, is that you can do so much with it. Long hair doesn't just have to hang there, it can be tied, knotted, plaited or simply pinned. Skill comes with practice and soon you'll have a whole collection of styles at your fingertips. Use your imagination – today anything goes. The nuisance about long hair is that it's more difficult to wash, to condition, to comb and to brush. It is, however, often easier to control as it can be tidied away.

1

2

3

4

1 One-sided effects can be amusing; here hair is pulled up to one side, held firm with covered elastic (never an ordinary elastic band, it ruins the hair) and secured in a loop. Good for fine hair.

2 Curly hair can also be coped with long; an idea is to layer it so it is a wild mop; it can be worn with a centre parting or brushed over the forehead.

3 A real little girls' look, long hair, long bangs. The cut is even all round and the best results are achieved with straight hair.

4 Wavy hair should be tapered, allowing it to undulate softly to the tips. Here it is swept from a side parting and held with a clip.

5 Hair can be draped like fabric, but you have to divide the hair into sections first. Take two sections either side of a centre parting; first roll each on its own, then roll into each other; secure with pins.

6 This is more complicated; hair is plaited by starting with a front section and continuously bringing in the rest of the hair.

7 For prim days, hair is pulled back and

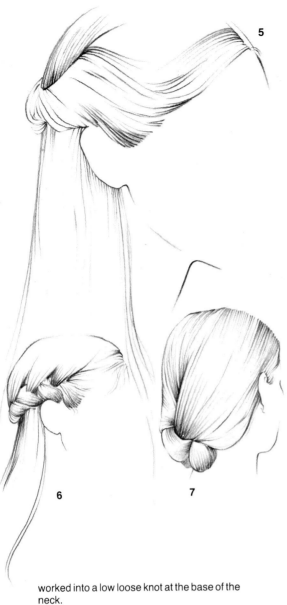

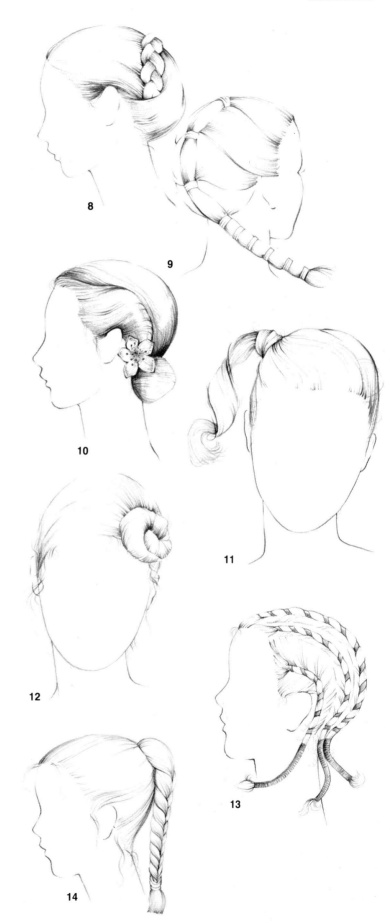

worked into a low loose knot at the base of the neck.

8 If you have enough hair you can plait the under section and secure it in a circle over the loose hair, which is then pinned at the neck. An easier way is to use a false braid.

9 A young and charming idea – hair tied back in sections and secured with bands, ribbon, wool or what you like.

10 For more formal occasions, roll back hair at the sides, plait a little if you like, but leave enough hair free to make a bun at the nape.

11 Quick and easy – hair is swept up to one side, and a few strands are wrapped around the securing elastic.

12 A knot almost on the forehead; hair is pulled to one side and twisted into a bun. The look is softened by allowing loose strands of hair to trickle round the face.

13 This works for straight or curly hair – the hair is sectioned and plaited or bound with ribbon. It can stay like this for many days.

14 A variation on the simple pony-tail: hair drawn back into a band, then plaited.

ARABELLA'S HAIR

Ten ways to do it
Infinite variety from a basic cut

Type: dark, thick, almost straight; with only a little coaxing it waves; it takes quickly to curl.

Cut: even length and bluntly cut; it naturally hangs straight from a centre parting. This is just about the most basic cut you can get, but so much can be done with it. It is trimmed every two months.

Care: washing every four or five days with a mild shampoo, plus a cream conditioner put on the ends only; a final rinse for shine: 1 tablespoon of cider vinegar in 2 pints of warm water.

Style: it looks fine just as it is, but it can be changed at the flick of a brush: it can easily be tied back into a high or low pony-tail; it can be held in place with a band; it can be lifted away from the face with clips or combs. Illustrated here are some of the more complex styles, but even these can be done on your own without the help of a hairdresser.

1

2

3

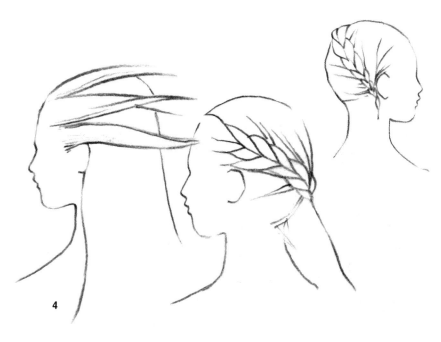

4

Photographs: Stefano Massimo
Drawings: Martin Welch
Hair: Pat of Vidal Sassoon
Make-up: Glauca Rossi

1 Hair swept smoothly to one side, held with covered elastic, then tied with a ribbon.

2 All hair tightly rolled up from a side parting, held in place with long pins.

3 Plaits at the side, where the hair is drawn in section by section, a knot at the nape.

4 Two ideas with plaits; two plaits from a centre parting to the nape, or one over the head.

5 Front and back view of a style with combs – the front section drawn up and back.

6 The front section, held by elastic, then secured on top with a clip or comb.

7 A change to curls – easily done by twisting small sections of hair into many knots, holding with long pins. After half an hour, brush out.

8 Back section is curled, front section kept smooth and swept up into an Edwardian top knot.

9 Almost curly, with front section swept away from forehead.

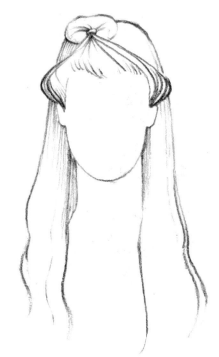

SCENT

Scent is intangible, yet it plays a very significant role in your everyday life.

You may well think there's too much fuss over fragrance, when surely it's just a matter of smelling good or bad. Actually it is much more complex than that and both the history and the modern use of scent present interesting facts.

The more you learn about fragrance, the more you'll realize how valuable it is. With scent you can create a mood and stir up emotions; you can stimulate or relax the mind and you can ease or revive the body. In fact, you communicate on levels that even scientists cannot understand.

First of all, our sense of smell is the sense with the most direct line to the primitive areas of the brain. It may be less sharp than that of animals, but it is a great deal keener than you imagine – and it has considerable influence on your behaviour. For a start it affects your memory – you remember smells as effectively as you recall pictures. If you think for a second, you can probably conjure up certain smells that remind you of a place, a person, a house, a holiday, a favourite food.

Odours affect us all the time and we react to the rotten smells as well as the pleasant ones. You receive 'odour' messages through the nose or through the rear of the mouth. They are picked up by the olfactory nerves and the information is then sent to the brain.

AROMATICS

They have been used for centuries for both health and aesthetic reasons

Do you know that . . .

Any spicy or fragrant substance that gives a pleasant smell is called an aromatic.

Aromatics are not just beauty aids but also agents that can stimulate mind and body.

The original aromatics were single, natural elements, mostly from flowers, leaves and stalks. Today they are complex compounds known as perfume, scent or fragrance.

The Greeks learned the aromatic arts from the Middle East and Asia. Hippocrates, the famous Greek physician, prescribed specially scented baths and massages as treatment for certain diseases.

Aromatics were thought to have the power to ward off evil and illness. For example, camphor, musk and other pungent scents were carried around by medieval physicians and held to the nose to avoid infections. During the Great Plague people wore scent-filled pomanders on ribbons around their necks and burned aromatic substances in the hope of warding off the disease. Smelling sweet was the prerogative of the rich in olden days. Although scented herbs, flowers and grasses were available to all, the perfumes were transient, and the processes used to make perfumes more stable involved ingredients from around the world. Scents, therefore, were luxuries; on the other hand they were almost essential for those living in cities and courts, to cover up the stench.

When explorers began to sail around the world, one of their main tasks was to find new sources of oils and spices. The Middle and Far Eastern countries provided exotic substances that had been used as health aids for centuries.

How is a perfume made?

In the tenth century an Arab physician first isolated the perfume of the rose and used this 'essential oil' to make rosewater. This was the beginning of modern perfume, though the art as we know it today was perfected in France two hundred years ago. Now the world centre is at Grasse, a French hillside town just inland from the Côte d'Azur on the Mediterranean.

It takes many years to create a new scent. The raw materials come from three sources – botanical, animal and chemical. The botanical (flowers, leaves, stalks, roots, grasses and barks) and animal elements (hormone extracts) are the traditional sources and have been used since the earliest times. The chemical ingredients are called aldehydes and have been developed over the last forty years. You may think it very strange that parts of animals are used, particularly when in their natural state the hormones often smell awful. However, in minute quantities they actually enrich a fragrance and often stabilize the aroma of the scent.

There are about three thousand 'smells' available to perfumers. The florals are very popular, particularly jasmine, hyacinth, May rose, lavender, carnation, narcissus, mimosa and tuberose. They have to be picked at a certain time of year, often at a certain hour of the day, to be sure they are harvested at their zenith. Flowers must be distilled within four hours of being gathered, otherwise they will dry and lose their fragrance. The quality and quantity of natural botanical essences can vary depending on growing conditions and climate. Just like wine, there are good and bad years. Enormous quantities of the natural source are required to produce just a little of the concentrated scented liquid known as the 'essential' oil. This is the main reason why perfume is so expensive.

A perfume is described in terms of 'notes'

The language of perfume is musical. You will hear of high or top notes, low or base notes and middle notes. It works this way: when you open a bottle of scent, the first strong whiff gives you the 'top note'. This lingers very briefly, because after exposure to air the chemistry of the perfume is altered and a much more subtle aroma emerges. This is called the 'middle note' and is really the main character. It can last several hours. Finally comes the 'base note', which is usually heavier because it reflects the fixative elements – and it is at this point that the whole impression of the fragrance can change, often becoming unpleasantly sweet or sour.

CHOOSING SCENT

How to see your way through the bewildering variety available

If you think sorting out the scents is confusing, you're absolutely right. Only the experts and the most experienced can claim a discerning 'nose'. In time you will discover the fragrances you like – and those that like you. That's the odd thing about perfume. A particular one may smell divine on your friend and not so good on you. Everyone has an individual reaction.

To make it easier, you need to know that most perfumes can be grouped into general categories according to their components and the impression they give. For example, a light floral scent will have a refreshing effect, while a sweet floral will lull the senses. These are the groups.

Single floral

The focus is on one note; they can be sweet or fresh.

Floral bouquets

A mix of flowers and seasons; many are a combination of jasmine, tuberose and gardenia; they can be very sweet.

Green

Ferns, grasses and barks; they are usually fresh and woody.

Citrus

Dominated by lemon, orange and bergamot notes; they are fresh and cooling.

Oriental

Made from aromatic eastern plants, and heavy with musk and ambergris; they are rich and exotic.

Modern

Made from synthetic materials; they are bright, cheery, fresh with a bracing air.

Unfortunately there is rarely any indication on the label as to what 'type' the perfume is, but you'll find the more you sniff, the more you notice that the perfumes you like have things in common.

Start at first with the flower and fruit smells – most people like them. Your choice of fragrance is highly personal and totally subjective. Response to scent is completely individual. One scent can bring a feeling of pleasure, another can leave you cold. Why? There's absolutely no answer!

The seven steps to perfume selection

There are hundreds of different fragrances and it will take a long time to determine which one is best for you. There are usually tester bottles available – they are specifically there for testing, so use them. Don't be shy. You are not

---

Do you know that:

Your sense of smell is less strong in bright light and at it's most powerful in the dark?

It's less acute in the morning, gradually increasing throughout the day?

expected to buy the whole bottle to find out if you like a perfume. Test, then buy.

1 It's best to evaluate a scent as a cologne or toilet water – a drop of perfume is a potent thing and can numb the nose.
2 Don't test more than two scents at a time.
3 Smell the scent in the bottle – this is its 'top note'.
4 Apply a bit to the inside of your wrist where body heat will bring out the fragrance. Put a different scent on each wrist.
5 After half an hour, smell the scent again; you now smell the 'middle note'.
6 Wait another hour, sniff again; this times it's the 'bottom note' that comes out.
7 Consider your reaction to all 'notes', particularly to the 'bottom' one, as this lingers on. Some perfumes turn sweeter. Do you like that? If not, find one that stays fresh and clear – it's often better for young personalities.

Perfume and personality

Your choice of perfume provides a good indication as to how you think about yourself. Are you a sporty, outdoor girl? The chances are that you will choose a fresh, clean scent from the green or modern groups. Are you sweet, fragile, feminine? Then your preference is likely to be one of the florals or citrus scents. How about the siren, the *femme fatale* personality? For you there's the mysterious attraction of the oriental and spicy fragrances. You see, scents can tell a lot – be sure they say the right thing!

What is the difference between perfume, cologne and toilet water?

A perfume can be very strong and too overpowering for a teenager – the other two are lighter and better for the young. Both colognes and toilet waters are diluted forms of perfume and contain a far higher percentage of alcohol, which explains their cooling and refreshing quality. The terms are more or less interchangeable, though in some cases the toilet water is stronger than the cologne. A good cologne or toilet water is half as concentrated as the perfume. Sometimes they are not merely diluted with alcohol, but can be composed of different ingredients. Perfume often has better-quality substances; for example, the perfume may include natural rose essence among its many ingredients, while toilet water or cologne has synthetic rose.

Your skin type and body chemistry greatly influence the effect of scent

Everyone has a different reaction to a particular scent. For instance, if you have a fair skin you'll get better results with a delicate fragrance than someone with dark skin. Dark skins are often oilier; although this means a perfume will last longer, it also tends to become sweeter.

DON'T use scent to counteract sweat – the chemical reaction smells dreadful.

DON'T put scent on clothes, as it is likely to stain; also scent that is not in direct contact with your skin doesn't take on its individual character.

DON'T wear scent when you are out sunbathing; some scents contain ingredients that have an adverse reaction to direct sunlight and can cause skin irritations and rashes.

DON'T overdo scent. Your nose gets used to a scent after you've worn it for a while, but others remain aware of it. Too much scent can be unpleasant, particularly at close quarters. And it *is* expensive.

DON'T keep scent in direct light. Put the bottles in a cool dark place; this helps preserve it.

WEARING SCENT

The final effect of fragrance lies in the way you use it

Learn to layer it. Scent is not just perfumes and toilet waters – it is also soaps, bath oils, powders and body lotions. If you follow through with one fragrance for all, you'll get the desired effect at less expense than a last-minute attempt with costly perfume.

Start with a scented bath oil and soap, follow with body lotion for arms and legs, a powder for your torso. You can finish with a cologne or eau de toilette – and that you can spray all over.

When it's very hot, you can use your fragrance for cooling down. The high alcohol content in cologne and toilet water acts as a natural cooling agent. Start at the extremities – the hands and feet.

How long does a perfume last?

It varies according to the individual, but a concentrated scent should last about eight hours, a toilet water or cologne about four hours. However, the hotter the climate and the warmer your body, the faster you burn off any scent.

Test the effect of fragrance on your mind

Some scents have a definite influence on mental attitudes. You can benefit by putting certain essences in your bath – the effects are not glaringly obvious, but they do have a subtle, positive effect. Use the essential oils which can be obtained from a herbalist and some pharmacies. Most oils only partially dissolve in water, so fill the bath with warm water and then drop in the essence.

Perfume – a memory that lingers on

Throughout history, scent has left its message and many heroes and heroines have contributed aromatic memories. Even Napoleon was sentimentally affected by fragrance. He died wearing a locket filled with violets he had gathered from Josephine's grave. He had planted them in living memory of the perfume she had worn to please him. The one she wore to please herself was musk, which the Emperor hated – but she used it so liberally that a century later her rooms at Malmaison still smelled of it.

COLOGNES, POTPOURRIS, SACHETS AND HERB PILLOWS

It's fun to make your own simple fragrances:

You can find the ingredients in a herbalist shop, in many health-food stores – or simply in your garden. The making is easy. You'll need glass bowls for mixing and airtight containers for storage. For the colognes use old perfume bottles or glass-stoppered vinegar bottles. Here's what to do.

Lavender toilet water

1 tablespoon oil of lavender
4 cups ethyl alcohol
1 dessertspoon rose water

Mix the lavender oil with a little alcohol until blended, then slowly add the remainder. Finally stir in the rose water. Keep in sealed jars and leave for six weeks to mature.

Cologne water

2 teaspoons oil of lavender
3 teaspoons oil of cloves
2 cups ethyl alcohol
2 tablespoons rose water

Blend the two oils with a little of the alcohol until everything is well mixed; beat in the remaining alcohol and add the rose water. Bottle tightly and allow to mature for six to eight weeks.

Basic cream perfume

½ cup grated beeswax
½ cup almond oil
4 tablespoons distilled water
4 teaspoons any commercial cologne (or those above)

Melt the wax in a double boiler, beat in the oil very slowly and then add the water. Remove from the heat and stir in the cologne. Whisk until thoroughly blended; pour into small flat jars.

Rose essence

3 handfuls of dried rose petals
3 tablespoons sweet almond oil

Put dried rose petals in a glass bowl or jar and cover with the oil. Place the pot in a pan of simmering water, heat until the oil has removed all the colour from the petals. Strain. Keep tightly lidded.

Easiest of all to make: potpourris

These are fragrant mixtures containing complete petals and leaves, perfumed with a fragrance. You have to add what is known as a 'fixative'. This is an ingredient that literally fixes the scent and prevents deterioration. Potpourris should be kept in large glass or china bowls and jars and they must be lidded. A potpourri can be ground down and put into sachets – small fabric shapes usually made of muslin, voile or calico. All leaves and petals must be absolutely dry before use. If you are gathering your own, flowers should be picked early in the morning and laid on drying racks in the dark – light will destroy the colour. You can buy packets of mixed dried flowers in most herbalists'.

You can make your potpourri in any glass or ceramic jar, but it must have a tight-fitting lid. The mixture takes six to eight weeks to mature and it needs an occasional stir during that time. Afterwards it can be transferred into decorative containers or sewn into sachets or pillows.

Rose bowl

4 cups dried rose petals
2 tablespoons ground orris root
2 teaspoons ground allspice
1 teaspoon ground nutmeg
1 teaspoon crushed cinnamon stick
1 teaspoon crushed cloves
1 tablespoon dried orange and lemon peel (broken into tiny pieces)
1 ground vanilla bean
½ teaspoon rose geranium oil
a little lemon verbena oil (optional)

Using a wooden spoon, mix the first six ingredients together very well, then add the bits of orange and lemon peel and the ground vanilla. Add the rose geranium oil. Stir very, very well. If the mixture appears too dry, add a little lemon verbena oil. Cover the jar, seal and leave for six weeks.

A simple lavender potpourri

1 cup lavender flowers and leaves
1 cup mixed dried flowers
1 tablespoon ground orris root
½ teaspoon oil of geranium

Put the flowers into a jar and stir in the fixative with a wooden spoon. Add the oil of geranium and stir very well. Cover and leave to mature for eight weeks.

INDEX